INTRODUCTION
TO
MILITARY HISTORY

AMS PRESS

NEW YORK

The Century Historical Series

INTRODUCTION
TO
MILITARY HISTORY

BY

ROBERT GREENHALGH ALBION, Ph.D.

Associate Professor of History, Princeton University

MAPS PREPARED IN COLLABORATION WITH

GIRARD L. McENTEE

Lieutenant Colonel, Regular Army

D. APPLETON-CENTURY COMPANY

INCORPORATED

NEW YORK   LONDON

Reprinted from the edition of 1929, New York

First AMS EDITION published 1971

"Reprinted from a copy in the collection of the
Cleveland Public Library"

Manufactured in the United States of America

International Standard Book Number: 0-404-00303-6

Library of Congress Catalog Number: 75-158240

355
A 337

AMS PRESS INC.
NEW YORK, N.Y.   10003

To

J. B. P.

PREFACE

This book is based on three years' experience in conducting a course in military history in the Princeton University unit of the Field Artillery Reserve Officers Training Corps. Since there seemed to be no single volume which could give the students the essential background and facts, the lectures in this course had to be crowded with details. It appears that if the student can obtain such necessary factual introductory information from a compact textbook beforehand, the lecturer will be free to devote his time to presenting important illustrative matter.

The volume has been written with the needs of senior and junior R.O.T.C. units particularly in mind. It should meet the official requirements in respect to the study of American military history and military policy prescribed for such courses. It is hoped that it may also prove of interest and value to reserve officers, to C.M.T.C. graduates, and to lay readers interested in military history.

Military history, lying as it does on the frontier between history and military science, requires a knowledge of both of those fields. This fact often presents a difficulty to the history teacher or the officer who undertakes a course in the subject, as he is apt to be best prepared in his own half of the field. An effort has been made in this book to combine both approaches to the subject.

The book is divided into three parts—The Development of Arms and Armies, American Military

Policy, and American Wars and Campaigns. The
second and third parts are definitely designed to
meet the official R.O.T.C. requirements. The nation's military policy in peace and war is analyzed
in two chapters, and the more important parts of
the National Defense Act are given in the Appendix. As for American military history proper, a
chapter is devoted to each of our three major wars
in order to guide the student in further study and
to show how such names as Saratoga, Yorktown,
Gettysburg, Vicksburg, St. Mihiel, and the Meuse-
Argonne actually fit into history. In addition, a
typical campaign of each of the three wars is analyzed to show the various tactical and strategical
principles in practice. The maps accompanying these
chapters have been designed to show all places
mentioned in the text without containing too much detail.

Some may question the advisability of Part I
in such a textbook, since its subject-matter is not
generally included in the conventional course. Its
purpose is to give the student a general background
for the study of military history by showing how
arms and armies have reached their present state of
development. It need not be studied with the same
thoroughness as the rest of the book, though the
chapter on strategy and command has particular
bearing on the later analysis of campaigns.

Individual student reports on particular campaigns, introduced into the Princeton course by
Professor T. J. Wertenbaker, have been highly
successful in bringing the students into actual contact with concrete examples of strategy and tactics.
These reports may be oral or written. A list of
suitable subjects, together with suggestions for the
preparation of reports, is appended. The Appendix

also includes a bibliography of the best books on various subjects, indicating to the general reader what he may expect to find in each. It is believed that there is no other critical military bibliography which performs just this service.

I wish to take this opportunity to acknowledge the help which I have received from many sources. My wife, Jennie Pope Albion, actually collaborated with me in the preparation of the book. At the expense of her own writing, she gave untiring assistance, rewriting a major part of the book and making many radical changes in organization. If the treatment is at all clear and interesting, she deserves the credit. My colleagues at Princeton have given helpful criticism on many parts of the book. I approached the subject as an historian, my military experience having been limited to "fighting" the World War in Kentucky as an infantry lieutenant in a depot brigade. Several officers of the Regular Army, including instructors at the Command and General Staff School, at West Point, and in several R.O.T.C. units, have generously given advice and criticism to check up on and fill out my own shortcomings in matters military.

Professor D. C. Munro, editor of The Century Historical Series, and Major J. H. Stutesman have given me invaluable assistance throughout the preparation of the book. They have both read the entire manuscript and have made a great many suggestions as to fact, interpretation, and treatment. Lieutenant-Colonel G. L. McEntee, who has frequently lectured on military history at Princeton, kindly prepared the maps on the basis of my rough sketches. For suggestions and criticisms on various parts of the work I am deeply indebted to Major E. R. Van Deusen, retiring head of the Princeton

R.O.T.C. unit, Major C. M. Busbee, Captain H. C. Holdridge, Captain G. I. Cross, Captain L. E. Babcock, and Captain R. W. Hasbrouck, all of the Regular Army; Professors V. L. Collins, T. J. Wertenbaker, W. P. Hall, H. R. Shipman, C. R. Hall, and S. J. Howe and Dr. M. J. Offutt of Princeton University; Mr. L. J. Lee, formerly lieutenant in the King's Royal Rifle Corps, B.E.F., Mr. Arthur Sachsse, Mr. M. E. Malone, and Mr. A. J. Powers. Mrs. S. J. Howe prepared the plates showing the development of arms. Captain T. J. Frothingham, O.R.C., kindly gave me permission to base two of my maps upon the excellent maps in his *Guide to the Military History of the World War*. If, in spite of the wide-spread assistance I have received, errors may still have crept into the book, I accept full responsibility for them.

R. G. A.

Princeton,
August, 1929.

CONTENTS

xi

FIGURES

MAPS

PART I

THE DEVELOPMENT OF ARMS AND ARMIES

CHAPTER I

FROM CLUB TO AUTOMATIC RIFLE

THE EVOLUTION OF SMALL ARMS

To understand how men fought in the past, one must first know about weapons. The type of weapons available has always strongly influenced the tactical formations of armies on the field of battle. For instance, the fighting was at close quarters at the time of the American Revolution, because of the short range of the guns. Infantry advanced in solid lines until almost upon the enemy. Heavy cavalry charged directly against these infantry lines. Artillery often opened fire within a few hundred yards of the enemy. Such tactics would be suicidal to-day because weapons have undergone tremendous changes.

We must, therefore, trace briefly the history of arms before turning to the study of tactics. The early centuries can be covered quickly. For a long time, men got along with a few simple weapons. The important changes have occurred fairly recently.

CLASSES OF WEAPONS—Weapons are frequently divided into two main classes according to their *purpose*. Many are intended for hand-to-hand fighting. These are contact or *shock* weapons. The other sort, *missile* weapons, are designed for use at a distance from the enemy. All arms may, again, be separated into two different kinds according to *size*. The heavier ones, such as cannon, are known as *artillery,* and are used only by that branch of an army which is also called artillery. This chapter will deal with the lighter weapons or *small arms* with which the infantry and cavalry fight.

PRE-GUNPOWDER WEAPONS

PRIMITIVE SHOCK WEAPONS—The origins of weapons are lost in the haze of prehistoric times. We can only guess, but it is likely the club was the earliest. Some primitive man, either deliberately or in an emergency, probably grabbed a heavy stick to increase the power of his right arm. The value of such a shock weapon naturally depended upon his muscular strength. The followers of this "shock" school eventually improved their club by substituting an oblong, chipped-edged rock as a "fist hatchet." Later a stick was attached, forming a real hatchet.

PRIMITIVE MISSILE WEAPONS—Before hatchets were made, the first missile weapon had undoubtedly appeared. Short and less brawny men do not like hand-to-hand fighting, at which they are at a noticeable disadvantage. Probably one day some small man was confronted by a husky adversary with a club. Perhaps, to his delight, the little fellow found that he could "get" his enemy with a well-aimed rock without coming to grips. Primitive fights of this sort are still seen in modern riots, when the mob throws bricks to hold off the night-sticks of the police. This missile fighting always seemed less heroic than hand-to-hand combat.[1] Yet it was apt to prove more effective, especially after the discovery that a stone would travel faster and farther if propelled by a sling. It is said that the Philistines probably considered David unsportsmanlike to use a sling. Still, small as he was, he easily put the giant Goliath out of commission.

[1] See pp. 46, 50, 52.

THE "BIG THREE"—The "big three" of weapons, down to fairly recent times, were the sword, the spear, and the bow. The sword was only for shock fighting; the bow was solely a missile weapon. The spear, in its various forms, served both purposes. These three weapons held the center of the military stage from the prehistoric Stone Age until about the time of the discovery of America.

MINOR EARLY WEAPONS—Other weapons, of course, existed during that time. The club survived in the heavy iron mace which bashed in helmets during the middle ages. A bishop swung one at the battle of Hastings because the rules of the church forbade him to shed blood. The hatchet became the battle-ax, which appeared in several deadly forms for centuries. Then there was the halberd, a cross between the hatchet and the spear. But none of these minor weapons had the long vogue or importance of the sword, the bow, and the spear. We shall take up separately the history of each of this "big three."

THE SWORD—The sword was the most important of the three, becoming, in fact, the symbol for war. It was actually an enlarged knife. It started as the chipped flint dagger of the early stone age. Afterward, men mixed copper and tin to make bronze. From this they could fashion swords with longer, thinner blades. The Assyrians, around 650 B. C., were able to hew their way to victory because they used tough iron blades from the Hittite mines against the bronze swords of their enemies. The short, thick iron sword was a favorite of the Greeks and Romans, who specialized in shock action. The Mohammedan Saracens between 700 and 1000 A. D. carried sword-making to a high degree of perfection with their exquisite scimitars fashioned at Damascus and Toledo. Against them came the Christian Crusaders, carrying some of the largest swords in history, huge two-edged broadswords six feet long. As time went on, these immense weapons gradually shrank into slender rapiers for thrusting rather than for slashing. The final developments were the curved cavalry saber, used for slashing, and the long, straight thrusting sword of our American cavalry. The introduction of rapid-fire weapons has reduced the sword to chiefly ornamental purposes. It still cuts the cake at military weddings, but few swords were in evidence on the Western Front in the World War.

LIGHTER SPEARS—JAVELINS—Several different weapons can be classed under the general name *spear*. Each of them in reality was a "knife on the end of a stick." The lightest forms were missile weapons, generally known as darts or javelins. These were hurled by hand and could be effective at a considerable distance. The next size, the spear of moderate length, was nearly seven feet long and could serve either as a missile or contact weapon, as its bearer chose. The Roman legionary, for instance, usually hurled his spear or *pilum* at the enemy ranks from quite a distance.[2] If he preferred, however, he could keep it in his hands and thrust with it much as one does with a bayonet to-day. The latter method was less common because the iron head of the *pilum* was fastened with a wooden pin, so that it ordinarily broke off at the first contact. At the same time, this insecurity of its head improved it as a missile weapon since it would break before the enemy could throw it back.

HEAVY SPEARS—PIKES—The heaviest forms of spear were the infantry pike and the cavalry lance. They were almost solely contact weapons. The heavy

[2] See p. 51.

FIGURE 1

SOLDIERS AND WEAPONS OF FORMER TIMES
a. Greek pikeman. b. Roman legionary with *pilum*. c. Crossbow-
man. d. Medieval knight with lance and sword.

infantry of Alexander the Great carried pikes more than twenty feet long. This same weapon was revived about 1300 by the Swiss, and remained important in most armies until about 1700. Groups of pikemen had to protect the early musketeers while the latter slowly reloaded their pieces.[3] This necessity led to the bayonet, which allowed the infantry soldier to convert his musket instantly into a pike. The idea of the pike thus survives in the bayonet, the grimmest of present-day weapons.

HEAVY SPEARS—LANCES—The lance, the heavy spear of the cavalry, has also lasted. The armored knights of the middle ages carried heavy lances with which to unhorse their adversaries. A dispute has come down to our own day as to whether the lance or the saber is more effective in a cavalry charge. Most European armies have kept cavalry regiments of lancers. The "cold steel" of the lance or bayonet has been the final test in many an encounter in recent times.

THE BOW—The bow, a purely missile weapon, did not survive as long as the sword and the spear, but it was important during its time. Although not considered as heroic as the shock weapons, it was too effective to be neglected. Arrow-heads are found in very early remains, along with stone knives and spear-heads. Most ancient Oriental armies had large bands of archers, either mounted or on foot. Their bows were generally simple arcs, made out of horn, bone, or wood. A volley from the archers usually preceded a hand-to-hand encounter, for they could frequently break up a charge at a distance. The warriors of Greece and Rome ordinarily scorned the bow. They prided themselves on their courage in close-range fighting, so the bow did not come into

[3] See pp. 55–57.

its own again until the break-up of the Roman Empire.

THE CROSSBOW—Two later forms of the bow held out against the first firearms for more than a century. The more common of these was the crossbow. In this, the old bow was now made of iron and fastened crosswise near the end of a staff. It appeared in Europe about 1100, and lasted until after 1500. The cord of the old, ordinary bow was simply pulled back by hand. This iron bow was so heavy that a crooked lever or little windlass had to be used for this purpose. It generally shot small bolts about ten inches long. Sometimes it was effective at 400 yards, but it was such a clumsy weapon that the rate of fire was slow.

THE LONGBOW—The crossbow's rival, the longbow, became known more suddenly than most new weapons. Of the primitive standard design and made of yew-wood, the longbow was about five feet high, and shot arrows a yard long. Sturdy yeomen, in their archery contests all over England, were achieving remarkable speed and accuracy with this weapon by 1300. The longbow could be deadly at 200 yards and could send off at least twenty aimed shots a minute. This record was not duplicated by firearms for a long time. The English first tried this bow on the Scotch, but it crashed its way into fame at Crécy in 1346. Here a small English army crushed the powerful cavalry of the French knights. One chronicler reported that the sky was darkened by the volleys of arrows from the longbows of the English yeomanry.[4] For nearly two more centuries, the bow was the principal missile weapon—the crossbow in Europe and the longbow in England. Even during the American Revolution, Benjamin Franklin

[4] See p. 53.

suggested that our troops be equipped with bows and arrows, but he may have been joking. The bow had passed into history by that time. So much for the "big three."

EARLY FIREARMS

"HAND GUNS"—Firearms did not make such a sudden dramatic appearance. We shall see, in the next chapter, that gunpowder was used first for the large guns or primitive artillery, between 1300 and 1350.[5] Smaller firearms are not mentioned until about 1375. "The ancestor of the musket and the rifle was a toy cannon, strapped to a pike handle." In the beginning, it was merely "a tube with a touch-hole, fired by a match." The lower end of the handle often rested on the ground to absorb the recoil, the handles were made shorter after 1400, and the soldier's shoulder received the "kick."

SLOW START OF FIREARMS—These early firearms made little impression on warfare. The longbow and the crossbow usually outclassed them in range, penetration, and rapidity of fire. Gunpowder is said to have made a first appearance at the battle of Crécy also, but it was far less sensational than the new longbow. The noise and smoke doubtless had some moral effect, and at least scared the horses. These original guns probably had their greatest influence in hastening the expansion of Europe over the world. The remarkable conquests of the Portuguese in India, and of the Spaniards in Mexico and Peru, owed much to these mysterious fire-tubes, which terrified the natives. Had the Europeans come with only swords, spears, and bows, they would have been met on more even terms.

[5] See p. 29.

Methods of Detonation

LOOSE MATCH—The early important changes in these crude hand guns centered about devices to produce a spark which would set off or "detonate" the powder charge. The loose match, or fuse, with which the first guns were ignited, was clumsy and got lost too easily, so several substitutes were tried in turn. Each of these created the spark *outside* the gun, setting afire loose powder in a little priming pan, attached to the barrel. This explosion was transmitted from the pan to the main powder charge inside the gun through a hole or "vent." All these early guns were loaded through the muzzle.

MATCHLOCK—The first improvement was the matchlock about 1500. This was a device which held the fuse firmly in a hollow frame or "lock" on the gun. The pressure of the trigger brought this match or fuse against the powder in the priming pan. It was hard to keep the match lighted even by blowing upon it.

WHEEL-LOCK—Friction was tried in place of the actual smoldering fuse. The wheel-lock, invented about 1600, was equipped with a little wheel with rough edges and a spring which had to be wound up carefully. When the spring was released the rough edges of the wheel struck against the side of the priming pan and made a spark, which ignited the powder. This was better than a lighted match, but it took too much time to wind up the wheel.

FLINTLOCK—By 1700, the wheel-lock had given way to the flintlock. In this new device, by the pulling of a trigger a piece of flint was brought against a piece of steel over the priming pan. The flintlock was in vogue until after 1800. We shall return to the subject of detonation later in connection with the percussion-cap. In the meantime, we can study the types of guns which were made possible by these various locks.

TYPES OF GUNS

ARQUEBUS—The arquebus was the first real hand gun which could be used with any kind of regularity. It was a small matchlock gun with a light, curved stock. It came on the scene about 1500 and lasted seventy-five years. The matchlock at that time was also used for the first horse-pistols.

MUSKET—Then came the musket. This was the general name for hand guns until after 1850. The original type was a heavy matchlock. It was more accurate than the arquebus, but it was clumsy and slow. The gunner had to go through ninety-nine separate motions to fire it once. The first muskets were so heavy that their muzzles had to be supported on a forked rest. Captain John Smith and Miles Standish have been pictured with these.

LIGHTER MUSKET—A lighter type of wheel-lock musket invented shortly after 1600 improved the regularity of the infantry volleys. The soldiers could move more rapidly with these lighter pieces, but it took time to wind the wheels. Consequently pikemen still had to be mixed in among the musketeers to protect them while they reloaded.[6]

THE BAYONET—The flintlock musket had come into general use by 1700. It could fire faster than its predecessors and was equipped with a bayonet, which fitted over the muzzle. The musketeer thus became his own pikeman. Every soldier had now the same weapon for both missile and shock action.

"BROWN BESS"—It is worth while to pause and examine "Brown Bess," as the English affectionately

[6] See p. 56.

FIGURE 2

FIREARMS

a. Primitive hand gun with loose match.
b. Musketeer with matchlock and rest.
c. "Brown Bess" musket.
d. Springfield rifle.

termed this old flintlock musket, for it remained the
chief weapon of most armies until a century ago.
The soldiers of Marlborough, Frederick the Great,
and Napoleon fought with it. It figured in our own

Revolution and in the War of 1812. It had a long, smooth-bore barrel and fired a round lead ball nearly an inch in diameter. Paper cartridges were generally used. They were simply pieces of paper inclosing the loose ball and powder. Some preferred to pour in the powder from a hollow cow's horn. As in all the early guns, the powder was dropped down the muzzle. The ball was then pushed home with the ramrod. It was practically impossible to do this lying down, so the soldier had to stand, presenting a full target to the enemy while he reloaded. Two shots a minute was the normal rate of fire until Frederick the Great changed the wooden ramrod for an iron one. This more than doubled the rate of fire, for the iron ramrod would not break in the hands of an excited soldier.

DEFECTS OF "BROWN BESS"—"Brown Bess" had several obvious defects. The chances were about one in ten that it would misfire—just like the modern cigarette lighter! Since the ignition was outside, the gun was sometimes useless in the rain. One always ran the chance of shaking the priming powder out of the pan. Even if the gun did discharge when the trigger was pulled, the bullet would not go far, and there was no telling what direction it would take. The ball did not fit the barrel tightly. This left extra space, which seriously affected the aim. The round ball might bound from side to side inside the barrel. It might come out high or low. The vent between the priming pan and the charge reduced the power of the gun by allowing the escape of some of the gas created by the explosion. As a result, the old smooth-bore, flintlock musket was seldom effective at more than 150 or 200 yards. That explains the frequent order: "Don't fire until you see the whites of their eyes." Shooting at longer ranges was simply a waste of ammunition. This short range must be kept in mind in studying the battles of the period 1700–1815, for it had a decided effect on the tactics of the infantry, cavalry, and artillery.

Six Important Changes

THE SIX STEPS—Several steps were necessary to transform "Brown Bess" into the present magazine rifle. The most important of these, in general order of development, were (1) the percussion-cap in place of the flintlock; (2) the rifled barrel instead of the smooth-bore; (3) breech-loading instead of muzzle-loading; (4) repeating mechanism instead of the single shot; (5) smokeless powder in place of black powder; and (6) the small-caliber elongated bullet in place of the large, round one.

REASONS FOR SLOW CHANGE—These changes spread over more than a half-century, from about 1825 to 1886. Several important wars were fought while the guns were in a state of transition. Some of these improvements had been known for three centuries. We wonder why they were not adopted sooner. One important reason was official conservatism, which resisted all change. Another main point was uncertainty as to the best type. The ordnance officers of every army had to consider many new inventions. Some of these worked, others would not. A government could not replace, or even transform the hundreds of thousands of guns in its armories overnight. The limitations of the manufacturing plants would prevent this, even if the expense did not. Usually, a new improvement was worked out in sporting guns before the armies adopted it. The sporting pieces were ordinarily so much better that gamekeepers would condemn a poor gun as "only fit for a sojer."

INVENTION OF PERCUSSION-CAP—The first step in the new changes was an improved method of creating a spark to set off, or detonate, the powder charge. This had been produced, as we have seen, by the loose match, the matchlock, the wheel-lock, and finally the flintlock. The new detonation came not from a lighted fuse or by friction, but from the sudden explosion of a chemical substance. Fulminate of mercury was discovered about 1799. Eight years later, a Scottish clergyman placed this fulminate in a tiny metal cap. This percussion-cap gave the necessary flash when struck a sharp blow. This was still ignition from *outside* the gun, however.

ADVANTAGES OF PERCUSSION-CAP—Before the musket was discharged each time, one of these caps had to be fitted onto a nipple outside the gun, in the same place as the old flintlock. The hammer, released by the trigger, struck this cap. The spark communicated as usual through the vent to the powder charge inside the barrel. There were three advantages of the percussion-cap over the flintlock. It was much less apt to misfire, it could be used in wet weather, and it increased the range of the gun somewhat by reducing the former escape of gas through the vent. On the other hand, it slowed up the rate of fire for a while, for the cap had to be placed carefully on the nipple. A flintlock musket could be converted easily to use percussion-caps. This transformation had taken place in most armies by 1835. The guns in our Civil War were provided with these external percussion-caps.

RIFLING—Next, the rifle came into general military use, about 1855, in place of the smooth-bore musket. *Rifling* was the name given to the series of straight or spiral grooves inside the barrel. These grooves made the path of the bullet more accurate

by sending it off in a definite direction instead of let-
ting it bounce around loose. The bullet had to fit
tightly into the gun, in order to follow the course
of the grooves. This increased the range of the
piece.

THE KENTUCKY RIFLE—The idea of rifling was
nothing new. It had been in use from time to time
for three whole centuries. The rifle had reached its
best development among the American frontiersmen, where it had a high reputation for accuracy.
They needed a sure gun against the Indians, and
could not trust their lives to the uncertainties of
"Brown Bess." The frontiersmen developed the
long-barreled "Kentucky rifle," with which they performed wonders. They could drive a nail or snuff
a candle with it at 100 paces. The British learned
the deadly effects of this backwoods rifle during the
Revolution. Perhaps the greatest victory won by
this weapon was the Battle of New Orleans in 1815.
There the frontiersmen picked off 2,000 of the redcoats with unerring aim. The American regulars,
fighting alongside them with their smooth-bore
muskets, did comparatively little damage.

THE MINIÉ RIFLE—One is surprised that such an
effective weapon was not adopted more quickly by
whole armies. The trouble with it was the difficulty
in loading a bullet that would fit tightly enough to
be affected by the rifling. This was remedied about
1854 by the invention by a Frenchman named Minié
of a bullet that would expand to fit the grooves.
Various armies immediately discarded the smooth-
bores for rifles. The rifle was deadly at 500 yards, in
contrast to the 200-yard maximum of "Brown
Bess." That is important to remember, for it affected tactics considerably. The extreme range was
now increased to about 1,000 yards.

RIFLES IN CIVIL WAR—This was the state of guns at the time of our Civil War. The United States had rifled its old muskets in 1857. Most of the troops had percussion-caps for their rifles. The guns of the two armies had almost no uniformity at first. Many States purchased rifles abroad to equip their troops or ordered them constructed on various models at home. One officer said that his men had seven types of rifles, requiring several separate kinds of ammunition. Finally, the North had its rifles bored out to a uniform caliber of .57 in., nearly double the present caliber. This matter of uniform caliber was a big forward step, because it greatly simplified the problem of ammunition supply.

BREECH-LOADING—The third change was breech-loading mechanism. This meant, of course, that guns were loaded from the rear or breech, instead of from the muzzle. It was, likewise, a very old principle, but the early breech-loaders were very complicated. One was never sure whether the force of the charge would come out at the muzzle or at the breech. The infantry of nearly every army continued to ram the powder and ball down the muzzle of the gun.

THE NEEDLE-GUN—A second discovery was necessary to make breech-loading practical. Some way had to be found to ignite the powder *inside* the gun. Hitherto, we recall, it had always been from the outside with the loose match, the matchlock, wheellock, flintlock, or percussion-cap. The Prussian army adopted as early as 1841 a breech-loading rifle, effective at 700 yards, and known as the *needle-gun*. For the first time, the detonation was inside the gun. This gun was a boon to the infantryman. He could at last load his gun easily while lying flat on the ground, instead of having to stand erect.

ADOPTION OF BREECH-LOADING—Strange to say, the Prussians had this breech-loader all to themselves for twenty-five years. The other armies did not seem to have taken it seriously. The needle-gun suddenly became famous at the battle of König-grätz (also called Sadowa) in 1866, where Prussia put Austria out of commission in a "seven weeks' war." The Union cavalry in our Civil War had eventually been provided with some breech-loading carbines, but the world did not awaken to the value of breech-loaders until that swift, dramatic Prussian victory in 1866. Then came a rush to get the new weapon. France had an even better breech-loader, effective at 1,300 yards, when she fought Prussia in 1870. The United States finally equipped all troops with breech-loading rifles in 1871.

REPEATING MECHANISM—Repeating mechanism was the fourth general improvement. It had always been necessary to reload guns after each shot. Now, several bullets could be loaded into the magazine at once. Colt, an American, perfected the revolver as early as 1835. The value of this "six-shooter" was realized in the Mexican War of 1846–1848. Colt also invented a repeating musket, but it was not a success. Another American, Winchester, introduced a much more practical repeating rifle during the Civil War. Metallic cartridges, containing bullet, powder, and detonator, made it more workable. The frontiersmen quickly took to the Winchester repeater for Indian fighting, but the regular armies were slow to adopt it. Its first regular use was by the Turks against Russia in 1877–1878. The Germans soon tried it, and in 1884 gave their troops Mauser repeaters. The home of the inventor—the United States—did not accept the repeating principle for its army for another eight years. Up to

1892, the American regulars still had the single-shot Springfields.

SMALL CALIBER—A Swiss officer, Major Rubin, turned out the first successful small-caliber rifle in 1883. The old muskets had fired heavy one-ounce balls. The Civil War rifles had a caliber or bore of .57 in. This was reduced to .45 in. in the 1871 Springfields. Rubin's rifles had a .30 in. caliber, which soon became the standard.

It was necessary to make the projectiles longer in order to give them sufficient weight to hold their course. A lead bullet, with the new heavy charge of powder, would have been stripped by the rifling, so the new bullets were given a covering of cupro-nickel. Their range and velocity were much increased. When they hit a man, they were apt to go straight through him with a small, clean hole. Unless they hit a vital spot, they made less serious wounds, naturally, than the jagged tearing of the older, larger balls. This feature, while more humane, made them less effective, for it was considered more advantageous to wound than to kill, as wounded men are an encumbrance to any army. It was found that clipping the nose of a bullet caused it to "mushroom" when it struck, leaving a gaping wound. Such "dumdum" bullets are now barred by international law.

SMOKELESS POWDER—The use of smokeless powder accompanied the introduction of the small-caliber rifle. We shall take up its properties more in detail in connection with artillery.[7] It exploded more slowly, giving more velocity to the bullet without dangerously increasing the pressure in the barrel.

[7] See p. 38.

Its tremendous tactical value was due to the obvious fact that a cloud of smoke no longer betrayed the exact position of the rifleman.

THE NEW RIFLES (1883–1892)—The combination of these three latest features—repeating mechanism, small caliber, and smokeless powder—led to rapid developments in several nations. The German Mauser, the French Lebel, the Austrian Mannlicher, and the British Lee-Enfield were among the models produced in rapid succession. The United States adopted the Danish Krag-Jörgensen rifle in 1892. It was the main infantry weapon in the Spanish-American War, though many of the volunteers and militia had only the old single-shot Springfields, which betrayed their presence with the smoke of black powder.

THE SPRINGFIELD RIFLE—In 1903, the United States Army introduced a rifle which many claim is the best of its kind in the world. It bears the name of Springfield, like many of its predecessors. The most noticeable innovation was its length. The new Springfield was several inches shorter than the Krag, and weighed less. This was a great relief to the heavily loaded infantryman. Its bullets carry several miles, and can be fired at a maximum rate of about twenty shots in sixteen seconds. Aimed shots, effective at a very long range, can be fired at the rate of one in two seconds. It is certainly a far cry from the "Brown Bess" of a century ago. She was not effective, it will be recalled, at more than 200 yards, nor capable of more than five shots a minute. This new Springfield has been the standard in the army since its adoption, but is now, in 1929, about to be supplanted by a semi-automatic rifle.

Machine-Guns and Automatic Rifles

DESIRE FOR INCREASED VOLUME OF FIRE—The gunmakers soon went further than the Springfield. Its rate of fire was limited to the speed with which a soldier could work the bolt action and pull the trigger for each separate shot. One purpose of infantry tactics is to produce the heaviest possible *volume* of aimed rifle-fire. The next step, therefore, was to get an automatic machine which could fire as many shots as a whole platoon or company with rifles.

THE GATLING GUN—A machine to meet these requirements was no new idea. Attempts to increase the volume of fire by mechanical devices had been made from the very first years of firearms. But no practical rapid-fire gun could be produced until breech-loading and metallic cartridges were invented. In 1862, Dr. Richard J. Gatling, an American, originated a successful rapid-fire gun consisting of ten parallel barrels, mounted on a carriage like a light field-gun. It was operated by turning a crank, and could fire about 350 shots a minute. It played little part in the Civil War. The United States government was slow about accepting it, but within ten years it had been introduced into several armies. It was more popular than the rapid-fire *mitrailleuse* prepared in secret by the French for their war with Prussia in 1870. The French tried to use the *mitrailleuse* as a substitute for artillery, but failed.

AUTOMATIC MACHINE-GUN—Sir Hudson Maxim did his bit to make war more deadly when he invented the automatic machine-gun. In this, it was no longer necessary to turn a crank to fire the gun. The gases caused by the explosion kept the mechanism going. The new gun had a cyclic rate of about 500 rounds a minute, using regular rifle ammunition. Such rapid firing naturally heated the barrel quickly, so cooling devices were necessary. Some guns were cooled by air, but a water-jacket outside the barrel became more common for these heavy machine-guns.

FAVORITE TYPES—The British Army introduced Maxim's machine-gun in 1889. Not long afterward, the French made use of the American Hotchkiss, while the United States Army had the Colt. The Germans had a gun known as the Schwarzlose.

DESCRIPTION OF HEAVY MACHINE-GUN—These early machine-guns weighed from fifty to seventy-five pounds, and rested on tripods of similar weight. They could be carried around by a small group of men, but horse, mule, or motor transportation was necessary for long distances. The Vickers gun next came on the scene. It weighed only thirty-eight pounds, and rested on a thirty-five pound tripod. This was the favorite model of "heavy" machine-gun during the World War. The still lighter American Browning machine-gun did not get into play until the end.

LIGHT MACHINE-GUN—The automatic principle was not limited to these "heavy" machine-guns. The World War saw two other types, the "light" machine-gun and the automatic rifle. Just before the war, Colonel Lewis, a retired American officer, invented a lighter machine-gun, about fifty-two inches long and weighing only about twenty-six pounds altogether. It rested on two slender legs, instead of requiring a heavy tripod. It was shaped like an ordinary rifle, except that the barrel was surrounded by a large jacket which cooled the gun with a steady stream of air. The ammunition was fed from little drums, each containing forty-seven rounds. It could fire 600 rounds a minute. In the World War, the British used great quantities of light Lewis machine-guns beside their heavy Vickers machine-guns. The Lewis guns were distributed freely among the infantry regiments. A squad or two in each platoon specialized in their use.

AUTOMATIC RIFLES—Finally the still lighter automatic rifle appeared. This gun could be fired from the shoulder like a regular rifle, instead of having to rest on the ground like the "heavy" and "light" machine-guns. The French had a poor gun of this type called the Chauchat. For want of something better, many of our infantry regiments were equipped with these until the last two months of the war. Then they received a weapon that surpassed all the others in lightness. It bore the name of the same Browning who had invented the lightest of the "heavy" machine-guns. This Browning automatic rifle weighed only about fifteen pounds, and it was just an inch or two longer than the Springfield rifle. It could fire nearly 500 rounds a minute. Also, when used as a semi-automatic rifle, it could fire 100 rounds a minute with a separate pull of the trigger for each shot. During its short service of two months at the end of the war, it was very successful. General Pershing refused to issue it for use until a large number were available, for fear the enemy might capture some and have them copied before the United States troops were themselves fully equipped. It is probably a gun of this type that will soon take the place of the Springfield rifle.

PRESENT TYPES—The infantry, therefore, have at present four different kinds of firearms. All have the same sort of ammunition. The difference is in *weight* and *rate of fire*. Lightest and slowest is the present regular rifle—less than nine pounds and capable at most of thirty shots a minute. As we said, it is soon to be discarded. Heavier and faster are the automatic rifle, the "light" machine-gun and the "heavy" machine-gun. Each of these four types has its special functions. The heavier guns are less portable, but they make up for this by their longer effective range, due to the chance for better aim.

AUTOMATIC PISTOL—The pistol has also undergone a change in recent years. The old "six-shooter" revolver eventually gave way to the automatic pistol. The "automatic" is easier to load and so can be fired faster, if not more accurately. It is used by cavalry, by artillery officers, and by others who do not carry the regular infantry weapons.

GRENADES

HAND-GRENADES AND RIFLE-GRENADES—The World War saw the revival of an old weapon, which had been neglected for nearly a century. This was the hand-grenade, a kind of small bomb which can be hurled a short distance before exploding. Grenades, filled with black powder, had once been fairly common. Grenadier companies held a position of honor in infantry regiments. But the grenade dropped almost completely out of warfare from 1800 to 1900. Its revival was due to the discovery of high explosives in 1886. It returned to favor in the Russo-Japanese War of 1904–1905. Then, in the first months of the World War, English soldiers turned their empty tin cans into crude bombs by filling them with explosives. Before long, these were developed into little iron grenades, the size and shape of a lemon. The release of the handle, in throwing, results in an explosion a few seconds afterward. They are quite important in trench warfare. There are also rifle-grenades, which are fired from the muzzle of a regular rifle.

THE GUN OF THE FUTURE—The last fifty years have thus seen tremendous changes in small arms. We have no reason to believe that they will stop here. No one can tell what the future holds, but developments will probably be in the direction of providing the individual soldier with an autoloading, semi-automatic rifle of smaller caliber (.267 in.). This will permit an increase in the volume of fire without the necessity, as is the case with the Springfield, of disturbing the aim by the operation of a bolt mechanism by hand each time a shot is fired. Such a gun represents the present climax of the long, slow evolution of the hand gun. Its bayonet makes it the equivalent of the ancient pike. The chances are that, in this era of rapid improvements, no single weapon will ever again enjoy the long vogue of "Brown Bess."

CHAPTER II

FROM CATAPULT TO "BIG BERTHA"

THE EVOLUTION OF ARTILLERY

Artillery is much younger than the other two main branches of the service, infantry and cavalry, or "foot and horse." Men could fight on foot or horse-back with simple weapons, but the rise of artillery depended upon complicated mechanical inventions. The word *artillery* has, of course, two meanings. It referred to the "big guns" themselves in contrast to "small arms." It also means the arm or branch of the service which uses the "cannon." We shall trace here only the growth of the *guns* themselves. Their *use* will be taken up in the following chapters.

SIEGE AND FIELD ARTILLERY—There have always been two main classes of artillery—heavy or siege and light or field. The heaviest guns have been used mainly in or against fortified places, as we shall see in connection with siege-craft.[1] They have been hard to move quickly. The lighter guns were made to be carried about with infantry and even with cavalry. Their use on the battle-field with the other two arms has increased steadily. This will be seen in the next chapter in connection with tactics.

PERIODS OF DEVELOPMENT—Artillery proper dates from the introduction of gunpowder about 1300, although the ancients had ingenious ma-

[1] See Chap. IV.

chines for throwing heavy weights. Since then,
its history falls into three big periods, which
closely follow the growth of small arms. The
guns of the experimental period, from about
1300 to 1600, were crude, imperfect, and lacking in uniformity. The middle period, from about
1600 to 1850, had a general type which changed
very little. The modern period has seen the influence
of the same inventions that transformed the smooth-
bore musket into the present rifle. The really vital
improvements in artillery date from about 1886.

PRE-GUNPOWDER "ARTILLERY"—In the pre-gunpowder days, certain weapons might be classed as
heavy artillery. They could throw weights with
force, for considerable distances. Simply large
frames of heavy timber, they worked in three different ways. The first class operated like a bow, a cord
being pulled back and then released. The most
famous of this style was the Roman catapult. In
others, such as the Roman ballista, the cord was
twisted instead of being stretched. The third class
used the principle of counterpoise. A heavy weight
was hung from one end of a long pole suspended
in the frame, while the other end—holding the missile—was pulled down toward the ground. Upon its
sudden release, the fall of the weight caused the missile to be discharged with great velocity. The chief
example of this kind was the medieval trebuchet.

These early pieces of artillery were ordinarily too
heavy and immobile for use on the battle-field. They
played, however, as we shall see, a big part in
sieges. [2] Some of them could hurl, with fairly accurate aim, stones weighing 600 pounds or more
for several hundred yards. The missiles sometimes
struck with enough force to batter down walls. One

[2] See pp. 72, 75.

such missile is said to have killed thirteen men. Even after the introduction of gunpowder, they were more useful than the first crude guns.

THE EXPERIMENTAL GUNPOWDER PERIOD

GUNPOWDER—No one knows who invented gunpowder. Modern historians generally reject the old idea that the Chinese used it for missile purposes centuries before Europeans knew it. About 1250, a monk, Roger Bacon, hinted at the formula of a mixture which would produce a flash and an explosion. This was what we know as gunpowder, though Bacon himself may not have been the "inventor." Saltpeter, sulphur, and charcoal, mixed together and then broken into small black grains, explode with a cloud of smoke if a spark is applied. We do not know who first employed it to propel missiles, but it was probably not so used until after 1300.

FIRST USE OF REAL GUNS—Artillery came on the scene about fifty years ahead of hand guns. An old manuscript of 1327 gives the first picture of a cannon. It shows why the earliest guns were called fire-pots or vases. The cannon was shaped like an earthen vase lying on its side upon a wooden frame, with a large, round body, narrow neck, and spreading mouth. The missile was a big iron-headed dart with the shaft padded to fit the muzzle. It is said that guns were used in an Italian siege in 1331. Vague accounts imply that they appeared even earlier. They gradually came into use during the Hundred Years' War from 1339 to 1453.

EARLY SIEGE GUNS—Artillery in its infancy was represented by too mongrel an assortment of guns to describe here fully. Siege guns became important more rapidly than field-pieces. The Turks, in their siege of Constantinople in 1453, supposedly had a huge gun which could fire 600-pound stone balls seven times a day. Many of these monsters of primitive siege artillery had calibers almost equal to those of our largest guns to-day. The powder was shoveled in loose with a long-handled ladle. These guns generally fired *stone* balls, because most of the gun barrels were merely strips of metal bound with hoops. A powder charge heavy enough to shoot iron balls would have burst their weak barrels. Siege guns had come to play an important part in history by 1500. They helped the kings of England, France, and other nations to break the power of their nobles by shattering castle walls which had been quite secure from attack.

CRUDE FIELD ARTILLERY—The lighter guns were of little importance until after 1500. They were mounted on stationary wooden frames at first. Once placed in action, they could be moved with only the greatest difficulty. Real field artillery—that is, easily movable pieces—could not become effective until the gun-carriage with wheels was invented. All through the sixteenth century, a bewildering variety of guns bore different names to denote their size and shape. There were bombards, falcons, falconets, minions, and sakers, to mention only a few from the long catalogue. Like the hand guns of the time, the moral effect of their noise and smoke was ordinarily more important than the physical effect of their shots. No such thing as accurate aim was possible. The gunners merely fired in a general direction and trusted to luck.

FIELD-PIECES, MORTARS, HOWITZERS, AND PROJECTILES OF THE MIDDLE PERIOD

INNOVATIONS OF GUSTAVUS—Shortly after 1600, artillery took on the general form which it kept with

little change until about 1850. This was partly the
work of the "father of modern warfare"—the Swedish king, Gustavus Adolphus. He reformed infantry,
cavalry, and artillery, to make them more mobile
and effective in battle, as we shall see in the study of
tactical formations. [3] He drew a sharp line between
heavy artillery, which has to move slowly, and field
artillery, which is light enough to be shifted about on
the battle-field. Gustavus limited guns to several
standard sizes, thus greatly simplifying the ammunition supply.

LOADING AND FIRING—We shall pause a moment
after these innovations of Gustavus Adolphus to
consider the guns of the period, as they remained
virtually the same down to the time of our Civil
War. This was also the era of the light musket—the
wheel-lock at first and later the "Brown Bess" flintlock. The cannon, like the muskets, were smooth-
bore muzzle-loaders.[4] The cartridges of wood, can-
vas, or paper were rammed home, followed by the
ball. The charge was ignited through the touchhole
or vent. This was filled with priming powder and
set off with a linstock or slow-match. Shortly after
1800, the percussion principle produced "friction
primers," which were inserted in the vent and fired
by pulling a cord, called the lanyard Two features
made the rate of fire slow. In the first place, after
each shot the piece had to be swabbed out, or the
smoldering remnants of powder and cartridge might
ignite the new charge prematurely. Second, the gun
usually recoiled several feet after each discharge.
It had to be dragged back into place and aimed
anew after the smoke cleared away. Also, the
loading from the muzzle, as we know from the mus-

[3] See p. 56.
[4] See p. 14.

ket, required the gunner to expose himself for each reloading.

SHORT RANGE AND INACCURACY—These old smooth-bore guns had the same deficiencies in *range* and *accuracy* as the contemporary musket. Few old field-pieces could do any damage at more than 1,600 yards, while their really effective range was seldom over 500. The siege guns had somewhat longer range. The balls, again like the smooth-bore musket, could not fit the barrel too closely or they would not go in and out easily. This left a margin of extra space, with considerable loss of gas from each discharge. This meant not only a shortened range, but also inaccuracy. The balls bounced around to such an extent inside that there was no telling whether they would leave the muzzle high or low. In addition, the aiming devices were too crude to secure any sort of accurate fire. Wedges were at first put under the breech to elevate the gun in order to obtain the proper range. Later the wedges were replaced by a screw. The gun was traversed, or moved from side to side, by ropes or a rod attached to the tail-piece or trail.

GUN-METAL—These early guns were ordinarily cast in one piece. The usual material for light guns was bronze or "gun-metal"—a mixture of brass with a little tin and sometimes zinc. The larger ones were often of cast-iron which was cheaper than bronze, but apt to be more brittle. Wrought-iron was tough, but it could not be molded with the same ease. The conventional gun-carriage with two wheels and trail was coming into general use. In transporting the gun, the trail was lifted and attached to the limber or light two-wheeled wagon containing an extra ammunition supply.

DESIGNATION OF SIZE—Military accounts of the period almost invariably refer to guns by the weight

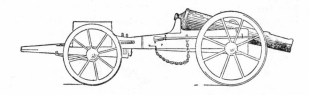

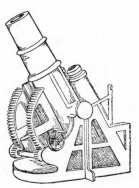

FIGURE 3

GUNS

a. Early cannon—about 1400.
b. Early mortar.
c. Smooth-bore field-piece with limber.
d. French "seventy-five."
e. Skoda howitzer.

of their solid projectiles. No longer were there culverins, minions, and sakers. They had become three-pounders, six-pounders, and twelve-pounders. These weights were based on the solid round iron shot, the common projectile. The following table will help one to visualize the standard sizes:

Weight of projectile in pounds	Diameter of bore of gun in inches	Weight of projectile in pounds	Diameter of bore of gun in inches
1	1.9	12	4.4
2	2.4	16	4.9
3	2.8	18	5.1
4	3.1	24	5.6
6	3.5	32	6.2
8	3.9	36	6.4
9	4.0	48	7.1

The bore of the gun was, of course, a little larger than the size of the ball. The length of the early guns was frequently twenty times their diameter, but this was gradually reduced to fifteen times or even less. Field artillery generally ranged between three-pounders and twelve-pounders, the eight-pounder or nine-pounder being the average size. Horse artillery, which accompanied cavalry, was particularly light.

MORTARS—The term *gun* is ordinarily applied to the conventional type of cannon which we have just described. Two other important kinds gradually appeared. The first of these was the mortar—a chunky little mass of iron with a total diameter far in excess of its bore. It was used mainly to hurl shells into the air at a much higher angle than that of the relatively flat trajectory of the regular guns. This made it valuable in siege work for firing over the walls of towns or into trenches.

HOWITZER—The mortar was, however, too heavy

to be moved easily. This fact led to the invention of the howitzer, a cross between the "gun" and the mortar. The howitzer was usually mounted on a carriage like a regular gun, but its barrel was considerably shorter, making it possible to fire a much larger projectile from a piece of the same weight. The range was naturally shorter. The howitzer became a regular part of the field artillery, and was also used by heavy artillery. The howitzer class was not always clean-cut, as it was sometimes hard to distinguish between howitzers and guns, or between howitzers and mortars. Howitzers and mortars were designated by their caliber rather than by the weight of their projectiles, because they fired shells rather than solid shot.

SHELLS AND CASE SHOT—Solid shot was gradually superseded by two other kinds of projectiles. A solid shot was effective only when it made a direct hit, or possibly caught something on the rebound. Shells and case shot were invented to increase the effectiveness of the projectile. Shells were hollow round shot filled with powder and exploded by a fuse. They were chiefly used against matériel such as buildings and wagon trains. Case shot or canister consisted of light containers filled with bullets, which scattered on leaving the gun. Grape-shot was of a similar nature, with a few large shot arranged in tiers. Case shot was ordinarily used against close masses of men, and was seldom effective at more than 400 yards.

SHRAPNEL—Shortly after the American Revolution, a British officer named Shrapnel combined the two ideas of shell and canister. It resulted in the deadly projectile which still bears his name. The bullets were enclosed in a light shell with a charge of powder which was exploded at the proper time by means of a fuse. This shell held the bullets together longer than the old canister, and scattered them with much force. A few other types of artillery projectiles, such as red-hot shot and chain-shot were used, but the "big three" of this middle period were *solid shot, shell,* and *canister.*

GRIBEAUVAL'S REFORMS—We have been describing the kind of artillery used in the wars of Louis XIV, Marlborough, Frederick the Great, and Napoleon, and in the American Revolution. The main improvements during the period were due to a French officer, Gribeauval, about 1770. He made the gun-carriages lighter and stronger, and further reduced the varieties of guns. His greatest achievement was in organizing artillery into efficient units. But the guns still remained the same old smooth-bore muzzle-loaders—quite harmless at a mile's range.

MODERN QUICK-FIRING, LONG-RANGE ARTILLERY

RIFLING—The improvements that led to our modern artillery started shortly after 1850. We remember that, in small arms, the rifle replaced the musket about 1855.[5] That same year the principle of rifling was applied to artillery by the British inventors, Whitworth and Armstrong. This rifling increased both range and accuracy, as in the case of small arms. The tightly fitting projectile lessened the escape of gas. This about doubled the effective range. No longer did a loose, round ball bounce around inside the barrel. The rifle projectiles were now pointed cylinders instead of round balls, and they started off in the right direction. We recall the popularity of the infantry's muzzle-loading rifle in our Civil War. Likewise, in field artillery one of the two

[5] See p. 17.

chief guns was the three-inch muzzle-loading rifled gun, which fired ten-pound cylindrical projectiles. The other common field-piece was the twelve-pounder, four and one-half inch smooth-bore "Napoleon" gun. These were preferred for rough country and short ranges. Their maximum range was 1,566 yards but they were uncertain at 600 yards. This was only half the range of the rifled guns. Smooth-bore howitzers were also used in large numbers. A visitor to Gettysburg can see dozens of specimens of these three kinds of field-pieces.

BREECH-LOADING—Breech-loading was the next step. It appeared about the same time as rifling, but, as in small arms, it was adopted more slowly. Too many breeches blew off at first. The Confederates had a few breech-loading rifled guns in the Civil War, just as the Union cavalry finally had breech-loading small arms, but these were exceptions. The Civil War was the last big contest of the muzzle-loaders. The Franco-Prussian War in 1870 saw the Prussians using only breech-loading rifled guns.

USE OF STEEL—A third change was the use of steel for the gun barrels. Bronze, the old favorite, was not hard enough for rifling. Cast-iron was too brittle. Wrought-iron was too difficult to work into shape. During the Civil War, many of the great pear-shaped siege pieces were of cast-iron with the breech reinforced by a band of wrought-iron, but this was only a temporary makeshift. The Prussians were using steel guns by 1870.

The improvement of artillery continued steadily. We shall not follow this progress "play by play" during the latter half of the century. It will be enough to see the results combined in the French "seventy-five" of 1897. This produced a veritable revolution in artillery. In the meantime, however, we must see how the chemists were contributing to the developments.

NEW EXPLOSIVE COMPOUNDS—Smokeless powder and military high explosive came on the scene in 1886, with Vieille's famous "Poudre B" and Turpin's "mélinite." The old black powder had been used both for propelling the missile and for bursting the shell. Now a special preparation for each purpose gave better results than the old black powder. The chemists produced *compounds* which gave a much more complete combustion than a mere mixture like black powder. The essential base of explosives is nitrogen. Saltpeter (potassium nitrate) provided this element in gunpowder. Nitric acid was now applied to various innocent substances to produce the deadly new explosives. In combination with cotton, it became nitrocellulose or guncotton. Applied to animal fats, it made nitroglycerine. With coal-tar, it produced picric acid and trinitrotoluene (TNT). The compound in each case was reduced into atoms so that combustion was complete.

SMOKELESS POWDER—Smokeless powder is a horny substance composed of either nitrocellulose or nitroglycerine. The white smoke which had accompanied the discharge of black powder resulted from incomplete combustion. Now there was simply a gas and a flash. Smokeless powder in the open air will burn as harmlessly as sealing-wax. Detonation by means of fulminate of mercury or electricity is necessary to make an explosion.

ITS INFLUENCE—The introduction of smokeless powder affected artillery in several ways. As in the case of small arms, it led to big improvements. Most important, perhaps, was the increased power it gave. It burned more slowly than the old black powder, giving a continuous shove to the projectile in the barrel of the gun, instead of a sharp blow. Its explosive pressure was several times greater. This helps to explain why the new artillery, like the new small arms, was to have so much longer a range. The smokeless quality of the new explosive enabled the gunners to fire again at once without having to wait for a cloud of smoke to clear away. This paved the way for the quick-firing gun. Naturally, smokeless powder did not reveal the position of the gun as black powder had done. The concealment of batteries soon became an art in itself.

HIGH EXPLOSIVES—High explosives were invented to produce an instantaneous and violent explosion. In this, they differed from the slow-burning smokeless powder. They are made of the same general materials as smokeless powder, with the addition of coal-tar derivatives, and greatly increase the destructive power of shells. Much larger holes could now be blasted than could have been with the old black-powder shells. Even the concussion alone could be destructive. Long experimentation was necessary in order to discover compounds that would not spoil and could be handled with comparative safety. Automatic devices replaced the lighted fuse for exploding the shell. Special names, such as mélinite, dynamite, lyddite, jovite, and TNT were given to various forms of high explosives.

REVOLUTION IN FORTIFICATION—Heavy artillery was first influenced by these new chemical compounds. By 1890, a profound change had been produced in the art of fortification. The long range of the guns and the terrific force of the high explosives showed that the old defenses were inadequate. We shall see in a later chapter how the concrete "ring" fortresses came as a result.[6]

QUICK-FIRING FIELD ARTILLERY—But even more

[6] See p. 82.

amazing was the revolution in field artillery. The
military world was startled in 1897 by the appearance of a new quick-firing French field-piece which
immediately put all other field artillery out of date.
The guns were made by the famous French munitions firm of Schneider at Creusot. A French engineer, Gustav Canet, probably did more than any
other man to bring about the changes. The various
new technical discoveries were combined, after long
experiments, with several very original devices.

THE FRENCH "SEVENTY-FIVE"—The new gun was
known as the "seventy-five" because its caliber was
seventy-five millimeters—about three inches. Its
most striking feature is its fixed position. The carriage remains stationary after the first shot, the
gun barrel itself recoiling in a fixed cradle. It is
easily pushed back into place by hydraulic or pneu-
matic pressure. Hitherto, the gunners had had to
stand clear of the gun when it was fired, for the
whole piece recoiled several feet and had to be
pushed back into place after each shot. Now the
gun-crew can remain steadily with the piece. They
are protected from enemy rifle-fire by a large shield.
Nor do they have to aim the piece anew after each
shot. The telescopic sight, attached to the carriage,
remains fixed on the target or aiming-point. The
rate of fire is thus much increased. The old guns
were doing fast work if they fired two shots a minute.
The new "quick-firing" pieces are capable of twenty
to thirty rounds a minute. The force of the smokeless powder gives a tremendous increase in range.
The old guns, we recall, had scarcely been able to
reach a mile, and were effective only at a fraction of
that distance. Smokeless powder gave the new pieces
an extreme effective range of 6,000 yards, more than
three miles. This was later increased to 7,500 yards

and will soon probably exceed 10,000. Improved sighting and aiming apparatus enables the gunners to attain accuracy at these new long ranges. The new guns, moreover, are capable of "indirect fire." The crews of the old guns had to see the actual target at which they were firing. The new artillery is directed from an observation post, and so can play upon targets invisible to the gunners.

Other new features are embodied in these guns. They are made entirely of steel, which is often hardened with nickel or some other alloy. The inner bore of the gun is usually a separate steel tube, and a hardened jacket is fastened outside of this. The larger tubes are sometimes wound with wire. Most of the smaller guns use fixed ammunition with the projectile, the powder charge and the detonator all combined in a copper cartridge case similar to the small-arms cartridge. Such a case would be too bulky for the larger guns. Round shot has passed away. The projectiles are cylinders, usually tapering at one end. The shell for the "seventy-five," for instance, is about three inches in diameter and nearly a foot long, weighing about sixteen pounds. The two common types of field artillery projectiles are shrapnel and high-explosive shells. Gas-shells also came into use during the World War.

WORLD-WIDE ADOPTION—The rest of the military world saw that France had stolen a march on them with the "seventy-five." They knew that their artillery was completely outclassed. The next few years saw all the principal nations adopting field-guns built on similar plans. The United States developed the three-inch gun; England, the eighteen-pounder; Germany, the "seventy-seven"; and so on around the world. These guns all approximated the French "seventy-five" in caliber, in range, and in weight of projectile. The French naturally had not revealed any more secrets than they could help. Their somewhat improved "seventy-five" was *the* field-piece of the World War.

"GUNS" AND HOWITZERS—These light guns were by no means the only new ones. Similar principles were applied to larger forms of artillery, which we cannot describe here in detail. They fall into the two general types of the old artillery—"guns" and howitzers. The "gun" proper has a long barrel and a long range. The howitzer is shorter, fires at a higher angle and has a shorter range. Its value lies in its ability to hurl a heavier projectile than a "gun" of the same weight into areas which cannot be swept by fire from the flat-trajectory guns.

CLASSIFICATION OF MODERN ARTILLERY—We find these two types side by side in the various sizes. As a companion to the "seventy-five," a howitzer of about 4.7 inches was invented. It is mounted on a similar carriage and is moved with the same speed. This and the "seventy-five" form the light field or divisional artillery. The next class consists of medium field or corps artillery with a 4.7-inch gun and a six-inch howitzer. These have considerable mobility, but are naturally slower than the divisional pieces. Then comes the heavy field artillery. Its guns are about six inches, and its howitzers about eight inches in caliber.

The howitzer in each case has the caliber of the gun in the next higher class, but weighs approximately the same as the gun in its own class. The larger pieces have increased range with lessened mobility. The substitution of motor tractors for horses has, of course, increased the mobility of artillery in general.

"BIG GUNS"—Above these regular classes are special large pieces of particular interest. For battle-ships, coast-defenses, and railroad artillery, "guns" with a length equal to fifty calibers or more have been perfected. Typical of these are the United States fourteen-inch coast-defense guns with ranges between twenty and thirty miles, depending on the weight of their projectiles. Such guns wear out quickly because of the high charge needed to fire them. The record for long-range artillery was established in 1918 by the German guns which bombarded Paris with 265-pound shells from a distance of seventy-six miles.

HEAVY HOWITZERS—Heavy howitzers are important in the reduction of fortresses, as we shall see in a later chapter. The problem with such guns is transportation and emplacement. As some heavy pieces are mounted on railroad trucks, their mobility is naturally limited to railway lines. The Skoda gunworks in Austria perfected a heavy siege howitzer which could be carried in three motor trucks at a fair rate of speed, and assembled very quickly. Some were rushed to the siege of Liége in 1914 and they quickly crumbled the city's powerful defenses.[7] Heavier and even more powerful were the Krupp "Big Berthas," with which the Germans battered Antwerp later that fall. These monsters had a caliber of forty-two centimeters (16.5 in.) and could fire 1,570-pound shells nearly six miles, but needed concrete emplacements. During and since the World War, the distinction between "guns" and howitzers has become less clean-cut. The howitzers have been lengthened from twelve to twenty-five calibers, with a great increase in range, while the guns have been arranged for higher angles of fire.

RECENT INNOVATIONS—The World War produced a few particular innovations in artillery out-

[7] See p. 301.

side the conventional type. Anti-aircraft artillery
is one of these. As the name implies, such guns are
capable of firing shells to a great height. They are
equipped with head shields and controlled by ingenious electrical devices for following the target.
The trench mortar, another product of the war, is
useful for throwing weights short distances.

EXTENSIVE USE IN WORLD WAR—The use of artillery in the World War has occasioned some surprising figures. Experts have estimated that the Allied
artillery on the Western Front in the last year of
the war fired 152,515,000 rounds, whereas the
Union artillery fired less than 2,000,000 rounds in
the heaviest year of the Civil War. In the four-hour
artillery preparation at St. Mihiel alone, the American guns fired more than 1,000,000 rounds. It was
found that the average field-gun in 1918 fired thirty-
three rounds a day, while the daily average for the
Civil War was four rounds. The total cost of artillery ammunition in the World War was reckoned at
thirty billions of dollars; in the Civil War, at only
ten millions.

The last two generations have seen the power of
artillery tremendously increased. Its problem has become infinitely more complex. The growth has been
more radical than it was during the whole two previous centuries. Gunners trained under Gustavus
Adolphus in 1630 could have handled Napoleon's
guns in 1815 with no great difficulty. Civil War artil-
lerymen suddenly transplanted into a battery of
"seventy-fives" would be bewildered and useless.
When one hears of guns firing seventy-six miles and
of anti-aircraft "Archies" picking targets out of the
clouds, the guns of Gettysburg seem almost as obsolete as the culverins and bombards of Columbus's
childhood.

CHAPTER III

MASSES AND THIN LINES

THE EVOLUTION OF TACTICS

Tactics as well as weapons must be studied to understand how armies fought. The word *tactics* is associated with the *battle-field* itself, in contrast to *strategy*, which deals with getting men to the battle-field under the most advantageous conditions. The management of the battle as a whole is "grand tactics," while the particular fighting methods of individual units comprise "minor tactics." We shall discuss here the history of both, leaving siege operations for the next chapter. During long periods of history, several distinct tactical formations have been in vogue. This chapter will take up a few of the most important, showing how certain problems kept cropping up again and again.

Rival Elements Influencing Tactics

THREE RIVALRIES—We must have in mind three rivalries in studying tactics: solid mass formations against the more elastic, mobile ones; shock versus missile action; and the shifts between infantry, cavalry, and artillery. The history of tactical formations is confusing because all three disputed issues are apt to be involved in every change. We have to watch for all these elements at every turning-point.

MASSES VS. THIN LINES—The two types of formation—masses and thin lines—have contended for supremacy down through the centuries. The reason for the heavy, solid mass lay in the crushing weight of its onslaught and its invincibility as long as it was unshaken. The other kind was more flexible and mobile, requiring better soldiers. It lacked weight, but could be maneuvered around more rapidly and so adapted itself better to the ever-changing conditions on a battle-field. We shall center our attention on a few outstanding examples of each sort. The principal mass formations were the Greek phalanx, the medieval cavalry charge, the Swiss phalanx, the Spanish square, and the French perpendicular attack. The leading flexible formations were the Roman legion, the innovations of Gustavus Adolphus, the "thin-line attack," the skirmish line, the advance by rushes and, finally, "infiltration." The flexible, mobile formations have proven far more successful in the long run.

SHOCK VS. MISSILE ACTION—Second, we have had both shock and missile action since the primitive days of club and rock. Some men wanted to fight at close quarters, while others preferred to keep the enemy at a distance. Many of the earliest armies relied heavily on their archers, slingers, and other missile fighters. Then came a very long period of shock action, when hand-to-hand encounters were considered the only heroic and effective way to fight. Gunpowder revived missile action. It has grown steadily more important for the last five centuries. To-day the artilleryman rarely sees the men upon whom he fires, and even the machine-gunner cannot ordinarily distinguish between individuals. War has become impersonal. The "cold steel" of the bayonet is still used for final decisive action, but rifles, machine-guns, and long-range artillery keep the combatants farther and farther apart.

THE THREE ARMS—Third, we must also take into account the shifts in importance between infantry, cavalry, and artillery. Infantry and cavalry—"foot and horse"—have been the two major branches or "arms" of the service in history. Artillery, the third principal arm, is of comparatively recent date, as we saw in the last chapter. Infantry and cavalry, on the other hand, have been side by side in most of the great armies. They have taken turns, during five long periods of history, in being the most important. The earliest armies were purely infantry. Then came a thousand years of cavalry supremacy. Infantry returned to the first place with shock action under the Greeks and Romans. During the middle ages, the man on horseback became the real power for another thousand years. Infantry has been the backbone of modern armies for the past six centuries, while artillery has, at the same time, gradually crowded cavalry out of second place.

INFANTRY—Infantry is the most versatile of all the arms. It can deliver destructive fire from a distance, and also give the shock of cold steel at close quarters. It has sufficient mobile power for the offensive, and can also stand firm on the defensive. Cavalry can travel faster and, formerly, dealt a more crushing blow. Artillery is more powerful in missile action. But neither cavalry nor artillery can do much beyond its own specialty. The infantry has usually been the most numerous and the hardest-worked part of an army. We can understand, therefore, why one of Napoleon's marshals exclaimed, "L'infanterie; c'est l'armée!"

CAVALRY—Cavalry used to have two functions.

It often decided the outcome of a battle, carrying the field by a charge, from its conventional battle position on the flanks of the infantry lines. Its superior mobility made it also invaluable for reconnaissance. Modern warfare has lessened these two main activities. Cavalry charges have become suicidal against modern rifles, machine-guns, and artillery. Much of the scouting is now performed more quickly and more thoroughly by aviation. Cavalry is still useful for screening an advance and for some reconnaissance work. It may be helpful in demoralizing a routed enemy. Its particular value is for fighting in large, unsettled regions. The horseman is not relatively as important as he was a thousand years ago.

ARTILLERY—Artillery, on the other hand, has increased tremendously in its tactical importance during the last two centuries, becoming essential as a supporting arm. It has sometimes won battles, but it could never win them alone. Infantry, or possibly cavalry, must be on hand to utilize the victory. One can find armies with nothing but infantry or nothing but cavalry, but never an army with only artillery.

HEAVY AND LIGHT TYPES—Infantry, cavalry, and artillery have all been distinguished as "heavy" and "light" according to their equipment and functions. Heavy infantry was used at close quarters for hand-to-hand fighting. Light infantry specialized in missile action. Heavy cavalry was used for charging, while light cavalry was developed for scouting and for rapid movements to cut off the enemy. Heavy artillery was principally engaged in siege work, and will be discussed elsewhere.[1] The only artillery with which we are concerned here is the light field in its co-operation with the other two arms.

[1] See Chap. IV.

ANCIENT ARMIES

INFANTRY AT FIRST—The earliest armies were composed solely of infantry for the simple reason that they had no horses. We have a picture of perhaps the earliest regular troops on record. They lived around 5,000 years ago in the Tigris-Euphrates Valley. They were heavy infantry in close formation, armed with spears and shields. About a thousand years later, a wild tribe from the eastern hills introduced the horse and defeated this infantry. The military value of the horse was thus quickly recognized.

PRIMITIVE CAVALRY—The horses used in early armies were very small compared to the average of horses to-day. They served principally to draw chariots for shock action. Sometimes they were assisted by elephants to add to the weight of the shock. Armed men were later mounted on horseback; generally as light cavalry. One writer has pointed out that, until stirrups and high-pommeled saddles were introduced, riders could be pulled off their horses too easily for shock work.

CAVALRY THE "CRACK" ARM—The cavalry became the cream of the armies of the Egyptians, Assyrians, Persians, and other ancient Oriental monarchies. It attracted the wealthiest, most important men, and those who could afford the costly equipment. The rest of the armies, more numerous but less effective, often formed an irregular mob of light infantry. They were usually archers or slingers, and suffered the heaviest casualties.

THE GREEK PHALANX—Heavy infantry came back for another nine centuries about 500 B. C. when the Greeks turned back the Persian invaders. The Greeks had the first important tactical formation—the phalanx. It was a solid mass of heavy infantry for shock action, in sharp contrast to the loose infantry hordes of the previous empires. The high quality of the Greek citizen-soldiery made them brave hand-to-hand fighters. From four to thirty ranks of foot-soldiers stood shoulder to shoulder in continuous lines in the solid, regular mass of the phalanx. Well protected by helmet, breastplate, and shield, and armed with both spear and sword, they made their phalanx a formidable body. Their front was one bristling, unbroken array of spears. This formation was almost invincible, provided the soldiers had time to form into its "hedgehog" mass.

IMPORTANCE UNDER ALEXANDER—The Greeks continued to improve the phalanx after their first great victory over the Persians at Marathon in 490 B. C. It reached its height under Alexander the Great of Macedon about 330 B. C. He conquered the whole Eastern world without losing a battle.[2] He had some heavy cavalry and some light infantry with missile weapons, but the backbone of his army was the heavy, solid, infantry phalanx. Under him, it was ordinarily sixteen deep, with the men standing so close together that six rows of their twenty-foot pikes stuck out beyond the front rank.

THE ROMAN LEGION—The next famous tactical formation was the more flexible Roman legion, also of heavy infantry. It supplanted the solid Greek phalanx, just as "open football" has taken the place of the solid "flying wedge" of thirty years ago. The early Roman citizen-soldiers, like the Greeks, were good at close combat. Their legion could be ma-neuvered more easily than the heavy phalanx. In con-trast to the continuous line of the Greeks, the legion was divided into several units, with spaces between

[2] See p. 129.

them. The Romans, in other words, gave the phalanx "joints" in order to secure flexibility. Each soldier had twice as much room for individual action.

TACTICS OF THE LEGION—The early legion had thirty units or maniples of about a hundred men each, arranged in three lines about 250 feet apart. This was changed about 100 B. C. to ten units or cohorts of 600 men each. The green men were put in the front line so that dependable veterans would be behind them in case they should break. The legionary was armed much like the Greek infantryman, but his spear or *pilum* was shorter—about six or seven feet long.[3] Ordinarily the units hurled their spears at fairly close range and then hacked their way through the enemy with short swords or *gladii*. The cavalry was used as an auxiliary arm on the wings of the infantry to complete the rout of an enemy or for scouting.

LEGION VS. PHALANX—With this successful legion, the Romans conquered in every direction until their rule was established over most of the known world. The legion and the phalanx actually came face to face in 197 B. C. at the battle of Cynoscephalæ—a disaster for the phalanx. The Greeks might have been all right if they had had time to form their solid front, but the mobile Romans caught them coming up a hill in broken formation.

DECLINE OF THE LEGION—The legion deteriorated in the latter days of the Roman Empire. Foreign mercenaries, especially barbarians, took the place of the earlier sturdy citizens. These mongrel bands, gathered from the ends of the earth, were a very inferior lot. They grumbled at the long, fast marches in heavy equipment. They carried stakes to

[3] See p. 6.

break the force of enemy charges. To avoid fighting at close quarters, missile weapons were revived.
Discipline was relaxed. The legionaries lazily settled
down in scattered frontier garrisons, and raids in
between these posts were repelled by cavalry, rather
than by the legions. The end of the Roman legion
came in dramatic fashion at the battle of Adrianople
in 378 A. D. Tired by a long infantry fight, the legions
were unexpectedly struck in the rear by a body of
Gothic horsemen. This won the day for the Goths.
The Romans were completely routed, and their emperor was slain.

A Thousand Years of Cavalry

CAVALRY PARAMOUNT IN MIDDLE AGES—The triumph of the Gothic horsemen started a thousand
years of cavalry superiority. The man on horseback
was the principal military feature during most of
the middle ages. This does not mean that the infantry disappeared at once. It lasted as the sole arm
in some regions. In fact, the legion itself was preserved for several centuries in the Byzantine Empire.
Also in many a medieval army the infantry outnumbered the cavalry two or three to one. But, like
the ancient Oriental infantry, it was generally a
loose horde of those men who could not afford a
horse and armor. A horseman's equipment frequently
cost as much as a small farm. The mounted knight
was thus *the* soldier. The terms *cavalier* and *chivalry*
indicate the high position of cavalry.

MEDIEVAL TACTICS—No standard tactical formation such as the phalanx or legion was produced during the middle ages. But we might class the heavy
cavalry charge of the mounted knights as a third
major tactical formation. This depended more on

the weight of its shock than on ability to maneuver, so it was a return to the solid mass type. Two bodies of well-armored knights would charge each other. Their purpose was to unhorse their adversaries with lances in the heavy shock. Long swords, maces, or battle-axes were kept as reserve weapons in case lances were splintered and fighting at close quarters was necessary. Occasionally, the horsemen dismounted for battle to fight as infantrymen, while the real infantry would support them with missile action.

Medieval fighting can be best studied in the Crusades, those great European expeditions against the Saracens in the Eastern Mediterranean region between 1096 and 1270. The cavalry was, as usual, the best part of the crusading armies. Many zealous Crusaders, however, could not afford horses. Others lost their mounts on the long, hard trip. So the infantry was apt to outnumber the cavalry. It has been pointed out that the Crusaders were apt to be successful as long as they used cavalry and infantry together. The infantry formed a solid mass upon which the horse could retire. Several of their defeats took place when their cavalry or infantry were caught alone by the Saracens.

THE REVIVAL OF INFANTRY IN THE FOURTEENTH CENTURY

LONGBOW AND PIKE—The thousand years of unquestioned cavalry superiority ended shortly after 1300. This was just the period when gunpowder was introduced, but, strange to say, it was not firearms that broke the rule of the horseman. Sturdy infantrymen, armed with the English longbow or the Swiss pike, did that. As we have seen, one turning-point

against cavalry was the dramatic victory of the longbow at the battle of Crecy in the Hundred Years'
War, but no new tactical formation was created by
this victory.[4]

MASS SHOCK FORMATIONS—The second blow at
cavalry, with the pike, actually brought back infantry
superiority. The pike consequently interests us more
here, since its appearance led to two important new
formations, which held the stage, in turn, for three
centuries. The idea of the Greak phalanx was revived in the Swiss phalanx, which was later modified into the Spanish square. The solid infantry mass,
relying on weight rather than mobility, was back
again. The longbowmen had defeated cavalry too, of
course, but being purely missile fighters, they were
not self-sufficient. Consequently it remained for the
revived phalanx to restore infantry leadership.

THE SWISS PHALANX—The Swiss phalanx could
look out for itself and win victories as long as its
ranks stood fast. This idea came from the Swiss,
because they were poor and hardy mountaineers.
Not only could they not afford horses and armor,
but cavalry would have been of little use in their
mountains anyway. They adopted this infantry form
to defend their liberty against their oppressive Austrian overlords. Their phalanx, like its Greek pred-
ecessor, had deep, solid ranks, protected by long
pikes. Their constant drill enabled them to advance
in perfect order. Through two centuries, this phalanx
was successful against mounted knights. Before long,
it spread beyond Switzerland. Various rulers began
to copy the formation or to hire Swiss troops for
their armies.[5]

THE SPANISH SQUARE—The Spanish square re-

[4] See p. 9.
[5] See p. 99.

placed the Swiss phalanx about 1525 and was domi-
nant for almost exactly 100 years. It helped make
Spain the first military power in Europe in the sixteenth century. It resembled the Swiss phalanx in
that it was also a heavy "human fortress." But it
did not depend on pikes alone. A typical square was
forty or fifty men wide and equally deep. The pikemen would be in the front ranks to withstand cavalry
charges. Behind them would be ranks armed with
shields and short swords like Roman legionaries. If
these men found a break in the "hedgehog" array
of the enemy pikes, they could hew their way to
success through the pikemen. While the square relied
chiefly on shock action, it also had some musketeers,
perhaps six deep, stationed at each corner. Firing
was so slow a process that the men would file to the
rear to reload. It has been said that the filing to
the rear interested them more than the firing. To
form a battle array, several of these huge squares
were often arranged in checker-board formation for
mutual support. They were assisted by the cavalry,
who now had learned a pleasant use for the newly
invented wheel-lock pistols. Instead of charging with
lances as before, all that the horsemen had to do was
ride up to the enemy, discharge their pistols, and
ride off to reload.

REFORMS OF GUSTAVUS ADOLPHUS

THE RETURN OF FLEXIBILITY—The slow, solid
Spanish square met defeat at the hands of the Swedish king, Gustavus Adolphus, at Breitenfeld in 1631,
during the Thirty Years' War. The evolution of
tactics had now come to a significant turning-point.
The vogue enjoyed by heavy mass formations, ever
since the close of the Roman Empire, was over. This

time the legion was to be the model. For the three centuries after Gustavus, progress continued almost unbroken toward flexible formations, which moved faster, maneuvered more easily and delivered a heavier fire. No wonder that Gustavus is called the "father of modern warfare."

THE THREE ARMS IMPROVED—His improvements affected all three branches of the army. In the infantry, he made the musket more important than the pike. Groups of musketeers, six men deep, were the main part of his line. Their guns were lighter, faster, and more effective than the old ones. In front of the musket units were placed detachments of pikemen to make or repel charges. While Gustavus thus emphasized missile action in the infantry, he did the reverse in the cavalry, where he revived the old shock function. His horsemen charged directly on the enemy with sabers, instead of merely firing pistols from a safe distance. Finally, Gustavus made his artillery lighter and more mobile. Field-pieces were brought right into the front line to be used against the solid masses of the squares. Then, and for long afterward, these lighter field-pieces were attached to the infantry units rather than to the artillery. The Spanish square did not long survive these innovations in the direction of flexible, mobile formations.

EIGHTEENTH CENTURY FORMATIONS

FREDERICK THE GREAT—A century of experimentation on Gustavus's new ideas followed. They were crystallized into the seventh great formation—the "thin-line" attack—in the campaigns of Frederick, the great Prussian king of the middle eighteenth century. The "thin-line" attack combined two noteworthy principles—effective fire and a steady advance. Frederick's infantry could deliver a much heavier fire than had been possible during Gustavus's time. First, the introduction of the bayonet about 1700 had made the musketeer his own pikeman. It was no longer necessary to tie up a third of the infantry for shock action alone, in order to protect the musketeers. Second, the musket was much improved, and third, Frederick's iron ramrods doubled the rate of fire.

"THIN-LINE" TACTICS—With this more effective fire, Frederick next combined a steady advance. He accomplished this by severely drilling and thoroughly training his infantry. His lines of infantry deployed from column about a thousand yards from the enemy. Then they advanced, in step to music, in a parade-ground formation of two or three long lines, three ranks deep and 250 yards apart. They did not fire until within a hundred yards of the enemy, where their shots would take effect. Then the companies would deliver volleys in rapid succession and advance a few more paces. Finally, if the enemy still stood its ground, they would rush the positions with bayonets. Frederick's mobile troops were so well in hand during the Seven Years' War that, at Leuthen in 1757, he was able to roll up the left wing of a much larger Austrian army by an oblique attack. This "thin-line" attack was Frederick's main contribution to the art of war. It was copied by most other nations and had a permanent influence on tactics.

TYPES OF CAVALRY—But infantry "thin lines" did not win his victories alone. Cavalry also played a significant part in more than one of them. At Rossbach in 1757, the Prussian cavalry charge was largely responsible for his brilliant victory over the French. Cavalry by this time had fallen into several standard classifications. Its battle position was still on the flanks of the infantry. The heavy cavalry were known as *cuirassiers* because of the cuirass or breastplate which they wore. They specialized in shock action —the cavalry charge on the field of battle. The light cavalry bore the name of *hussars*. They wore no armor and traveled faster. Their chief function was scouting and detached action. The *dragoons* were a type of mounted infantry. They frequently fought on foot, using their horses principally to move rapidly from place to place. Finally, there was the so called *partisan* cavalry, informally organized and loosely disciplined. Like the hussars, they were valuable for reconnaissance and independent service. Typical of these partisans were the Russian Cossacks, the Croats in the Austrian Army, and our own Southerners under Marion and Sumter in the Revolution, and Ashby and Mosby in the Civil War. They were destructive to enemy communications, but were less dependable than the three regular kinds on the battle-field. Frederick used those three—cuirassiers, dragoons, and hussars—for well-disciplined shock action on the battle-field along with his "thin-line" attacks.

SKIRMISHERS—The eighth step in tactical formations came from America. It was the light skirmish line, sent in advance of the formal line attack to "feel out" the enemy and prevent surprise. In 1755, the British general, Braddock, found the "thin line" suicidal against the French and Indians in the forests near Fort Duquesne. His men marched to the attack, helpless targets for their hidden enemies. Soon after, in the Revolution, British regulars suffered time and again from similar irregular attacks of the American minute-men and frontier riflemen, who fought from behind trees and stone walls. On the other hand, the well-trained "thin-line" attack of the regulars had the decided advantage in pitched battles. The British soon added a so-called "light infantry" to their regular line infantry so that they would be ready for hidden attacks as well as for fighting in the style of Frederick the Great. French officers, over here also, saw the wisdom of having this skirmish line go in advance, and introduced it into their army on their return. In this way, skirmishers spread through European armies and became a permanent feature. The skirmish line was extremely loose and mobile—a far cry from the Spanish square and a long step toward more flexible formations.

THE PERPENDICULAR ATTACK—Shortly after our Revolution, these skirmishers were combined with a solid formation, which seemed a return to old mass tactics. This was the "perpendicular attack," used in the armies of the French Revolution and Napoleon between 1793 and 1815. The army of the French revolutionists was the first of the great national armies. It was made up not of a few regulars, but of hundreds of thousands of wholly untrained and enthusiastic patriots. The "thin-line" attack was out of the question because of the high discipline essential for its success. Forced to find a substitute, the French returned somewhat to the old phalanx principle, but modified it by the skirmish line. The skirmishers went ahead to "feel out" the enemy positions. The main attack was then made in columns of battalions—not "thin lines." They did not deploy until the last minute, so that the recruits were carried along by the momentum of the mass, and their lack of training became less of a hindrance. The sheer force of numbers alone was often enough to carry the "thin" enemy lines.

NAPOLEON AND ARTILLERY—In addition to the development of this temporary infantry formation, field artillery was made of real tactical importance during these wars. Napoleon started his career as an artillery officer, and he strongly believed in the value of "a whiff of grape-shot." The most striking thing he did was to concentrate guns in large groups. No longer were they scattered among the infantry regiments. Instead they were put in artillery brigades, which stayed directly under the general's control. He could thus center a heavy fire whenever and wherever he chose. Part of this reorganization had been started by Gribeauval,[6] as we saw, some time before. Napoleon steadily increased the use of artillery, particularly in his later campaigns after his infantry surplus had been cut down by heavy casualties. Artillery was at last as important as cavalry. From Napoleon's time onward, one speaks of "the combined tactics of the three arms."

NAPOLEONIC TACTICS—The formula for Napoleon's later battles has been described as follows: A preliminary attack was made by skirmishers all along the enemy line to "feel out" any point of weakness. When that was found, Napoleon concentrated his guns there. The field-pieces were brought up to a point 400 yards from the enemy—quite out of range of the "Brown Bess" muskets. With grape and canister, this artillery literally blasted a hole through the opposing regiments. Then cavalry and infantry were sent through this hole to finish up the job.

A CENTURY OF TRANSITION

VARIED TACTICS IN CIVIL WAR—The nineteenth century was a period of constant change in all phases

[6] See p. 36.

of military art, caused by the radical improvements in weapons.[7] Our Civil War, coming as it did in the 1860's, is the best example of this transition. The old conventional tactics were upset in this general upheaval, leaving a mongrel assortment. Eighteenth century formations lasted on almost unchanged, alongside features which were considered novelties in the World War.

CIVIL WAR INFANTRY TACTICS—The infantry in the Civil War borrowed two formations from the past. The standard infantry attack of the war was an informal version of Frederick's "thin line," with the addition of skirmishers. Some generals copied instead the French "perpendicular attack," but the rifled artillery raised havoc with such dense masses. A third and the most successful infantry attack, however, was a foretaste of modern tactics. In this, the enemy was approached by a series of rapid *rushes* instead of a steady advance. These halted each time the enemy fire grew too hot, and went forward again as soon as it slackened. Another hint of the future was the infantry's readiness to "dig in" for temporary shelter from rifle bullets.[8]

CIVIL WAR CAVALRY AND ARTILLERY—Cavalry had an exceptionally prominent part in this war. One general said that it "could fight anywhere except at sea." It was still invaluable for reconnaissance and raiding, but its old charges on the battle-field were impossible against the new weapons. Infantry rifles also kept artillery from offensive action at close quarters, so that it was only useful on the defensive, during this transitional period.

THE ADVANCE BY RUSHES—The interval between the Civil War and the World War saw a new forma-

---

[7] See pp. 15–21; 36–40.
[8] See p. 87.

tion develop. The infantry, once it had the breech-loader, took advantage of the chance to lie down for shelter. This finally led to a fairly standard attack. It consisted of several waves, each advancing by a series of platoon or squad rushes. The remainder of the line was meanwhile trying to silence the enemy with rifle-fire. This plan insured a minimum of exposure and a maximum of fire, until the point for the final assault was reached. The invention of the quick-firing field artillery and the machine-gun led to constant tactical experimentation with them. Above all, they forced the infantry to spread out and avoid mass formations. The Boer War (1899–1902), the Russo-Japanese War (1904–1905), and the Balkan Wars (1912–1913) taught a few lessons, but it remained for the World War to show the real importance of the new weapons.

WORLD WAR TACTICS

TRENCH WARFARE—The main fighting on the Western Front of the World War saw a close alliance between artillery and infantry. Cavalry was hardly in the picture at all. The old conventional "warfare of maneuver" was replaced by a "warfare of position," as we shall see in a later chapter.[9] The warfare of position was really a four-year siege of strongly intrenched positions, where flanking operations were practically out of the question. The armies dug themselves in in trenches and there they stayed. Great drives dented the lines one way or another, but the "break-through" did not come until the end.

MACHINE-GUNS—The significance of the machine-gun was one of the first lessons of the war. The in-

[9] See p. 303.

fantry had been taught that an effective rifle-fire was the principal way to overcome enemy resistance. But here was a machine that could tremendously increase that rate of fire. The Germans realized this sooner than their enemies. The German machine-guns took a terrific toll of the conventional dense infantry formations of the French attacking forces in Alsace in the first weeks of the war. Thereafter, the machine-gun—the heavy at first, and later the light and the automatic rifle—became essential arms for infantry fighting.[10]

THE TYPICAL ATTACK—The conventional offensive of the Western Front, down to the last months of the war, consisted of attacks with large numbers on limited fronts. The attacking force would throw one heavy wave after another against the enemy trench lines. The enemy would do their best to hold firm on those lines. The assailant's artillery had to clear the way for the infantry attack, as the trenches were protected with barbed wire in front. A heavy bombardment would sometimes last two whole days. This would generally demolish the wire and smash in most of the trenches. The infantry attack was then launched, preceded by a rolling barrage from the field artillery to lay a curtain of shells just in front of the infantry waves. The success of the attack largely depended upon the thoroughness of the artillery preparation and accompanying fire. If it had put the defenders' machine-guns and field artillery out of commission, the attacking infantry had a fairly clear field; but it generally happened that many of the defenders had taken shelter in deep dugouts during this bombardment, and emerged after the barrage had passed. Then, those few remaining machine-

[10] See pp. 22–24; 301, 350.

guns of the defenders could raise havoc with the advancing waves of infantry. The dead were often found mowed down by the scores in front of such single machine-gun nests. Naturally this type of fighting was costly to the defenders, but even more so to the infantry attacking against such odds. Knowing nothing better to do, each side tried to wear down the enemy's man-power in attacks of this sort. Reserve man-power was heavily reduced as the war progressed. Economy became necessary.

THE TANK—To meet this situation, each side introduced new tactics. The British invented the "tank" to assist the infantry and make the attacks more decisive. The tank was an armored car with caterpillar traction, so it could move over almost any kind of ground and straddle trenches. It was large or small in size and was equipped with machine-guns or light field-guns or both. Its great value lay in its ability to accompany or precede the infantry, as it could crush those defense machine-gun nests which had hitherto been the bugbear of the infantry attack. It also revived the possibilities of surprise attacks. Artillery preparation had smashed the enemy, but, at the same time, it gave warning of what was coming, so reserves could be moved up to meet the coming infantry attack. Now the tanks could look out for the barbed wire and the trenches while they were accompanying the infantry attack. They were a valuable moral as well as material support to the infantry.

FLEXIBLE GERMAN INNOVATIONS—The Germans made more fundamental tactical innovations in the last year of the war. These were the extreme forms of the flexible, mobile formations, which had started with Gustavus Adolphus. The Germans saw why trench warfare had been so costly. The defenders had massed on a narrow series of lines, which they had tried to hold at all costs. The attackers, at the same time, had thrown fairly dense masses of men in continuous lines against these defenses. The Germans, therefore, introduced the deep, elastic defense in 1917 and in 1918, the last of our series of loose formations—infiltration.

THE ELASTIC DEFENSE—The elastic defense meant that the positions were held "in depth." The Germans no longer depended upon a series of trench lines close together. Instead, they established a lightly held front line, which would resist only long enough to spread a warning to those behind. The whole region, to a considerable distance to the rear, was sprinkled with concrete "pill-boxes." These were veritable little forts containing machine-guns. The enemy would spend their initial force against the outer positions, which the Germans planned to sacrifice anyway. After that, the farther the enemy advanced, the more costly his progress. There was no "thin line" to break through, and so the attack would sink deeper and deeper into the yielding resistance. A narrow attack could even be taken in flank by the defenders. The French copied a form of this elastic defense by 1918. Of course, one had to have plenty of reserves in the rear before thus abandoning one's outer lines without a fight.

INFILTRATION—The Germans applied this same flexible principle to their final great drive in the spring of 1918, after trying it out on the Russians the year before. The new process for attack was known as "infiltration." Instead of smashing a series of dense lines against the enemy defenses, they adopted a looser formation. Small groups, operating on their own, were to hunt out weak points in the enemy positions, worm their way through, and attack the defenders in the rear and flank. Thus the whole defense would be honeycombed. No attempt was made to maintain straight, formal lines in the advance. Successive units followed up the original infiltration, and went through the disintegrated defenses as far as possible. The whole force was now a glorified skirmish line.

SPLITTING-UP OF COMMAND—This new type of attack threw most of the responsibility in action upon the junior and non-commissioned officers in command of platoons, squads, and sections. The war had shown the impossibility of larger groups remaining under the direct control of one man in battle. The compact units of Frederick the Great and Napoleon could obey the commands of captains, majors, and even colonels. But, in the World War, airplanes, artillery, and machine-guns would have wiped out infantry which stayed closely enough together for whole companies, battalions, or regiments to respond to the voice of one man. The last months saw in the infantry the loosest and most informal regular tactical system in history.

PRESENT TENDENCIES—The various armies in the last ten years have drawn their models from the fighting of 1918 rather than from that of the earlier years of the war. Little groups armed with automatic rifles will probably be an outstanding feature of future infantry attack. Field artillery is modifying its tactics to support the new types of attack and defense. The future of cavalry is in question. Cavalry screens were valuable during the first weeks of the war before the armies settled down to trench fighting. Cavalry also played a large rôle in outlying regions like Palestine, where distances were great. But the tank has now taken over the old shock function of the cuirassiers. New kinds of tanks are being turned out constantly. They range from little one-man tanks to huge ones armed with field-pieces and machine-guns. Aviation is now the main reliance for reconnaissance and raids behind the enemy lines. Motor-cycles and trucks have so increased the mobility of the infantry that the old dragoons or mounted infantry are becoming superfluous. All this, however, is merely speculation on present tendencies. This book is meant to deal with history, not prophecy.

TREND TOWARD LOOSE FORMATION—As for history, we can draw a few lessons from the facts which we have just reviewed. Victory has gone, time and again, to the side that could create new tactical formations or revive old ones to meet changing circumstances. There have been numerous dramatic turning-points in the past—Marathon, Cynoscephalæ, Adrianople, Crécy, Breitenfeld, and the German drive of 1918. The increased power of firearms has led to the substitution of loose, mobile formations in place of the earlier "human fortresses." The German "infiltration" represents the opposite extreme from the Greek phalanx and the Spanish square. That seems to be the present tendency. Naturally the tactics of the future will inevitably be influenced by the constant succession of mechanical inventions.

CHAPTER IV

FORTS AND SIEGES

THE EVOLUTION OF FORTIFICATION AND SIEGECRAFT

FIVE TYPES OF FORTIFICATION—Fighting has not been limited to battle-fields. The defending and attacking of fortified places has also played its part in military history. This second kind of warfare has its own peculiar technique, distinct from regular battle-field tactics. The methods have undergone fewer fundamental changes, so the subject is simpler than tactical formations. Instead of a dozen different significant types, we need study but five. Four are permanent land defenses: the walls of the ancients, the medieval castles, the "bastioned" fortresses of early modern history, and the rings of separate fortresses in recent years. The fifth includes temporary field fortifications. In connection with each of these, we shall consider the principles of both *defense* and *attack*.

RACE BETWEEN DEFENSE AND ATTACK—We shall find a never-ending race between these rival sciences of fortification and siegecraft. Defense has depended largely on construction, while attack has centered around artillery or other means of battering down walls. An improvement in one science might give it superiority for a long while, but sooner or later this was bound to be offset by an advance in the other.

Medieval castles were almost impregnable until gunpowder came in to batter them down. Then defense lagged far behind attack until a new sort of fort was devised that, in its turn, was forced to improve by a new successful system of attack. Forts and siegecraft have thus gradually kept pace with each other down through the centuries. From ancient brick walls to modern concrete "land battle-ships" has been the construction record, while instruments of attack have progressed from battering-rams to huge howitzers.

PURPOSES OF FORTIFICATIONS—Defenses have been built for various reasons. Some cities, like capitals or trade centers, are of such consequence in themselves that their security is essential. Other places of less apparent importance have been fortified for strategic reasons. These are generally situated along routes by which an invader would enter the country. They would delay him, as he could not afford to pass them by, lest they threaten his lines of communication. The forts of Liége and Namur slowed up the Germans in this way in 1914. Key points along a seacoast are usually fortified against naval attack. Many medieval castles were built simply for the protection of the owner and his followers. Temporary defenses have frequently been thrown up on battle-fields, particularly since the days of high-powered rifles.

DISTINCTIVE FEATURES OF SIEGES—Sieges differ in several ways from battles in the open field. Mobility naturally counts less. Dashing, impetuous courage helps only in direct assault or in occasional sorties. The ingenuity of engineers and the ability of gunners is vital to both the besieged and the besiegers. Patience, endurance, and constant vigilance are needed both inside and outside the fortifications.

ANCIENT FORTIFICATIONS—WALLS

WALLED CITIES—A long wall with occasional towers was the standard form of defense in ancient times. In the very beginning, men may possibly have thrown up rude fences or hedges of logs or other materials to check the onrushing attacker; but by the time written history commences, regular walls were in common use, for the science of fortification was well developed in the ancient Oriental empires. Important cities were generally defended by continuous walls, sometimes miles long, and capable of sheltering the whole population of the region. These walls were originally built of sun-dried brick, but of stone later. Towers which served as sentry-posts, barracks, and rallying-points for the defenders were placed at close enough intervals for the archers to sweep the intervening walls with their arrows. Frequently a moat or dry ditch was dug outside the walls to keep the attackers and their siege machinery from getting too near. If they did close in, there was still a chance for the defenders to pelt the attackers with missiles, to set the wooden siege apparatus afire, or otherwise to make the most of their more protected position. The only entrances to a city were a few well-defended gates, from which the defenders often made energetic sorties to dislocate the siege operations or perhaps, with luck, to disperse the enemy completely.

FRONTIER WALLS—But the ancient defenses did not stop with city walls. The Romans partially defended their frontier with Hadrian's Wall across Britain and the "Devil's Wall" between the Rhine and the Danube. Even those ambitious miles of masonry shrink into insignificance compared with the Great Wall surrounding China, built in 200 B. C. It was a continuous stone wall about twenty feet high, twenty feet wide, and 1,400 miles long!

ANCIENT SIEGECRAFT

METHODS OF ATTACK—Various methods were devised for attacking these ancient walled cities. The simplest way was to get some traitor to open a gate or at least to throw a dead dog into the water supply. A city might also be surrounded and starved into submission if the besiegers' patience and supplies lasted. The actual military methods of attack were more significant.

STORMING THE WALLS—It was first necessary to get close to the walls by filling the moat or ditch with bundles or sticks or baskets of earth. Once across the ditch, one could use scaling ladders to storm the walls. This was risky business unless the defenders were completely surprised.

MAKING A BREACH—Ordinarily, a breach had to be made through which the infantry might enter. The earliest instrument for this purpose was doubtless a rude form of battering-ram—a long pole with a sharp or heavy head. With it, the besiegers picked and poked away at the wall until a portion crumbled, unless the defenders could stop them by grappling for the head of the ram or by lowering mats over the wall to soften its blows. The same result might be achieved by another familiar siege device, sapping and mining, or digging a hole under part of the wall to undermine it. This method sometimes worked well, but might be offset by countermining, in which the defenders dug a hole of their own and fought, smoked out, or drowned the attacking miners.

ROMAN SIEGECRAFT—The Romans carried siegecraft to a high state of perfection. Under them, the attack was ahead of the defense. Their soldiers were trained to dig as well as fight, as both were requisite for successful siege work. They were patient, laborious, and thorough. At the same time their siege methods were so ingenious that no defenses were secure against them.

EARLY SIEGE "ARTILLERY"—We have already mentioned the catapult and the ballista, the pregunpowder "heavy artillery," which hurled huge missiles several hundred yards.[1] The battering-rams of the Romans were sheltered under movable sheds, which usually were covered with rawhide to prevent the defenders from setting them on fire.

MOUND AND TOWER—If the walls were strong and the defense stubborn, the Romans would build a huge mound of earth and logs right up near the wall. Rows of little sheds sheltered the mound-builders from the defense fire. Next, a movable wooden tower was rolled along the completed mound. This tower was provided with a drawbridge by which armed men could be landed on the wall itself. This thorough system resulted in the fall of one stronghold after another to the legionaries as they extended the frontiers of the empire. The capture of the powerful Jerusalem defenses in 70 A. D. was an outstanding example of their methods.

PERMANENT FEATURES—Some of these devices of ancient siegecraft lasted down through the centuries. The scaling ladder became a permanent part of siege apparatus. Moats and ditches continued to be filled up by the attackers wherever possible. Mining and countermining were to be even more effective when gunpowder and high explosives were invented. The capture by surprise or treachery has not by any means been limited to the ancients, nor

[1] See p. 28.

has the surrounding of fortresses in the hope of
starving out the defenders. The price of rats soared
in many a later siege. Moreover, beleaguered garrisons in all periods have sent out energetic sorties in
the hope of improving their situation.

Medieval Fortifications—Castles

REASONS FOR CASTLES—The castle, rather than
the walled city, characterized medieval fortification.
The decline of the Roman Empire and the coming
of the barbarians changed the problem of defense.
Every man had to look out for himself now. The
more powerful fortified their estates for protection
against marauding bands. The weaker threw in their
lot with those who could look out for them. The
central government dwindled away. Many local po-
tentates thus secured full power in their little regions.
Their strongholds were to become the medieval
castles.

PROGRESS OF CASTLE-BUILDING—Castle-building
passed through several successive stages during the
middle ages. The earliest castles were merely rude
wooden palisades surmounting a mound of earth.
They were easy to burn, and so, after several centuries, solid masonry replaced the inflammable
wooden structures. The first stone castles were simply "keeps," square towers several stories high, rising straight from the ground. Shortly before 1100, a
new feature appeared. The keep was surrounded by
a wall, which served as a first line of defense. The
Crusaders (1096–1270) were deeply impressed by
the highly developed fortifications of the East, and
came home determined to improve their own.

CASTLES IN 1200—As a result, castle-building

reached new heights by 1200. The keep, by this time, was a fort within a series of forts. Elaborate systems of high outer walls were designed to provide a step-by-step defense. Consequently, even if attackers should breach one wall and carry the outer ward, they would have to repeat the whole process before reaching the final stronghold. Curved lines replaced the early squares, for the corners had been sources of weakness. The walls were provided with overhanging galleries, from which missiles could be dropped on the attackers, and with towers, from which archers could command the intervening stretches of wall. The sketch on page 78 shows the combination of these features in one of the masterpieces of castle construction, the Château Gaillard. It was built in 1196 by Richard the Lionhearted to protect Normandy from the French king.

NATURAL DEFENSES—Medieval castles differed from most forts of the other periods in the matter of natural defenses. Ancient and modern fortifications were generally built for the protection of particular cities, towns, or strategic points. This restricted the choice of site. But the castle-builder had more freedom. Primarily interested in picking a place that would be secure from attack, he was likely to select an out-of-the-way site, where nature would assist in the defense. "Ideal situations were an island a short distance from the shore, the spur of a hill, a bit of firm ground in the midst of a bog, or a narrow tongue of land at the junction of the two rivers." If such natural defenses were unavailable, a moat was dug to keep away siege machinery. The peculiarities of the site, of course, determined the size and shape of the fort.

Medieval Siegecraft—Ineffectiveness

ATTACK METHODS FALL BEHIND—The stronger castles were practically impregnable. For once, the methods of attack had not kept pace with the development of defense. There was still no great difference in attack from that of the ancient times. The trebuchet, to be sure, could hurl great stones; the "cat," an effective new battering-ram, might pick loose the masonry so as to undermine the walls. The Château Gaillard, powerful though it was, was captured in 1204 by the French. They laid siege to the place, and finally undermined the tower in the outer defense. The next walls were carried by lucky assault. Mining was used again to get into the inner ward. The half-starved little garrison had to surrender before they had time to take refuge in the keep.

THE BESIEGERS' DIFFICULTIES—But such success in sieges was rare. Clumsy siege machinery was of little use on a steep hillside or in a swamp. Mining and sapping operations beneath the defenses could not progress through solid rock or under the water of a swamp or moat. The walls were generally too high for scaling. If surprise or treachery failed, little remained except a patient siege to starve out the defenders. That was a difficult affair in the middle ages, when armies usually held together for only the required forty days of feudal military service.[2] The weaker party almost always went quickly into its castle, so sieges were much more common than pitched battles. The average noble, once he had raised his drawbridge, had lowered his portcullis, and was safely within his well-manned, well-supplied

[2] See p. 98.

castle, could defy a large army. Many a "virgin fortress" resisted all attacks for centuries. This made it particularly difficult for kings to extend their authority over rebellious nobles, and retarded the growth of strong national government.

INFLUENCE OF GUNPOWDER—Then, at the very end of the middle ages, the attack caught up with the defense and went ahead of it. Gunpowder made itself felt in siegecraft before either small arms or field artillery became effective. Heavy siege pieces were beginning to batter down castle walls by 1450. The capture of the powerful defenses of Constantinople by the Turks in 1453 was an especial instance of this.[3] The old type of feudal castle was before long doomed as a stronghold. The siege gun robbed the noble of his strength.

FORTIFICATIONS IN EARLY MODERN HISTORY— BASTIONED FORTS

STRATEGIC PLACES—This naturally had far-reaching influence on fortification. As the private castle lost its prominence, interest centered, after 1500, on the defense of cities and towns once more. Places like Paris were not the only ones to be powerfully walled. Great strategic significance began to be attached to certain frontier towns on the main highways between France, Germany, and Belgium. Typical of these were Metz, Toul, Verdun, Mons, Charleroi, Liége, and Namur. The nation controlling such key positions could defend the approaches to its own territory and had a good jumping-off place for invading enemy regions. Consequently, from this period to the present, military engineers in generation after generation have made those places and

[3] See p. 30.

others like them as strong as possible, while siege after siege has tested their defenses.

IMPORTANCE OF NEW FEATURES—We shall examine the new type of fortification carefully. Its general principles remained in vogue for about three centuries. We should know a few terms of the jargon of the military engineers, in order to understand better the forts and sieges. The whole continuous line of fortifications surrounding a town, or a part of a town, was known as the *enceinte*. We shall study this first in its cross-section and then in its ground-plan.

CASTLE WALLS NO LONGER ADEQUATE—Artillery had revealed two defects in the old castles. Their high stone walls presented too vulnerable a target, and they were not suitable for mounting guns. At first the old walls were cut down and modified to meet the artillery situation. Before long, however, a whole new system of construction—the bastioned fort—replaced such temporary makeshifts.

THE NEW CROSS-SECTION—The new walls were "sunk in the ground." They were thus much lower, and were as little exposed as possible. The diagram shows such a typical cross-section. The main wall, known as the *scarp*, was backed with earth and other material. Earth also covered it to form the *rampart*, from which the guns were fired. A ditch, often 100 feet wide, was dug in front of the scarp. Its far side was walled to form the *counterscarp*. Part of the earth from the ditch had gone to make the rampart. The rest was thrown up on the outer side, making the *glacis* or bank. This sloped up almost to the height of the rampart. The glacis intercepted the enemy artillery fire. The balls buried themselves in its soft earth without reaching the masonry. A passage, called the *covered way*, was inside the glacis.

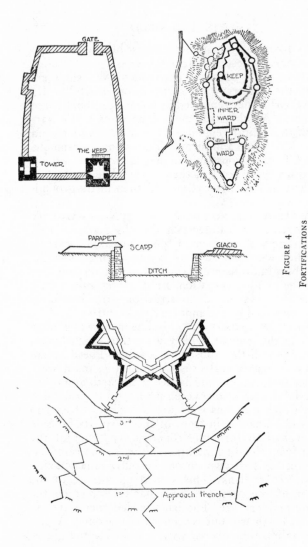

FIGURE 4

FORTIFICATIONS

a. English castle about 1050.
b. Château Gaillard about 1200.
c. Cross-section of fortress about 1600.
d. Typical Vauban approach by parallel lines.

Here the defenders could assemble to beat off an infantry attack or to make a sortie of their own. These low walls made the new fortress much less conspicuous than the proud old medieval castle.

BASTIONS—The outline, or *trace,* of the fortress also underwent a change. The old castle walls had been built in a fairly straight line. This left considerable "dead space" which could not be covered by the defending artillery. As a result, if a breach was made in one part of the wall, it could not be defended from the other parts. The new fortifications were designed on the principle that "each part should defend its neighbor and be defended by it." This was secured by the construction of projections known as bastions. They were often shaped like an ace of spades. Later, they resembled more a broad, short spear-head. In each case the point was toward the enemy. The enceinte consisted of several such bastions, arranged so that their guns would cover each other. The walls between the bastions were known as curtains. The military engineers invented many elaborate and intricate systems based on these principles. Their designs are a bewildering mass of geometric figures. Most forts, however, had five or six bastions. These were often called star fortresses because of their general shape. Defense had once more stolen a march on attack.

Siegecraft in Early Modern History—Vauban

VAUBAN—Siegecraft finally caught up again between 1670 and 1700 through the clever idea of a brilliant Frenchman, Marshal Vauban, an officer of Louis XIV. He was the greatest military engineer in history. He invented a systematic method of attacking the bastioned fortresses. He was so successful in both attack and defense that the saying arose, "A fortress attacked by Vauban is doomed; a fortress defended by Vauban is impregnable." His method of attack is of particular interest to us, since it long served as a model for most armies. It was known as the *approach by parallel lines*.

THE VAUBAN ATTACK—PRELIMINARIES—The first step in Vauban's attack was the surrounding or "investing" of the fortress with cavalry and infantry to cut off communications from the outside. The attack was directed against one side of the fortress only. Batteries of heavy siege artillery were brought up to points about 600 yards from the walls. They were placed so that they could be fired along, or could "enfilade," the sides of the bastions. Just behind these batteries, a trench was dug *parallel* to the fortress walls. The purpose of this parallel was to shelter the infantry so that they could protect the batteries from capture by a sortie of the defenders. While these batteries were trying to put the defense artillery out of commission, several "approach" trenches were being dug toward the walls. They were in zigzag form, so they could not be swept by the guns of the fortress.

THE NEAR PARALLELS—A second parallel was then dug nearer to the walls. The batteries were now brought up to this closer position. The diggers of the "approach" trenches were coming within musket range of the walls by this time. Specially trained men, called sappers, dug slowly ahead under shelter. Fifty yards a day was considered good time. Finally, the third parallel was dug just beneath the glacis or outer mound. From there, the sappers continued to dig their way up along the slope to the top of the glacis. The attacking artillery from this new vantage point overlooked the ditch and could fire directly at the masonry of the scarp. It was ordinarily breached in a short time.

THE BREACH—A fortress was apt to surrender as soon as its scarp was breached. Further defense was generally hopeless. If the fortress commander was stubborn, another group of diggers, or "miners," burrowed their way beneath the glacis and across the ditch. Then the infantry, with scaling ladders, stormed the breach made by the artillery. This was usually very bloody work. If a fortress held out after its scarp was hopelessly breached, the attackers frequently massacred the whole garrison for forcing the unnecessarily costly storming of the walls.

SYSTEMATIC METHOD—The whole approach was thoroughly systematic. It could almost be carried out according to schedule unless the defenders put up too energetic a resistance with sorties and repair of damages. Fortresses were often classified according to the number of days which they could be expected to hold out, unrelieved. Vauban took thirteen days to capture his first fortress, Maubeuge, in 1673.

LATER MINOR CHANGES—With these general principles of defense and attack in mind, we can understand most of the sieges in the next century or two. There was comparatively little change in the method of attack or in the cross-section of the defenses with their scarps, ramparts, ditches, and glacis. Mortars were introduced to bring vertical fire to bear upon places which ordinary guns could not reach.[4] For protection against the vertical fire, the defense guns were later housed in casemates—masonry vaults covered with earth—instead of being exposed on top of the ramparts. Occasional modifications were made in the outlines or traces of forts between 1700 and the radical innovations after 1886, but they

[4] See p. 34.

were too intricate and not important enough to follow in detail. For a long time, attack and defense were about on a par.

RECENT FORTIFICATIONS—RING FORTRESSES

INFLUENCE OF NEW EXPLOSIVES—A revolution occurred in European land fortifications about 1886. That, we recall, was the year when the French produced smokeless powder and high explosive.[5] Some mélinite shells were tried on one of their forts. It crumbled to pieces. Every one at once recognized that forts must be built on a new plan. Defense had again fallen far behind attack, and Europe had to renovate its defenses.

NEW FEATURES—The modern fortifications show two important features. First, a "ring" of separate forts replaced the old enceinte or continuous wall. Second, the new forts were regular "land battle-ships" of concrete and steel. The old enceintes had been built in a day when armies were small and guns could seldom reach a mile. By 1886 universal military service had vastly increased the size of armies.[6] Larger spaces were needed to shelter them. Smokeless powder and rifling, moreover, gave the new guns a range of several miles. The defenses were therefore pushed out in order to keep the besieging artillery at a distance. Some detached forts had been built earlier, but after 1886 they became universal.

BRIALMONT—Typical of the new system was the "ring defense" started at Liége in 1890. This was constructed by General Brialmont, a great Belgian engineer, who was the Vauban of his day. He surrounded Liége with a ring of twelve forts. They

[5] See p. 39.
[6] See p. 109.

were placed at an average distance of four miles
from the city, at intervals of about two and one-half
miles apart. Brialmont surrounded Antwerp and
Bucharest with even more numerous forts. In case
of war, he planned to join them with a ring of infantry trenches. That was never done, as we shall see.

"LAND BATTLE-SHIPS"—The military engineers
engaged in a hot dispute over the proper construction
for the new forts. Some said that it was folly to place
the big guns in permanent positions. The enemy
would know their exact location; they could not be
moved to meet special conditions. This party preferred to limit the forts principally to infantry and
machine-gun defenses, while the big guns would be
moved around in temporary field positions. Brialmont, however, thought otherwise. He proposed to
guard the heavy defense artillery with concrete and
steel. He devised disappearing cupolas and turrets
so the guns would be exposed only when they were
fired. The magazines, troop shelters, and other portions of the defense were encased in concrete, heavy
enough to resist eight-inch shells. Half the Liége
forts were large five-sided affairs, while the other
six were smaller triangles. These forts looked innocent enough from the outside with their grassy
slopes. Inside, they were labyrinths of elaborate
mechanism.

FRENCH FORTRESS SYSTEMS—The other nations
built great defense systems on similar lines. Some
improved upon Brialmont's particular designs.
France defended its German frontier with four
powerful fortress systems, arranged in pairs. Belfort
and Epinal guarded the passes of the Vosges Mountains in the east, while Verdun and Toul covered the
Meuse Valley in the center. These defenses were so
strong that Germany in 1914 made her main effort

through Belgium instead of against this barrier.[7] The French had planned a similar series of fortresses behind the Belgian frontier, but gave up the idea because of the cost. Paris, of course, was a strong "intrenched camp" with dozens of forts. The Germans, on their side, spent millions in Alsace and Lorraine on the defenses of Metz, Thionville, and Strassburg to guard against French invasion. Verdun and Thionville served as very important pivots for the French and German lines respectively in the World War. Germany also had a mighty fortress system in the east at Thorn for defense against Russia. Dozens of other such systems were built throughout Europe. Some half-completed Russian ring forts at Port Arthur were reduced by Japanese howitzers in 1904–1905, so Europe still further strengthened its defenses.

RECENT SIEGECRAFT—HOWITZERS

LIÉGE AND NAMUR—Brialmont's defenses were put to the test in the opening act of the World War. His fortress systems at Liége and Namur lay along the route by which the Germans decided to advance upon France. They planned to pass through Belgium in six days.[8] This could not be done as long as those fortress guns commanded the railroad lines. On August 4, the Germans appeared before Liége. The Belgians felt that their forts were quite impregnable. They neglected in their haste an important defense feature which Brialmont had planned. They relied on guns and concrete without digging *trenches* for infantry between the forts. The Germans tried to rush the lines with their infantry. The first attack was beaten off, but on August 6th they passed be-

[7] See pp. 300, 301.
[8] See pp. 301, 302.

tween two forts and took the city. The Austrian twelve-inch Skoda howitzers had been rushed to the scene by that time.[9] The high-explosive shells of these howitzers crumbled the concrete walls, built to withstand eight-inch shells. One after another, the forts fell. The last one surrendered on August 16th. Liége had delayed the Germans two weeks. Namur fell more quickly, for this time the Germans waited until they had brought up their howitzers. Again the Belgians failed to build trenches or to break up the attack by energetic sorties. Five of the nine Brialmont forts were in ruins in twenty-four hours. Within four days, the rest were taken. In contrast, the obsolete French fortress system at Maubeuge, much weaker than Liége or Namur, held out for eleven days this same month because of energetic infantry sorties.

RIVAL DEDUCTIONS—Two opposite conclusions were drawn from these rapid conquests of supposedly impregnable defenses. The Germans had spent nearly three weeks instead of six days in passing through Belgium. This gave the French and British time to rally for the defense. In a way, the Brialmont forts may be said to have prevented Germany's immediate victory. On the other hand, the powerful howitzers had reduced the "impregnable" fortresses to ruins in surprisingly short order. A general reaction set in against the permanent "land battle-ships." The big guns in many other forts were removed from their concrete defenses to more mobile positions outside the forts.

VERDUN—The defense of Verdun proved that the experts had gone too far in declaring the regular fortress systems out of date. Verdun, we recall, was one of the four most powerful French systems of

[9] See p. 43.

ring fortresses. After watching Liége and Namur, the French stripped the Verdun forts of their heavy guns, removing the guns to open positions. They foolishly allowed the whole fortress system to run down. They depended almost entirely on trenches and temporary field defenses. After the terrific German bombardment, it was found that most of the emplacements of the forts were still intact. They had been built of better concrete than the Belgian forts. Verdun held firm, but it was at terrific cost. Its defenses, of course, had been made a part of the regular field trench system, but the results did something to restore confidence in the old forts.[10]

OTHER TESTS—Fortresses were not put to such severe tests away from the Western Front. The Russians, on the Eastern Front, invaded Austrian Poland and came up before the unpronounceable and powerful Austrian fortress, Przemysl. They lacked heavy siege artillery, such as the Germans had. Consequently, they had to detail part of their army to settle down around Przemysl for a long, slow, old-fashioned siege.[11] At Gallipoli, the Turkish coast-defenses proved strong enough to beat off an allied fleet, containing one of the mightiest battle-ships afloat.[12]

OPPOSITE CONCLUSIONS—The experts, therefore, have been able to draw opposite conclusions about the value of conventional fortresses in the World War. The fact that many of them were battered to pieces is offset by the fact that they frequently detained the invading armies. Attack had grown so powerful, however, that they were no longer real defenses unless backed by field fortifications.

10 See pp. 315, 316.
11 See p. 310.
12 See p. 313.

FIELD FORTIFICATIONS

TEMPORARY DEFENSES—The fifth main type of fortification consists of temporary defenses, thrown up in time of war. Though less elaborate than permanent strongholds, they have finally become the most important defenses of all. Ordinarily they have been earthworks, sometimes reinforced with timber or even concrete.

TRENCHES NO NOVELTY—Field fortifications are nothing new. Trench warfare was hailed as an innovation in the World War, but soldiers had dug and defended trenches for centuries. The Roman legionaries used to "dig in" whenever they encamped for the night. Trenches were dug to break the force of medieval cavalry charges. In front of these ditches was often found an abattis of sharpened stakes or similar obstacles—the forerunner of barbed wire entanglements.

ELABORATE FIELD DEFENSES—Military engineers in the "early modern period" learned to improvise makeshift substitutes for bastioned fortresses. Two special terms were applied to field fortifications of this period. The redoubt was ordinarily a small outlying defense with a wall of earth and timber all the way around it. A redan was an open angle, shaped like a V with the point toward the enemy. Cities, unprovided with permanent fortifications, frequently built temporary defenses of this sort as the fighting came their way.

INFLUENCE OF RIFLE—Modern rifles gave a great stimulus to field fortifications. Troops used to grumble at spade work, but after the introduction of the rifle, they were generally glad to dig little "foxholes" on the battle-field, even if their stay in the place was to be only a short one. The intrenching tool, as we know, became a regular part of the infantryman's equipment.

THE WESTERN FRONT—It was only natural, therefore, that trenches should play an important rôle in the World War, for machine-guns and quick-firing artillery had increased the need for shelter. Where the region was too wet for trenches, piles of sandbags had to be used for protection. The Western Front became a continuous line of rival trench systems for the whole 600 miles from the Alps to the sea. For more than three years, the fighting on that front was in reality a gigantic siege.

TACTICS OR SIEGECRAFT?—We are faced with a complicated question here, whether the special features of the trench system of the Western Front—drives, rigid defense, elastic defense, and infiltration—belong to tactics or to siegecraft. It is almost impossible to draw the line. In the three years after the two sides dug in, the fighting, as we just said, was actually a siege; but the very first and the last months saw more open warfare. We have arbitrarily divided our discussion of the trench system. Here we shall consider nothing but actual *construction* of the defense systems, as we took up trench warfare under tactics.[13] We must keep in mind that, for more than three years, defense was far ahead of the attack.

TYPICAL TRENCH "POSITION"—The diagram of any small section of the trench system has a surprising resemblance to the scheme of Vauban's attack by parallel lines. The average position in the trench system was about a mile in depth, with four parallel trenches, connected by so-called communication trenches. Barbed wire entanglements protected the front of the trenches. The outpost line was nearest the enemy; the main line of resistance and its sup-

[13] See pp. 63, 303, 304.

ports were in the center; and the reserves occupied
the rear. Artillery was posted behind the lines, still
farther to the rear. This was the "rigid" defense, in
which the purpose was to keep the enemy from getting past the second or third line.

THE "ELASTIC" DEFENSE—Toward the end of the
war came the "elastic" defense which we noticed in
connection with tactics. The Germans built the so-
called "Hindenburg Line" in the rear of their regular trench system and retired to it early in 1917.
They used much ingenuity and a great deal of concrete in constructing the most elaborate system of
field fortifications in history. A unique feature was
the "pill-box"—a little concrete shelter for machine-
guns. Hundreds were sprinkled in all sorts of places
to hinder the enemy infantry. Behind them were occasional trenches and dugouts, reinforced with concrete to withstand artillery bombardment. These
defenses were scattered over a depth of several
miles, so that, according to the purpose of this yielding defense, the force of the enemy's onslaught would
gradually waste itself.[14]

TRENCHES AND PERMANENT FORTS—Not only
were tactics and siegecraft brought closely together
in the war, but other conventional divisions were also
broken down through the prevalence of field fortifications. For instance, the great ring fortress of Verdun was merged into the regular trench system, while
the "Hindenburg Line" was far more elaborate than
many former permanent defenses built in time of
peace.

FORTIFICATIONS AND SIEGECRAFT IN AMERICA

FEW INLAND STRONGHOLDS—Before leaving fortifications and siegecraft, we shall glance at their

[14] See pp. 65, 320.

history in America. Due to peculiar conditions, this country's experience with them has been different from Europe's. Our relations with our immediate neighbors have not made it essential to guard our frontiers with fortresses of the type considered necessary by European nations.[15] There have not been many of these permanent land fortifications here. At the time of the Revolution, we had a few defenses on this order, such as Ticonderoga, Crown Point, and the Hudson forts like West Point. Our usual inland forts have been western frontier posts built for protection against the Indians. Fort Leavenworth, Fort Riley, Fort Sill, and many others got their start that way. They were outgrowths of the colonial wooden "blockhouses." More elaborate construction was not required, since the Indians had no artillery.

AMERICAN FIELD FORTIFICATIONS—American military history, therefore, has little to say about conventional permanent inland fortifications. American troops, however, have had plenty of experience with two other kinds of defenses: temporary field fortifications, and permanent coast-defenses. The absence of permanent land-defenses resulted in an unusual amount of field fortifications in our various wars. In the Revolution, these progressed from the trenches at Bunker Hill to the intricate British defenses at Yorktown, which were captured by the Americans and French with methods which recall Vauban.

TRENCHES IN THE CIVIL WAR—The Confederates in the Civil War had field fortifications on a much larger scale in the sieges of Vicksburg and Petersburg. In the front of the latter, there was almost a year of actual trench warfare. In both, the Union

[15] See p. 147.

forces blew up portions of the defenses with mines—
a familiar old device in siege warfare. Infantry
trenches were also common. We have already seen
how the increased power of the rifle made them
necessary for shelter. Grant learned the value of
such defenses when he lost 12,000 men in a few
minutes, while trying to storm the Confederate
earthworks at Cold Harbor.[16]

COAST-DEFENSES—Our coast-defenses are the
highest type of fortification which this country has
seen. They were built to ward off possible attacks
from our principal ports. In general features, they
resemble contemporary European models, but of
course they were designed to fight warships and not
infantry. Their progress during the last century can
be easily studied by any one who visits one of our
older seaports. In the earliest forts, he will see occasional granite scarps peeping from behind grassy
mounds often arranged in elaborate geometric
figures. Fort Sumter, built just before the Civil War,
rose straight from the water in a solid mass of brick.
Its weakness was proved by the guns which opened
the war. Because of this, its twin, Fort Gorges in
Portland Harbor, was never completed. The latest
forts are far less conspicuous. They are usually located several miles from the city which they defend.
Their huge disappearing guns are sheltered in concrete pits. Other essential parts of the defenses are
strongly encased in concrete and steel. They are
modern forms of the ring fortress system with its
"land battle-ships."

THE FUTURE OF FORTIFICATIONS—The forts of
the future are still a matter of doubt. These Brialmont "land battle-ships" are out of date, but some of
their features may be consolidated into new systems.

[16] See pp. 256, 260.

The World War showed at least that reliance cannot be placed on guns and concrete alone for defense, but that infantry and trenches have an important part to play. The increase in aviation may further alter the problem. In the meantime, the United States keeps her coast-defenses, but no real forts worthy of the name are found away from the salt water. Our experts are following the new developments, but the question is not the simple one of a century ago, when defense and attack followed pretty much the conventional example of Marshal Vauban. The balance between the strength of defending walls and the destructive power of siege weapons has shifted back and forth so many times that the chances are that some new invention may again change the old systems overnight.

CHAPTER V

PROFESSIONALS AND AMATEURS

THE EVOLUTION OF MILITARY PERSONNEL

Soldiers may be divided into two great classes—professionals and amateurs. We shall see here how various nations have decided which sort should compose their armies. Both kinds have their advantages and disadvantages.

PROFESSIONALS—Professionals were formerly called mercenaries and more recently, regulars. They are men who make soldiering their regular business in peace as well as war. Their great advantage is *discipline*. Frequently a handful of professional soldiers has defeated a large body of amateurs because the regulars were used to obeying orders and did not lose their heads. The main drawback to a professional or standing army has been its cost. It is a steady charge against the government in time of peace.

AMATEURS—The amateurs might better be called part-time citizen-soldiery. They are sometimes known as militia. They may be partly trained or totally green. Their service may be compelled by a levy, conscription, or draft, or they may be volunteers. In any case, they earn their livings in non-military occupations in time of peace, and so are less expensive than professionals. As a result, a nation can secure at the same price more amateurs than pro-

fessionals for its army. It is a matter of quantity
against quality.

EFFICIENCY VS. FREEDOM—The question involves
the consideration of the interest of the nation and
that of the individual. The ideal method from a
purely military point of view is to give every able-
bodied man enough training so that he will approach
the efficiency of the professional. But such training
takes time and interferes with a citizen's private
business. In prosperous countries, a citizen's time is
valuable. Consequently, rich nations, especially those
with far-flung imperial possessions, often prefer professional armies, because they leave the citizens as a
whole free to pursue their own business. At the same
time, those who prefer soldiering are paid for it.
The main difficulty lies in efficiently expanding a little
professional army to war-time proportions.

HISTORICAL PERIODS—Armies of professionals
and amateurs have been about equally common
throughout history. Greece and Rome started with
citizen-soldiery and both ended with regulars. The
middle ages also originally had general military
service, but gradually swung toward mercenaries.
The five centuries from 1300 to 1800 formed the
great period of the professionals. At first they were
mercenaries fighting for any one who would pay
them: later they were organized into "standing
armies." Most European countries, during the last
century or so, have tried to give amateurs the efficiency of regulars. This universal military training
produced huge armies made up of practically the entire adult male population. England and the United
States are the only important nations which have
clung to the small standing army. We shall trace the
experiences of Europe in this chapter. Later, we
shall see how the United States has experimented

with both professionals and amateurs, and is at present trying to combine the best parts of both systems.

ANCIENT ARMIES

PRIMITIVE PERSONNEL—In ancient times, some tribes and countries expected every able-bodied man to turn out for war—and wars were very frequent. Other tribes had a distant warrior class, which somewhat corresponded to a regular professional army. The Persians and other ancient oriental peoples commonly used such a system. The small group of warriors lived off the rest of the community and generally lorded it over them. In a crisis there might be a levy of all the men. These others were usually formed into a huge unorganized mass of infantry, which suffered the casualties and received few honors. The leading warriors were ordinarily the chief men of the nation.

GREEK CITIZEN-SOLDIERY—The Greeks and Romans, as we said, both started with a citizen-soldiery and ended with professionals. The early Greek city-states expected every citizen to render military service. Boys were so trained from a very youthful age. Such service was universal for "citizens," but this meant only certain upper classes. It was considered a privilege and an honor from which slaves and some others were barred. This militia idea was carried to an extreme in Sparta, where everything gave way to the military policy of the nation. They had a universal barracks existence, which produced a harsh, hard people—and victories.

GREEK PROFESSIONALS—These citizens, in their phalanxes, made splendid soldiers. They had plenty of practice, too, not only in defending their lands from the Persian hordes, but also in many wars between their own little city-states. The system worked as long as wars were short and one could "commute" to the battle-field. Athens, however, developed widespread commerce and an empire. Citizen-soldiers could not very well be drafted for long garrison duty on distant islands. The state was prosperous, so it began to hire professionals who enjoyed soldiering. Other states soon took up this scheme. These "soldiers of fortune" even sold their services outside Greece. Xenophon's famous "Ten Thousand" were Greek professionals in Persian pay. The armies with which Alexander the Great conquered the Eastern world were made up for the most part of such long-time regulars.

ROME'S SIMILAR EXPERIENCE—It was the same story with Rome. The legionaries of the early Republic were upper-class citizens. These soldiers gradually brought most of Italy under Rome, and defended the country against the Carthaginian professionals under Hannibal. Then Rome began to spread her influence beyond Italy, especially in Spain, Asia, and Africa. Naturally, long-time regulars were needed for such long-distance wars. By 100 B. C. the legionary was a professional. Cæsar spoke slightingly of a certain legion because it was made up of green troops—its men had been in service only nine years. Men often spent their lives in military service. There was a chance to rise from the ranks to the command of a cohort or even higher. The sons of prominent men usually had the inside track to officers' commissions even in that day, but they had to make good. The early professionals were Italian Romans, but as time went on the bulk of the army was made up of men from the outlying provinces. Even barbarians were recruited from outside the

Empire. Hadrian's Wall in Britain, for instance, was manned with legionaries from all parts of the known world. More than one professional in the later days of the Empire was raised to the throne as Emperor by the legions. We have already seen how this influx of foreign mercenaries so sapped the strength of the legion that it gave way before the onrush of Gothic horsemen at Adrianople.

MIDDLE AGES

THE FRANKISH LEVY—Now we see the whole cycle starting again in France. The Franks had their old Germanic traditions when they settled down at the fall of the Roman Empire. Theirs was a citizen-soldiery. Every free man had his weapons and turned out for annual inspection at the "March field" or the "May field." In wartime, the *Heerban* or levy called out all this militia. The trouble was that, with every man at war, no one was left to keep agriculture and business going. To remedy this, the service was adjusted on the basis of income. Those who could afford to do so bought horses and became cavalry, just as in ancient times when the cavalry was the rich man's outfit. The "middle classes" fitted themselves out as infantry. The poor clubbed together. For instance, five men might purchase soldier's equipment for one of their number. No well-organized state existed to provision and equip armies. This was the sort of army that built up Charlemagne's empire around 800.

THE FEUDAL SYSTEM—The Germanic militia idea gradually developed into the feudal system, which flourished during the height of the middle ages. This feudal system may be defined as a "system of land-tenure based on military service." The king or lord would grant part of his land to a lesser lord or vassal. The vassal had to furnish a certain number of armed men to fight in his lord's service for not more than forty days a year. No one had enough ready money ordinarily to hire men for longer periods, so the campaigns were naturally short. The weaker side usually sought shelter in a castle,[1] because they knew the attacking army was very apt to melt away before the castle would have to surrender.

SCUTAGE—This led to a return to professionals. The Crusades to the Holy Land between 1096 and 1270 meant long-term service. One old chronicler remarked that whoever went to Jerusalem had to stay out a long time. Forty-day service was no good in campaigns which lasted two or three years at the least. The kings and vassals all saw the value of long-time service on their return to Europe. Some lords decided to call on their vassals for money instead of the forty days' free service. This money would hire soldiers who would stay on the job as long as paid. This system was called "scutage" or shield-money. The lord, instead of furnishing so many men-at-arms, now sent a bag of gold. Those who enjoyed fighting could do so in the lord's pay, while the others paid in gold. The old feudal levy continued for a long time after scutage appeared, but the paid professionals became constantly more common.

THE FREE COMPANIES

THE CONDOTTIERI—From about 1300 to 1650, war was a regular business proposition for most soldiers. Bands called free companies appeared all over Western Europe. An able captain would gather a group of men-at-arms who were attracted by his

[1] See p. 75.

reputation. Then he would bargain with some king, noble, or city to sell the services of his company. The leaders consequently became known as *condottieri* or contractors.

INTERNATIONAL SOLDIERS—These mercenary troops were a thoroughly international class. A single army might contain free companies from a dozen different countries. The Swiss were famous as mercenaries. These hardy mountaineers, we remember, revived the old phalanx to overcome medieval horsemen. After defending their own country, they sold their services wherever the best price was offered. The German *Landsknechte* were also selling their services broadcast at this time. Likewise plenty of free companies were made up of English, Scotch, Irish, Flemish, French, and Spanish. The result of this mixture of races was that the soldiers were seldom stirred with patriotic enthusiasm for the cause for which they were fighting. Sometimes they would strike for pay on the very eve of battle. "No money, no Swiss," was a byword.

THE BUSINESS OF FIGHTING—This influenced their fighting. They were quite efficient as a whole. It paid to be. The captains copied the latest improvements in arms and tactics, because the better the reputation of his company, the higher price it commanded. Free companies frequently carried on a very pleasant sort of war against each other. There was no particular advantage in killing or in being killed. It was more profitable to take prisoners who could be ransomed. As a result, casualty lists in important battles were often surprisingly low. The mercenaries, moreover, did not ordinarily favor decisive action. They were paid by the month, not by the job. The longer they could make it last, the better for them. It was like a sort of international "soldiers' union" with mutual understandings on professional etiquette.

THE REAL VICTIMS—The real victims of this mercenary warfare were the defenseless civilians. Their women and property were seldom safe when a free company came along. Many of the soldiers fought only in anticipation of plunder. Time after time, towns were savagely plundered, with atrocities of the worst type. During "off seasons" or between jobs, free companies cruised around the countryside, spreading terror and desolation, and taking whatever they wanted.

FAMOUS FREE COMPANIES—The first of these free companies, and a famous one, was made up of Spaniards, who started out at the end of certain local wars to hunt new fields of action. They finally reached Greece, killed the feudal lords and became lords in their places, taking over their wives and castles. This showed the possibilities of "free-lance" warfare. Much of the fighting in the Hundred Years' War between France and England (1339–1453) was carried on by such mercenary bands. Conan Doyle, in his novel *The White Company*, tells the experiences of a typical free company. Italy was the greatest field for the free companies. The rich cities wanted to beat their rivals, but seldom cared to do their own fighting. Some *condottieri*, like the Sforzas at Milan, even became rulers.

The Thirty Years' War (1618–1648) was the last one in which free companies figured largely. Each side hired companies from any source where good soldiers could be found. On one occasion, a regiment of Scots in Swedish pay attacked a regiment of Irish in Austrian pay. Probably the largest wholesale contract on record came in 1631. Wallenstein agreed with the Holy Roman Emperor to raise, command, and pay 30,000 men, to fight in the Imperial service. He counted on making the war pay for itself by plunder and the like. Able soldiers from all parts of Europe flocked to his standard, for his high military fame led to hopes of many profitable victories.

PROFESSIONAL STANDING ARMIES

THE KING'S REGULARS—The next step was the creation of professional standing armies. They were the general thing from about 1650 to 1800. A country would keep a permanent force in time of peace instead of having to hire job lots of soldiers when war broke out. This made it possible to secure a degree of discipline, which had been out of the question with free companies. The soldier was still a professional under this system but he was now in the permanent service and pay of a particular ruler, except in the case of a few isolated mercenary forces, like the Hessians. A soldier no longer simply followed a captain who might sell his services anywhere. The word *regulars* always suggests discipline, steadiness, and dependability. These professional standing armies resembled the Roman legions at their best. Frederick the Great could rely on his "crack" Prussian Guard, just as Cæsar had been able to depend on the seasoned veterans of his favorite Tenth Legion.

GENERAL VOGUE—The French took the first step in the direction of standing armies in the later middle ages. Such armies did not become common until about 1650. Gustavus Adolphus [2] had a standing army in Sweden at the time of the Thirty Years' War. By its close, most of the principal countries had adopted the idea. The larger nations maintained

[2] See pp. 55, 131.

armies between 50,000 and 150,000 strong. They generally had, in addition, a partly organized militia for home defense, which was apt to be a joke and was of little service in war. The professionals usually fought all the battles. This was the period of "Brown Bess," smooth-bore cannon, "thin-line" attacks, and Vauban siegecraft. The armies of Louis XIV, Frederick the Great, and the British in the American Revolution were mostly of this professional kind. To-day, the regular armies of England and the United States are modeled upon it. Consequently, its features are well worth studying.

RECRUITING—Military service was ordinarily a life job for the "regulars." Generally they entered the army voluntarily. Recruiting officers, with a few men all dressed up in their gayest regimentals, would settle in a town, with headquarters at the inn. They would attract the yokels by the drum and treat the bystanders to free drinks. The officers and sample soldiers would all talk about the joys of a soldier's life. Then, when a prospective soldier looked ready, an officer would slip a coin into his hand. Once a recruit accepted this "King's shilling," he was in the army—perhaps for life unless he lost an arm or a leg. In time of emergency the recruiting was not always voluntary. Able-bodied vagabonds were forced into service. Jailbirds were freed to become soldiers. Still, armies seldom went as far as the navy press-gangs, which literally kidnapped men for the fleets. The international element still remained in the armies. A French or Prussian army might contain hundreds of Irish, Scotch, Poles, and soldiers of other nationalities.

DISCIPLINE—The recruit, once in the army, had plenty of time to become a seasoned soldier, as terms of enlistment seldom expired. The "thin-line" fighting required the strictest sort of discipline. Men had to be trained to advance in the face of enemy fire with an unbroken line. Frederick the Great considered at least two years necessary to make seasoned troops out of his recruits. Punishments for even minor offenses were brutal. Flogging on the bare back was common. For all this, the pay was low. The British private in the American Revolution received sixteen cents a day, from which his food and supplies were deducted. As a result, little if any cash was left over for pay-day. Desertions were naturally common.

OFFICERS—The officers were all noblemen, or at least "gentlemen." An almost impassable chasm lay between them and the enlisted men. The man in the ranks, no matter what his ability, had no chance at all of rising above the grade of sergeant. The French Army finally became so strict that a man could rarely get even the lowest commission unless his ancestors had been nobles for several generations. Even then, promotion was ordinarily out of the question without special influence at court. Boys of fourteen were sometimes given command of regiments containing gray-haired captains, of the lesser nobility who had lacked "pull." Commissions had to be bought in the British Army as late as 1871. The cheapest, a second lieutenancy of infantry, cost about $2,250—equivalent to about a year's pay. A lieutenant-colonelcy in a "crack" regiment cost more than $30,000. An officer could sell this again when he decided to retire. In peace time, it was usually a more social than military life. Many officers were then placed on half-pay, forming a reserve to be called in the next war.

The officers, like the men, were still a fairly international group. Hundreds of "soldiers of fortune" sold their swords wherever the fighting or the pay was good. A Scotchman rose to high command in the Prussian army. An Irishman became an Austrian general. One of France's ablest commanders was Marshal Saxe, one of the 300 children of a Polish king. The American Revolution was supposedly a "private fight" within the British Empire. Yet among the American high commanders were Lafayette, von Steuben, Kosciusko, de Kalb, and Pulaski. England, on her side, had von Knyphausen and von Riedesel among the numerous German leaders of the hired Hessian troops.

ORDERLY WARFARE—The nature of these standing armies influenced the warfare of the time. Probably no other period of modern history saw the people as a whole less affected by wars. The armies fought in the pay and in the interests of the monarchs— Bourbons, Hapsburgs, Hohenzollerns, or others— rather than for the nations. The people were seldom called upon for military service. The well-disciplined troops rarely ravaged the countryside as the free companies had done. The armies were relatively small because of the expense necessary to keep them up. Campaigns and battles were fought along conventional lines except when an occasional original genius came on the scene.

NATIONAL CONSCRIPT ARMIES

TWO NEW FEATURES—The French Revolution produced a new type of army during its long wars from 1792 on. It was distinguished by two features which were to have a permanent influence on the military systems of Europe. First, it was a *national* army, representing the whole country and not simply the monarch. A new spirit was appearing in warfare. Second, it became a *conscript* army, with compulsory military service for all men between certain ages. Much larger numbers were thus possible than under the old system.

THE NATION IN ARMS—France was invaded by the professional armies of Austria and Prussia in 1792. The revolutionary government could no longer depend on most of the old French regulars. It, therefore, declared the country in a state of danger, and summoned the men of the whole nation to its defense. They came by the hundreds of thousands— raw, green amateurs as a whole, singing the *Marseillaise* and burning with patriotic enthusiasm. Their greenness was offset by their numbers and spirit. They were no international group, fighting for the Bourbon king. They were Frenchmen, fighting for France. The heavy mass attack, we recall, was introduced to utilize these men against the "thin lines" of the disciplined enemy regulars. They not only threw the invaders out of France, but, under Napoleon, conquered most of Europe. The *nation in arms* was a success.[3]

COMPULSORY SERVICE IN WAR—Conscription was the next step. It was argued that a country does so much for the individual that he owes it military service in time of need. The original patriotic fervor had died down in France by 1798. Volunteers were no longer pouring in. The government declared that all able-bodied men between twenty and twenty-five were liable for military service, and would be conscript or drafted as the government saw fit. "There is perhaps no law on the statute books of any nation which has exercised and is destined to exercise a more far-reaching influence on the future of humanity," wrote a modern general. Conscription gave Napoleon 30,000 new men a month for his campaigns.

[3] See p. 132.

THE BATON IN THE KNAPSACK—A third feature helped the French armies to succeed. Any private might become a general. Napoleon told his armies that every man of them carried a marshal's baton in his knapsack. He did not insist on noble ancestry. Sons of innkeepers and small lawyers commanded army corps. Many of his marshals would never have been more than sergeants in the old armies. This showed how much talent had been wasted in the past. After Napoleon's day, the chasm between officers and men widened once more. But the idea of the national conscript army spread to other nations. France was victorious until this happened. One of her enemies, Prussia, went even further along these lines.

UNIVERSAL MILITARY TRAINING

CONSCRIPTION EXTENDED TO TIME OF PEACE— The modern military systems of the leading European countries are modeled on an experiment made in Prussia between 1807 and 1813. This was universal military training. The French had raised a national conscript army in time of war. The Prussians extended this idea to include the training of its citizens in time of *peace*. Napoleon had completely crushed Prussia at Jena and Auerstadt in 1806. He intended to keep her weak, so that she would not threaten his influence again. He made Prussia agree to limit her army to 42,000 men. The Prussians knew that they could never do much to throw off Napoleon's power with so small a force. At the same time, he was too strong to be defied. They got out of the dilemma by a clever ruse. They decided to train the army very intensively for a few months. Then most of the men would be discharged and a new lot put through the same drilling. A few officers and non-coms were kept as a permanent *cadre* to conduct the training. In this way, they kept the size of the army within the required limit. Yet they built up quickly a powerful reserve of trained men. The system was made compulsory. Every man was to go through it at a certain age. The Prussian army trained in this way played its part in the final overthrow of Napoleon.

PRUSSIA'S SUCCESS—Prussia continued the system after the war was over. The country was too poor to train every one, but the law was at least on the books, and so the policy of universal service did not die. It was revived about 1860. Prussia secured large numbers of trained men, who fought their way to victory over Austria in 1866 and over France in 1870. Prussia made herself the leader in the new German Empire, and kept up her successful system. Other nations followed suit either in self-defense or in hopes of accomplishing similar results. This accounts for the huge number of trained men who were instantly mobilized when the World War broke out.

THE SYSTEM—The German system of universal military service was so far-reaching in its effects that it is worth studying. It was, as the name implies, compulsory. The French had originally held a man liable for service in time of war. The German army kept its grip on a man for at least thirty years. Let us follow the military career of a typical ablebodied German citizen. He was called to the colors at twenty. For three years he served in the active army and was thoroughly trained. Then, for four years more, he was in the reserve. Here he had to show up twice a year for muster, and spend about six weeks at a training camp. At twenty-seven, he passed into the *Landwehr,* which means "national guard."

He received less frequent training for twelve years. Finally, he went into the *Landsturm,* where until after fifty, he was still liable for special service, such as garrison duty and guarding railroads.

SELECTION OF OFFICERS—Many of the officers were selected from educated Germans corresponding to our college men. Three-fifths of the regular Army officers were picked from men in the active Army, recommended by their colonels. The remainder were graduates of cadet schools, similar to our West Point. Candidates for commissions in the reserve or *Landwehr* could take a one-year course at their own expense, instead of the usual three years' compulsory training. It was not enough, however, to be recommended for a commission. A prospective officer could not secure a command until the other officers of a regiment accepted him. A single blackball would disqualify the candidate. This was an important social restriction, as it generally limited officers' positions to "gentlemen." Many of Napoleon's marshals under such a plan would undoubtedly have been blackballed by snobbish lieutenants before they had a chance to rise.

PREPAREDNESS TO THE LIMIT—Germany thus acquired a huge standing army on active service, in addition to a tremendous number of well-trained reserves. The reserves, *Landwehr* and *Landsturm,* were divided into regiments and divisions like the active army. Every officer and man knew exactly where he was to report as soon as mobilization was declared. It was found to be too expensive to train more than half of the citizens in this way. Many were put without training into a special reserve, which might be called upon for special duties. Also the period of active service was reduced from three to two years, so that more could be trained for the same amount of money. This meant a still larger army, but with somewhat less training.

OPPOSITION TO THE SYSTEM—Universal service was quite an ideal system from the purely military standpoint. The "Junkers" or landholding aristocracy, who dominated the government, supported it strongly. To the workman it was less satisfactory. He had to spend two or three years in a non-productive occupation just at the age when men in other countries were getting a good start in life. Not only was a large part of the population irritated, but the productive wealth of the country was cut down with so many men tied up as economic liabilities instead of as assets. The workmen did not have much influence in the government—the Junkers did. Germany remained, therefore, a nation in arms. The individual was subordinated to the state, not only in a crisis but in peace as well.

EUROPEAN "ARMED CAMP"—As a natural result, Germany's neighbors did the same thing, partly for defensive reasons, partly perhaps because they saw the possibilities of such a system. Europe became a vast camp with millions of trained men. France lived in fear of the German army and also wanted revenge for her 1870 defeat. So she introduced a similar plan. She had to require a longer term of active service in order to have as large a standing army as Germany because her population was a third smaller. This also meant that she had fewer reserves. Russia could afford to train only a part of her vast population, but even at that her army outnumbered any other. Austria, Italy, and several smaller nations also took up the system. Switzerland went in for it in a modified form. She wanted no standing army for offensive purposes, but needed soldiers to defend her neutrality. Every Swiss, therefore, spent

six months in military training and passed into the
militia.

ENGLAND AN EXCEPTION—England alone stayed
out of the system. The English Channel and the
British Navy defended her from these huge continental armies. All that she needed were troops to
defend her empire and to maintain order at home.
Like the United States—also protected from land
attack—she kept a highly proficient professional
army.[4] Territorials, like our militia, supplemented
her home defense.

SIZE OF NEW ARMIES—The size of the principal
active and reserve armies in 1911, on the eve of
the World War, was a striking contrast to the previous centuries when 100,000 men were thought a
large army. The official figures, which grew larger
by the outbreak of the war in 1914, were:

	Peace-time standing armies	Fully trained reserves ready for war	
Germany	806,000	4,000,000	
France	818,000	2,300,000	
Russia	1,284,000	3,800,000	
Austria	370,000	1,600,000	
Italy	305,000	1,250,000	
England	255,000	215,000	(Territorials)
United States	92,000	128,000	(National Guard)

THE TAXPAYER'S BURDEN—Naturally, the cost of
such armies was tremendous. Between 1873 and
1913, it is estimated, the six great powers of Europe
spent twenty-seven billions of dollars on their armies
and ten billions on their navies. France was spending
nearly half her government income for military pur-

[4] See Chap. VII.

PROFESSIONALS AND AMATEURS

poses in 1913. The citizen paid for the new systems in taxes, as well as in services. It was small wonder that many came to America to dodge the double burden, and then dared not return.

THE NEW SPIRIT—The spirit of the new national armies was different. The old professional soldiers often cared little about the cause for which they fought. Frequently it was merely a monarch's desire to grab or to defend some small piece of territory. The new soldier certainly had a more definite interest in a war even if the military service itself appealed to him less. Besides, we saw that the old professional armies might contain soldiers from a dozen different lands. The new armies, except for special units like the French Foreign Legion, were composed wholly of nationals. The German army was all Germans, the French all Frenchmen, and the Russian all Russians. The whole population was affected, for almost every household had some member liable for service.[5] Deliberate propaganda stimulated enthusiasm for one's own army and hatred or fear of the enemy. The hate between many of the nations spread throughout the armies and the peoples. This system, in addition to its cost in money and time, also led to a vaster, more bitter and more thoroughgoing war of peoples against peoples.

THE PRESENT SITUATION—The World War did not settle the problem of universal training as opposed to the professional system. France still has her universal service, and is training African blacks to offset her lack of population. Many European nations still compel all their citizens to train, and keep them in a reserve ready for future complications. The peace treaty forced Germany to reduce her army, which is now about the size of our own. Eng-

[5] See pp. 295, 296.

land and the United States learned the immense difficulty of expanding a small professional army overnight into a "nation in arms." Yet the people of those two countries would probably never consent to adopt compulsory universal training. A compromise between the two systems seems necessary. We shall see in later chapters how unfortunate experience is guiding the United States toward a military policy which may combine efficiency and security with individual liberty.[6]

[6] See Chaps. VII and VIII.

CHAPTER VI

WAR ON THE MAP

THE EVOLUTION OF STRATEGY AND COMMAND

Strategy is a hard word to define. Literally, it means generalship. It has been called "war on the map" and "the application of common sense to war." Briefly, strategy may be called the art of directing armies; tactics, that of leading troops on the battle-field.

POLICY, STRATEGY, AND TACTICS—Strategy occupies the important middle position in war between policy and tactics. Determination of national *policy* is the work of the civil government. Its statesmen determine when, with whom, and for what purpose a war is to be fought. They also generally decide the number of men and amount of materials available for the war. Then comes *strategy*. The commander takes the troops and supplies made available for him. Then he plans and directs the operations during campaigns in such a manner as to meet to the best advantage the purposes and conditions of the national policy. The whole idea of war is to impose the will of one nation upon another. The commander tries to move his forces so that they can force the enemy either to submit without a battle or to fight under the most unfavorable circumstances. Finally *tactics,* as we have seen, is the arrangement of troops for the battle itself and their direction and control on the battle-field.

UNCHANGING PRINCIPLES—The study of strategy is important in military history because its general principles never change. Weapons and tactical formations come and go, but the main teachings of strategy hold good throughout the ages. Yet, unchanging as they are, the successful strategical methods are hard to explain. The trouble is that strategy is an *art,* not a science. A science has definite, exact rules, an art merely general principles. Success depends upon the genius of the individual who puts them into practice. Napoleon explained this difference clearly. "Tactics, maneuvers, military engineering, and the science of artillery," he said, "can be learned from a textbook almost like geometry, but the grand art of war can be learned only from the history of the wars and battles of the great captains, and by experience. There are no definite, precise rules at all. Everything depends upon the character which nature has given to the general, upon his ability, his defects, the quality of the troops and weapons, the season, and a thousand circumstances which prevent things from ever repeating themselves exactly." The best training for a general, Napoleon said, is to "read and reread the campaigns of the great masters of the art of war."

THE APPLICATION OF MILITARY HISTORY—It is out of the question for any general to take some previous campaign as a model and follow it slavishly, "play by play." The conditions, as Napoleon said, would never repeat themselves exactly. As soon as some little change came, the general would be lost. Napoleon's approach to Austerlitz in 1805 resembled Marlborough's in the Blenheim campaign during the War of the Spanish Succession in 1704 just as "Stonewall" Jackson's Shenandoah campaign of 1862, in our Civil War, was like Napoleon's Italian campaign of 1796.[1] In each case the general had studied the successful elements of the earlier campaign, and had genius enough to apply them to his own somewhat different circumstances. Success requires a clear idea of the general principles—and an able man. We shall take up the principles first, and the men afterward.

THE PRINCIPLES OF WAR

THE NINE PRINCIPLES—Strategists have tried to analyze the campaigns of history to discover what things produced success or failure. Many have tried to explain them. General Forrest, the illiterate but able Confederate raider, did it most briefly. He said that strategy consisted in "gitting thar fustest with the mostest men." That definition hits most of the essential truths, but it is not enough. On the other hand, we have not time to weigh all the arguments in the heavy volumes of von Clausewitz, Jomini, von der Goltz and the other great writers on strategy. The lessons to be learned from history have been boiled down to nine general principles—the *objective,* the *offensive, mass, economy of force, movement, surprise, security, simplicity,* and *cooperation.* These can be applied in any campaign as a test. They are closely interrelated, so that an even shorter list would be possible. They are not absolute like the laws of science. But they are on the whole the principles which have led to victory. When they have been successfully violated, it has generally been for very special reasons that were carefully considered beforehand.

[1] See Chap. XII.

STRATEGICAL TERMS—The most satisfactory way to get an idea of the chief points in the art of war is to take up these nine elements one by one. Before that, we must understand some of the terms used in strategy. Military men, like so many other classes, have their own technical vocabulary. The first step in war is called *mobilization*. This means the change from the state of peace to the state of war. It leads to the concentration of troops and supplies for action. A series of closely related actions in a particular region is known as an *operation*. Several connected operations, in turn, compose a *campaign*. A *plan* must be drawn up before starting upon an operation or a campaign. This should include the *objective,* at which the campaign is aimed. It should also designate the *base of operations*. This meant, in the old days, the particular place where supplies were stored. With the improved transportation of recent warfare, it refers to the whole district from which supplies are drawn. The *line of operations* is the route by which an army moves from its base toward its objective. That portion of the line of operations between the army and its base becomes known, as the army advances, as the *line of communications*. Such lines, in earlier wars, were usually roads or rivers, but now railroads are most important for this purpose. The district in which operations take place is the *theater of operations,* while the whole region affected by the contest is the *theater of war*. A country or an army fighting as a single unit against enemies who operate from different directions is said to occupy *interior lines*. Thus, Germany in the World War had interior lines between France and England on the west and Russia on the east.[2] Her enemies, of course, held *exterior lines*.

[2] See p. 300.

1. THE PRINCIPLE OF THE OBJECTIVE

THE PROPER MAIN OBJECTIVE—With these terms in mind, we shall now take up the nine principles of strategy. The principle of the *objective* comes first. The nation and the commander have to decide what is the most important thing to do. There is but one answer. The main object should always be the *principal armed force of the enemy*. There is a temptation to fritter away energy trying to capture some geographical point. At times, of course, the fall of the enemy's capital has a great moral and political importance. But that rarely means victory as long as the enemy's main army is still intact. Go straight for that army and beat it; the geographical points will come easily after that. Napoleon once remarked, "There are many good generals in Europe, but they see too many things at once. I see the enemy's masses and I destroy them." The British violated the principle of the *objective* in the American Revolution. They should have centered their efforts on crushing the main American army under Washington. Instead, they scattered their energy in seizing seaports and trying to occupy territory. Washington's army, foolishly spared, led finally to their defeat.[3]

MINOR OBJECTIVES—Particular operations, of course, may frequently have geographic points as objectives. It may be desirable to capture an important railroad center in order to cripple the enemy's line of communications or improve one's own. Certain enemy strongholds may have to be reduced before a safe advance can be made. Even the most limited operations should have definite objectives. Their goals should be worth what they cost in time, men,

[3] See Chap. IX.

and material. No troops must be used which could be employed to better advantage elsewhere. Finally, these lesser objectives should work in connection with the main objective—and that, we remember, is the principal enemy force.

2. PRINCIPLE OF THE OFFENSIVE

WHEN TO ATTACK—The principle of the *offensive* comes second. In most fighting, one side attacks on the offensive, and the other is on the defensive. The commander has to decide whether or not to take the offensive. The rule is to *attack whenever possible*. Military history shows that victory generally goes to the attacking side. Like football, one has to have the ball in order to score. But it is not always possible or advisable to attack. That is why the question of the offensive is an all-important strategical problem.

RIVAL CONSIDERATIONS—Both offensive and defensive have distinct advantages and disadvantages. The side which attacks has the important advantage of *initiative*. It can decide what to do next and the the defense has to conform to its movements. With this freedom of action, the attackers can pick their own objectives and the other side has to guard them. The offensive has a strong moral effect. Troops, keyed up for the attack, fight with more spirit, as they are going out to get something. They are carrying the war into the enemy's country while their own is spared. But there are certain drawbacks. The defenders know their own region well enough to take advantage of its strong points. The attackers have to guard long lines of communications through hostile country. They nearly always lose more men than the defenders, who are sheltered behind defenses. The offensive, therefore, is an expensive game. One has, as a rule, to be the stronger in order to undertake it successfully.

FABIAN STRATEGY—Consequently, the weaker side often has to take to the defensive. But it should only be a temporary defensive, sparring for time until conditions are right to seize the offensive. The name of the old Roman, Fabius Maximus, a dictator in the Second Punic War, is often attached to this kind of defensive fighting. He avoided battle with Hannibal's "crack" troops, but by harassing their flanks delayed their advance as much as possible. Washington adopted such Fabian defensive methods in the Revolution when he retreated across New Jersey before a vastly superior British force in the fall of 1776. To offer battle at the time would have been suicidal. By the end of the year, however, he was able to assume the offensive. He defeated the British at Trenton and at Princeton, and cleared New Jersey all in ten days.[4] In the same way, the French and the British in 1914 retired before the Germans as far as the Marne, where they were in a favorable position to seize the offensive. A purely passive defense, which merely tries to ward off attacks without planning an offensive of its own, can never win victories. It is lucky to stave off complete defeat. In fact, usually "the best defense is the offensive."

THREEFOLD APPLICATION—The terms *offensive* and *defensive* can be separately applied to wars as a whole, to strategy, and to tactics. This permits many strange combinations. The Civil War, for instance, was a *defensive war* for the South because the North was trying to force it to stay in the Union. The Southern general, Lee, assumed the *strategical*

4 See Chap. X.

offensive, however, in the fall of 1862 when he invaded Maryland. In the course of this same campaign, he was on the *tactical defensive* when the Northern army attacked him in the battle of Antietam in that state.[5] These various distinctions do not alter the main teaching of the principle of the offensive, *attack whenever possible.*

3. THE PRINCIPLE OF MASS

STRATEGY AND STRENGTH—The principle of mass, (called concentration by the British) could well be translated, "Be superior to the enemy at the decisive spot." Mass in this connection means combat power, and refers not only to the number of men, but also to weapons, fighting ability, discipline, morale, and leadership. Though numbers are not everything, they are the most obvious element of strength. Napoleon said, "God is on the side of the biggest battalions." His enemies often had much larger armies in the theater of war, but he generally managed to have equal or superior numbers in his *battles.* In this, he achieved one of the most brilliant things that strategy can do. A general rarely has the power to determine the number of men in his army. It is not his fault if the enemy's army is larger. But this need not mean that he has to be outnumbered by the enemy in battle. We shall see a very brilliant illustration of this in "Stonewall" Jackson's Shenandoah campaign in the Civil War. With 17,000 men, he was successful against 70,000 Northerners.[6] He nearly always managed to have equal or superior numbers on the battle-field, although outnumbered more than four to one in the theater of operations.

[5] See p. 246.
[6] See Chap. XII.

Jackson had studied Napoleon's comments on war, and he put them into practice. Napoleon urged that every possible man be brought into a battle and used where he would count most. A single battalion might, he said, turn the tide of victory.

4. The Principle of Economy of Force

PROPER DISTRIBUTION—This principle deals with the proper distribution of strength. Its main teaching is, "To have superior strength at the decisive spot, economize elsewhere." It is thus the corollary of the principle of mass. Seldom can an army concentrate *every* man and all its resources on the decisive spot. War is not that simple. Frequently secondary objectives cannot be ignored. Other hostile armies may have to be watched. Communications may have to be guarded. The problem is to withdraw as many men as possible from these secondary objectives for the decisive blow, and yet not endanger the security of the army in any place. There are no definite rules for this. It is a matter of judgment.

ONE BIG THING AT A TIME—But one thing the commander must *not* do, and that is, he must not try to accomplish big things in several places at once. If the offensive is to be taken with maximum force at the decisive spot, he must defend with minimum force elsewhere. Thus the Germans in 1914 assumed the defensive with a small force against Russia in the east while they concentrated against France in the west. They reversed the process in 1915 by keeping just enough men on the Western Front to be secure against attack.[7] They could not afford to run two big offensives at once. If a general attempts too much, his army runs the risk of being

[7] See pp. 300, 309.

defeated in "damned driblets." A "side-show" of-fensive is folly when a concentration of force is needed at the critical spot. Too often, the generals "send a boy to do a man's work." As a result, several "boys" are apt to be destroyed without accomplishing anything. It is better to wait until the "man" has finished one job and can center his superior force on the next one.

5. THE PRINCIPLE OF MOVEMENT

"KEEP MOVING"—The principle of *movement* insists that operations should "keep moving" until they get decisive results. The ability to move rapidly and steadily naturally increases the power of an army. Napoleon wrote, "The force of an army, like the quantity of momentum in mechanics, is evaluated in terms of mass multiplied by velocity." Too many offensives "peter out" before reaching their objectives. An attack can be compared to throwing a pail of water on the floor. At first the water rushes swiftly on, but the further it spreads the slower it goes. It stops at last, unless another pailful has been thrown. That is where reserves come in. They have been called the "fuel of all operations." A commander who has properly practised economy of force will have fresh troops on hand to keep things moving before this lull comes.

HISTORICAL VIOLATIONS—Countless battles in history have been tactical victories, yet did not bring decisive strategical results because the victors failed to follow up their gains. They often simply stayed on the battle-field for several days while the beaten enemy retired in safety. Meade, the Northern commander at Gettysburg, has been roundly criticized for his failure to pursue Lee's defeated army immediately after the battle. It was claimed that he might have won the war then and there if he had not given the Southerners a chance to retire into Virginia.[8] Most of the great drives on the Western Front in the World War failed because the advance over the shell-torn waste slowed up their momentum after the initial victory, and forced them to stop short of their main objective.[9]

SEIZING THE INITIATIVE—That critical moment —when the attack has spent its force—may even give the other side a chance to grasp the offensive. We shall study in detail how the tide of war turned on July 18, 1918. The Germans had launched their last great offensive three days before. It lost momentum and slowed down. Barely had it stopped when the Allies seized the offensive. The American and French drive at Soissons that day gave the Allies the initiative and they never lost it.[10] The constantly increasing reserve force of American troops kept things moving without let-up. The British call this "mobility," but it means more than simply the ability to move easily and rapidly from place to place. *Movement* is the ability to move steadily and uninterruptedly in the decisive direction.

6. THE PRINCIPLE OF SURPRISE

FORMS OF SURPRISE—The principle of surprise is quite obvious. Some sort of surprise is necessary in order to secure maximum results with minimum loss. Surprise has a great moral effect in addition to the actual strategical and tactical advantages it may secure. It may take the form of new tactical forma-

[8] See p. 250.
[9] See pp. 304, 310, 316, 327.
[10] See pp. 330, 345, 350, 354.

tions or instruments of war, planned long in advance. The needle-gun was a successful surprise at Königgrätz (Sadowa) in the Austro-Prussian War of 1866. Poison gas was a complete one in 1915, but its effect was wasted because the Germans were not ready to follow it up. The "tank" in 1916 was intended as such, but the secret leaked out and the tactical employment was imperfect.[11]

MOBILITY AND SECRECY—More often surprise is the result of a sudden, unexpected movement. It multiplies the power of the offensive by catching the defender off guard. Secrecy is naturally all-important. The fewer that know the plans, the better the chance for success. In the Civil War, when "Stonewall" Jackson's army approached a crossroads, even his staff seldom knew whether the course lay to the right, to the left, or straight ahead. Mobility is, of course, a great ally of surprise. A slow approach is apt to give everything away. Modern warfare has made surprise more difficult, but just as necessary for success. Aviation has given armies new eyes. Wireless telegraphy spreads news more rapidly than ever. Yet the Germans time and again in the World War made great concentrations of troops and artillery against an unsuspecting enemy.[12] Also, the Americans, as we shall see, concentrated with sufficient speed and secrecy to catch the Germans off guard at Soissons.[13] With all its advantages, surprise is a dangerous weapon in unskilful hands. If it fails, the material and moral effect on the "surprisers" may be a powerful boomerang.

[11] See pp. 18, 19, 314, 319.
[12] See pp. 311, 315, 324, 327, 337.
[13] See pp. 346, 349.

7. The Principle of Security

PRECAUTIONS—*Security* is a passive but very important principle. It is the direct opposite of surprise. It seldom brings victories, but it can prevent defeats. Even the boldest generals cannot afford to ignore it. Every plan naturally involves risks. Nothing is absolutely sure, but there is no excuse for failure to take proper precautions. Measures of security range all the way from powerful fortress systems down to the pickets which guard outposts from surprise. Constant vigilance is one essential of security. Napoleon was not the man to be caught napping. Two of his maxims deal with this point. "An army should be ready every day, every night, and at all times of the day and night to oppose all the resistance of which it is capable." "A commander-in-chief should ask himself frequently in the day, what should I do if the enemy's army should now appear on my front, on my right, or on my left? If he has any difficulty in answering these questions, he is badly posted, and should seek to correct his dispositions." Special care has to be taken for the protection of the flanks, the rear, and the lines of communication. They are the vulnerable parts of an army and the enemy know it.

THREE EXAMPLES—The Civil War shows three different illustrations of security. The Union general, McClellan, carried it too far.[14] He lost chance after chance because he wanted to be sure that nothing would go wrong. Grant, on the other hand, nearly wrecked his career at the outset. He neglected the most elementary precautions against surprise, and through sheer carelessness his army was

[14] See pp. 245, 274, 290.

caught unawares at Shiloh.[15] The Southerners, Lee and Jackson, took well-considered risks with great success. They knew how extremely dangerous it is to divide an army in the face of superior numbers. Yet they did this several times deliberately because they saw that chances could be taken with the poor Union generals.[16] But the principle remains—take no *unnecessary* risks.

8. The Principle of Simplicity

SIMPLE PLANS ESSENTIAL—The simpler a plan is, the more likely it is to succeed. War is so uncertain that it is useless and even dangerous to plan everything beforehand in minute detail. The whole operation may be thrown out of joint if one or two parts of a complicated plan go wrong. That means a change of plans—a demoralizing and risky procedure. A simple general plan, which can be adjusted to meet varying circumstances, is better. A sensible decision, once made, should not be altered unless absolutely necessary.

UNITY OF COMMAND—For simplicity and success, there should be *one head* with one plan—not two or twenty heads, each with its own plan. "Unity of command is the first requirement of war," wrote Napoleon. He was the unquestioned head of all his forces. His clear plans were easy to understand, and his marshals were trained to carry them out. He usually kept his army together or within easy call, so that he could operate on "interior lines." His enemies, who often lacked unity of command, were apt to be defeated one by one.

In the Civil War, both sides were slow to appoint

[15] See p. 253.
[16] See pp. 245, 247, 282.

supreme commanders. The North finally did so in 1864 and the South not until 1865. At one time in 1862, six independent Union armies were in northern Virginia.[17] It was the same in the World War. It took a severe crisis to bring about unity of command on each side. The Central Powers achieved it in 1916. The Allies did not appoint Marshal Foch as generalissimo until the critical days of the German "Peace Drive" in the spring of 1918.[18] In every case unity of command has paid.

9. THE PRINCIPLE OF COÖPERATION

TEAM-WORK—Coöperation has been described as the "cementing principle." As the name implies, it calls for team-work. Such team-work must range all the way from the tactical performances of a squad to the combined operations of several different nations in the field. Tactically, of course, it requires the intimate relations of the various arms of service in battle. The artillery barrage for the advancing infantry is an example. On the larger, strategical scale, it applies to the conduct of armies which lack unity of command. Thus France, England, and Russia coöperated against Germany and her allies during most of the war. Russia attacked quickly in 1914 to relieve the pressure on France. The French and English attacked in 1915 to help Russia. The situation was improved when Foch became generalissimo in 1918, but until such simplicity was secured, coöperation was absolutely necessary.

ARMY AND NAVY—Coöperation also applies to "amphibian" operations where the combined forces of army and navy are essential. A good example of

[17] See pp. 258, 272.
[18] See p. 328.

this can be seen in the operations of the Union armies and gunboats on the Mississippi River in the Civil War.[19] An example of poor coöperation was Gallipoli in the World War. The Allied military and naval forces attacked the Turkish positions separately, when a simultaneous action would probably have been successful.[20]

SUMMARY OF THE PRINCIPLES OF WAR

1. Objective—Strike at the enemy's chief force.
2. Offensive—Attack whenever possible.
3. Mass—Be superior to the enemy at the decisive spot.
4. Economy of force—Defend with minimum force in most places to have maximum force at the decisive spot.
5. Movement—Keep operations moving.
6. Surprise—Strike where you are not expected with secrecy and speed.
7. Security—Take no unnecessary risks.
8. Simplicity—Avoid complicated plans.
9. Coöperation—Show team-work with the others on your side.

GENERALSHIP

ESSENTIAL QUALITIES—Any one can understand such general principles. But it takes genius to apply them properly. That is why the *great* generals of history can be counted on one's fingers. Generalship requires many things of a man. Intellect is one big essential. He must have a keen, clear mind, which can size up a complicated situation quickly. It is not enough to follow plans drawn up in advance. A general must keep in constant, close touch with everything happening and must be able to make quick, sen-

[19] See pp. 251, 252.
[20] See pp. 312, 313.

sible decisions. He must be able to imagine himself
in the enemy's place and to forestall the enemy's
plans. He has to have, moreover, a strong will to
dominate subordinates and to enable him to keep on
in the face of tremendous difficulties. Organizing
ability is essential because of the countless details
requisite for success. Finally, moral qualities are
needed to give him the confidence and enthusiasm
of his men. The mere presence of some generals on
a battle-field is said to have been worth thousands
of men. The great general has to be studied not only
as a strategist but also as a battle tactician, an organizer, a leader of men, and sometimes even as a
statesman.

THE GREAT GENERALS

"THE BIG SEVEN"—A few men stand out in history as really great generals. They reveal real genius
in their systematic conduct of war. The list of those
in unquestioned first place is short—Alexander, Hannibal, Cæsar, Gustavus Adolphus, Marlborough,
Frederick the Great, and Napoleon.

ALEXANDER—Alexander, King of Macedon, overran the whole known Eastern world between 334
and 323 B. C. He inherited an enthusiastic, well-
trained, well-equipped army. With Greece and the
Danube region securely his, he determined to con-
quer the vast Persian Empire. He did—in five years.
His generalship was evident after his first victory
over the Persians at Issus on the Mediterranean.
Next he conquered the whole eastern coast of the
Mediterranean, including Egypt, to deprive the
powerful Persian fleet, which threatened his communications with home, of all its sea bases. Then
with his rear safe, he struck eastward at the main

army. He completely crushed it at Arbela, where he followed up his victory with relentless pursuit. With the main opposition out of the way, it was easier for him to extend his conquests far into Central Asia to the Indus River. He was only thirty-three when he died. He excelled not only in strategy, but also in battle tactics, siegecraft, and organizing ability. His personal magnetism was a vital factor in his success.

HANNIBAL—Hannibal, "the father of strategy," led the Carthaginian forces against Rome in the Second Punic War, 221–202 B. C. He took the Romans by surprise, coming over the Alps into Italy in winter, and thus kept them from launching an attack against Carthage. He had about 35,000 men; the Romans could raise twenty times as many. He more than made up for his deficient numbers by maneuvering. In two years, he whipped in succession four Roman armies. He caught the enemy by lying in ambush at Lake Trasimenus. At Cannæ, the most decisive victory, he wiped out a larger army by his famous enveloping maneuver.[21] The tide turned before long. Badly supported by the Carthaginian government, he was too greatly outnumbered to offer battle. Yet for thirteen years he outwitted the Romans time and again with his unexpected movements. These later years added much to his reputation, although he won no more victories. Finally recalled, he was defeated at Zama, near Carthage, by Scipio Africanus.

CÆSAR—Julius Cæsar has been called the ablest man in history. He was a combination of the statesman and soldier, securing supreme power in Rome by using his military skill. Beginners in Latin are familiar with his first successes in Gaul between 58

[21] See p. 307.

and 49 B. C. Then he turned his forces against
Pompey, his rival at Rome. Pompey's regular
legions were in Spain, but he himself crossed to
Greece for new forces. He thus expected to catch
Cæsar in Italy from both sides. Cæsar rushed to
Spain, where, outnumbered, he maneuvered Pompey's legions into a surrender without even fighting. Next, he speedily crossed the Adriatic to surprise Pompey. Saved from several tight places by his
constant luck, he eventually crushed Pompey's army
at Pharsalus by a clever surprise arrangement in his
battle-line. He continued victorious campaigns
against the enemies of Rome and of his own supreme
power in Asia, Africa, and Spain almost until his assassination at Rome in 44 B. C. As a general, Cæsar
was exceptionally resourceful. No one ever knew
what he would do next. He was active, energetic,
and quick to size up a situation. His veteran legions
were utterly devoted to him, and, as we said, he was
extraordinarily lucky.

GUSTAVUS ADOLPHUS—In the 1,700 years after
Cæsar there were plenty of outstanding warriors,
but no general contributed much to the art of war
until the Swedish king Gustavus Adolphus (1611–
1632). This "father of modern warfare" standardized the methods of fighting on a new basis, after
centuries of irregularity.[22] He made infantry, cavalry, and artillery more mobile, as we know, and
gave them new functions in battle. His application
of intellect to warfare led to the efficient organization of supplies and communications. Gustavus
worked out many of his reforms during his early
wars with Denmark, Poland, and Russia. He is remembered more, however, for his campaigns, and
for his victories at Breitenfeld and Lützen during his

[22] See pp. 30, 55, 101.

two years' fighting in the Thirty Years' War. His fame rests rather on his tactics and organization than on his strategy.

MARLBOROUGH—The Duke of Marlborough led the armies of England and her allies against the French forces of Louis XIV in the War of the Spanish Succession (1701–1713). His original and forceful strategy was particularly noticeable in his Blenheim campaign in 1704. He dashed across Europe, to the enemy's bewilderment, and crushed part of their forces before the others could come up. He was also remarkably tactful in the way he secured coöperation from the numerous allies.

FREDERICK THE GREAT—Frederick the Great of Prussia won his reputation in two long wars, the War of the Austrian Succession and the Seven Years' War, between 1740 and 1763. Like Alexander, he inherited an excellent army from his father. He disciplined it severely, and introduced the "thin-line" attack, which we have studied.[23] His best work was against superior enemy numbers when his little army faced the forces of nearly all Europe in the Seven Years' War. He made able use of "interior lines" in keeping his enemies apart. His victories at Rossbach and Leuthen in 1757 were masterpieces of tactical maneuvering. His perfectly trained troops executed difficult and decisive movements on the field. Frederick did suffer some bad defeats, but he was able to hold his own in the face of overwhelming opposition.

NAPOLEON—Napoleon Bonaparte is rated by many as the greatest general in history. He rose rapidly from lieutenant of artillery to Emperor of the French. He sprang into fame with his Italian campaign of 1796–1797. He darted about Italy, defeat-

[23] See pp. 56, 57.

ing one bewildered Austrian general after another. In 1805, he hurried across Europe like Marlborough in the Blenheim campaign. He picked off one surprised Austrian army and then crushed the combined Austrians and Russians at Austerlitz. Other brilliant campaigns, Jena and Wagram, followed, and made him master of Europe for several years. The tide turned against him in his invasion of Russia. He was finally defeated at Waterloo in 1815. Jomini, one of the first scientific writers on strategy, explained Napoleon's success, like Frederick's, as being largely due to the use of "interior lines" against divided enemies. His "maxims," as we have seen, still give us the best concise statements of the principles of war. He showed bold originality in strategy, gaining constant victories against his more conventional opponents. He was equally successful as a battle tactician and as an organizer. His influence on his soldiers was tremendous.

THE "NEAR GREAT"—In addition to these men, many "near great" generals are frequently placed on a par with them. It is, of course, impossible to draw the line. We have room to mention only a few of them. In ancient history Scipio Africanus, who defeated Hannibal, has been recently hailed as a "greater than Napoleon," but many disagree with this judgment. Jenghis Khan, the Tartar chieftain from Central Asia, showed superlative strategical skill about 1240, when his rapidly moving armies swept over most of Asia and part of Eastern Europe. Turenne, who led the French armies of Louis XIV between 1660 and 1675, was a strategist of rare ability. The combination of Turenne for campaigns and Vauban for sieges led to the steady success of the French for several years.[24]

[24] See p. 79.

Then, about 1700, the tide turned against them. We have already seen what Marlborough did. With him, it is usual to mention his brilliant ally, Prince Eugene of Savoy. The English have much to say about Wolfe who captured Quebec in 1759, and Clive, who did wonders against overwhelming numbers in India about the same time. They also boast of the Duke of Wellington, with his Peninsular campaign against Napoleon's marshals in Spain and Portugal and his defeat of Napoleon himself at Waterloo.

THE OUTSTANDING AMERICANS—Probably the two greatest generals produced in America were the Confederate leaders Lee and Jackson. They will be discussed in detail later.[25] We must remember that the greatest generals are not always the victorious ones. Lee and Jackson are rated higher than their successful Union adversaries, just as Hannibal has a higher place than the Romans who defeated him. Grant and Sherman were good generals, but they scarcely merit a place among the leaders in history. Neither does Washington. He was a good strategist, but his principal contribution was the moral strength with which he held the army together.[26]

RECENT EUROPEAN GENERALS—Contemporary with Lee and Jackson, there was in Europe von Moltke, the scientific Prussian, who won rapid victories over the Austrians in 1866 and the French in 1870. The World War produced no genius of the Napoleonic type. The best strategists were probably Foch and Ludendorff, who were the real "master minds" of the opposing forces at the end. We are still too close to that war, however, to form an estimate as we can for earlier contests.

[25] See Chaps. XI and XII.
[26] See pp. 197, 208, 216, 217, 218.

These various names naturally by no means exhaust the list. Everyone will have his own nominations for the position of honor. Various nations have "favorite sons" who are lauded to the skies by enthusiastic supporters. Nevertheless, it is to the campaigns of the outstanding commanders we have named that we should look in particular for the proper way to conduct war.

STAFFS

THE NEED FOR STAFFS—Brilliant commanders alone are not enough to bring victory in modern war. There must be means of translating their ideas into action. To round out this subject, we must consider staffs in addition to the principles of war and the men who have applied them most successfully. One man cannot look out for the multitude of details involved in large-scale military operations, nor can he himself maintain adequate contact with the various subordinate units in a large command. Consequently, the commander of large forces has ordinarily gathered about him a group or "staff" of men to relieve him of the burden of details. He then has the time for really important problems and decisions. The staff officers may give strategical and tactical advice, but they have no authority to give orders except in the commander's name. He alone is responsible for the performance of his forces.

INFORMAL EARLY STAFFS—Early staffs were generally very informal affairs. A few specialists, generally engineers, would attend to reconnaissance and the like. The commander also had a "personal staff," made up of aides-de-camp who often served as orderlies. But there was no division of functions, no adequate means of regular contact with the subordinate units of a command, and very little staff training.

NAPOLEON AND BERTHIER—The national armies produced by conscription were too large to be managed with staffs of the old type. Napoleon organized separate staffs for the corps and divisions under his command. He had an invaluable "chief of staff" in Berthier. He merely had to tell Berthier what he wanted done and could rest assured that foolproof orders would be issued to the corps and divisions. Incidentally, Berthier was not present in the Waterloo campaign when two French corps went astray. But Berthier was in reality only a supersecretary. The ideas and plans all came from Napoleon. He was such a military genius that he could look out for details of strategy, tactics, administration, and supply in a way that would be impossible for the ordinary commander.

PRUSSIA'S CONTRIBUTION—The modern "general staff" as we know it to-day dates from about 1809. Prussia invented it after her defeat at Jena by Napoleon. Along with universal military training, it was part of her remarkable military reorganization under Scharnhorst. He realized that great generals, being geniuses, cannot always be produced when needed. Efficient staff preparation can eliminate some of the risk by giving ordinary generals every possible advantage.

THE GENERAL STAFF—The Prussian general staff system deserves careful study. It was not only the first, but for a long time was the most successful system. It served as a model for most modern general staffs in other armies, including our own. At the head of the system was the "Great General Staff" which coördinated the work of the whole army.

Its chief of staff was the principal adviser of the commander-in-chief. But, instead of being a Berthier who merely translated the ideas of a Napoleon into intelligible orders, he was very often the man who really directed the army. The Prussians frequently placed royalty in command of their forces. Since the Hohenzollern family has not produced a second Frederick the Great, this left the real work to the chief of staff. The chief had several assistants, each in charge of some particular function. The "general staff" included also the similar staffs in the divisions, corps, and higher units. These were in close relation to the Great General Staff, so that the whole army could function as a smoothly running machine under a single head.

STAFF OFFICERS—General staff officers of various ranks were selected from the different arms of the service and sent to schools which were started to give them a thorough training in the science and art of war. Prussia passed many officers through short terms with the general staff, returning them to duty with troops. This had two advantages over the original French system of permanent staff officers. First, the Prussian staff kept in touch with actual conditions instead of living entirely in a world of theory, while the "line" had a sprinkling of officers who understood the workings of the higher command. Second, it provided a large reserve of officers who would be qualified for general staff work when war increased the size of the army.

FUNCTIONS IN PEACE—The general staff had plenty of important work in time of peace. Plans for mobilization and concentration were worked out in detail. Every officer and man knew just where he was to go as soon as mobilization was ordered. Supplies were arranged in advance. Strategic railways were often built to hasten the movements of troops and supplies to vital points. Technical experts followed the latest improvements in ordnance, tactics, and other branches of warfare. The Prussians, for instance, had the needle-gun twenty-five years before the other armies adopted breechloaders.[27] Elaborate maps were made for every region where the army might possibly be called upon to fight. The staff officers tested their skill in war games. They were given imaginary conditions and took opposing sides. Then they worked out their moves step by step. Sometimes this took the form of field maneuvers with real troops. More often it resembled a game of chess played on a map. Such war games afforded opportunity for practice in the application of the principles of war in concrete situations, strategical and tactical. These games could not create genius, but they could give valuable training and could reveal incompetents before their blunders meant the loss of thousands of men and, possibly, decisive battles. Finally, and most important, the strategists of the Great General Staff carefully considered all the various wars which the diplomats and statesmen might call upon them to undertake. This meant that plans did not have to be thrown together hurriedly after the beginning of a war. One simply had to reach into a pigeonhole for the well-developed campaign against that particular enemy nation.

FUNCTIONS IN WAR—In war itself, the Prussian general staff simply reaped what it had sown so carefully in time of peace. It was naturally in an excellent position to take charge of the troops in the field. The close connection between the Great

[27] See pp. 18, 19.

General Staff and the general staffs of the higher
units ensured unity and coöperation.

THE FIRST REAL TESTS, 1866 AND 1870—The
Prussian general staff came into the limelight with
the rapid victories over Austria in 1866 and France
in 1870. In the latter case, the Germans mobilized
rapidly, while the French soldiers sometimes
traveled 1,500 miles—even from one corner of
France to another—picking up uniforms and guns
in different places. Officers and soldiers roamed
around the front for days and even for weeks to
find their proper organizations. Also, the French
commanders distrusted the permanent staff officers,
who were out of touch with real conditions. While
the French were blundering around, the German
Army advanced like clockwork toward its speedy
victories. The Prussian King was commander-in-
chief, but credit for the unusual series of victories
goes to von Moltke, head of the Great General
Staff.

WIDESPREAD IMITATION—The other nations soon
copied the Prussian (by that time the German) general staff system. They all worked out mobilization
schemes and plans of campaign, years in advance,
modifying them constantly to meet changing conditions. The French staff in particular became highly
efficient. The result was that Germany in 1914 did
not enjoy the same staff superiority that she had had
in 1866 and 1870.

THE AMERICAN GENERAL STAFF—The United
States did not adopt the general staff system until
1903, nearly a century after it had been started by
Scharnhorst. Our old "General Staff" was simply
the list of generals. In the meantime our army had
been seriously handicapped without such an organi-

zation.[28] Our General Staff was, however, organized in time to help our participation in the World War.[29]

THE CHIEF OF STAFF—Our present general staff system was modified after our experience in the World War, but we can see that it closely resembles the Prussian organization. At the head is the Chief of Staff. In peace, he is the ranking officer of the Army—a full general. He is the immediate advisor of the Secretary of War, who in turn is the military executive of the President—the Commander-in-Chief. The Chief of Staff issues his orders in the name of the Secretary of War. In time of war, there is also a commander of the field forces. In the World War, for example, General Hugh L. Scott and General Peyton C. March served in turn as Chief of Staff, while General John J. Pershing commanded the American Expeditionary Force.

WAR PLANS—Next in the system comes the War Department General Staff—the equivalent of the Prussian Great General Staff. It coördinates the work of the whole army. It contains five sections. One of these is the War Plans Division, which, as the name implies, works out problems of national defense and prepares for all possible war contingencies. In time of war, it would form the nucleus of the general headquarters (G. H. Q.) staff of the army in the field. This is the group which has most to do with strategy proper.

THE OTHER FOUR FUNCTIONS—The other four sections represent a division of the functions of command which extends down through the army organization as low as battalions. They are known as G-1, *Personnel* (or Administration); G-2, *Mili-*

[28] See pp. 185–187.
[29] See pp. 154, 188.

tary Intelligence; G-3, *Operations and Training;*
and G-4, *Supply.* (In the lower staff units—brigades,
regiments, and battalions—they are called S-1, S-2,
S-3, and S-4.) The G-1 section handles everything
concerning individuals, in such matters as assignment, promotion, discharge, replacements, discipline,
and morale. It also has charge of sanitation and
prisoners, and prepares administrative orders,
strength reports, and casualty lists. G-2 collects all
possible information concerning the enemy, analyzing and reporting such findings. Its chief function
is to keep the commander and others informed of
the enemy's situation and probable plans. G-3 is
principally concerned with training in time of peace.
In war, it has the very important function of managing the actual fighting. It selects, assembles, and
equips the troops for operations, makes necessary
tactical dispositions, prepares field orders, and main-
tains direct supervision of the fighting. G-4 has
charge of procuring, storing, and distributing all
necessary supplies, including ammunition. It also
supervises shelter, hospitals, and transportation by
land and water.

STAFFS IN THE ARMY UNITS—The higher army
units, down to the division, contain all branches of
the Army and have general staffs with officers from
the General Staff Corps. Brigades, regiments, and
battalions are composed of but one arm of the service, so have less elaborate staffs made up of officers
from that arm instead of general staff officers. The
four-fold division of function is kept in all these subordinate staffs, but the War Plans Division, as we
said, is not copied in the lower units. Unity and co-
ordination are ensured from top to bottom.

THE GENERAL STAFF CORPS—About 215 officers
are now in the General Staff Corps. By this, we

mean the War Department General Staff and the general staffs of the units down to divisions. The officers serve four years and then return to duty with their particular branch of the service. Training for staff work is given at the Command and General Staff School at Fort Leavenworth to graduates from the lower schools.

SPECIAL STAFF—Alongside this general staff system, each unit has a "special staff." This is a sort of advisory council, consisting of experts in the numerous combat, administrative, technical, and supply branches of the army. Unlike the general staffs, they have no definite staff functions of management, but are merely called upon for advice about their specialties. A general staff officer, as such, has no authority to command, but the special staff officers are often also in command of the troops of their special branch in the corps division. Brigades, regiments, and battalions have naturally a simpler organization of "special staffs" just as they do with regular staffs.

The complexity of modern war, with its huge numbers and elaborate equipment, has made this staff organization absolutely necessary. There would be chaos under staffs of the old type. They relieve the commander of a vast burden of detail, but he still is personally responsible for results.

The whole subject of strategy and command is so general that we have been able here to see only certain high points. As Napoleon said, strategy cannot be learned from a textbook. It will be well, nevertheless, to apply, as he suggests, some of the points which have just been reviewed, when we read and reread the great campaigns of history. The big, unchanging principles of war can be a test of any campaign. The personal quality of the commander is a vital factor, though at times it has been overemphasized when the work of subordinate officers and troops is not taken into consideration. Finally, especially in more recent history, we can study the efficiency of staff work as a cause for success or failure. Organization, as well as strategical genius, is a requisite for victory.

PART II

AMERICAN MILITARY POLICY

CHAPTER VII

A HANDFUL OF REGULARS

AMERICAN MILITARY POLICY IN PEACE

The first peace-time standing army of the United States contained eighty men! Ever since, our professional standing army has been small in time of peace, and backed only by a rather uncertain quantity of militia. Indians, coast-defense, and overseas possessions have made a regular army necessary, but it has been just barely large enough for normal peace-time duties. To make matters worse, it was also non-expansive. Trouble always came when war forced the handful of professionals to increase a hundredfold overnight. Until recently, no provision was made for that; and, as we shall see, costly blunders resulted.

REASONS FOR SMALL ARMY—America had several reasons for following this example of England's in the matter of a small standing army. In the first place, no powerful hostile nations are just beyond our frontiers, so we have not felt the need of huge standing armies on the European model.[1] When our nation was founded, moreover, the separate States were jealous of a strong central government. It was only natural, therefore, for them to object to giving that central government a powerful army. They thought that they would be much safer relying on their own militia. That period of jealousy and suspicion passed, but the tradition of a small standing army continued.

[1] See pp. 90, 108, 109.

MILITARY PROVISIONS OF THE CONSTITUTION—
The Constitution is important in the study of our
military policy, because of the authority which it
gave to different parts of the government. The highest power in military affairs was given to civilians, as
was natural in a republic. Briefly, Congress has the
power of forming the military policy, while the
President carries it out. Congress is "to provide
for the common defense; to declare war . . . to
raise and support armies . . . to make rules for
the government and regulation of the land and
naval forces . . . to provide for calling forth the
militia to execute the laws of the Union, suppress
insurrections, and repel invasions." The Constitution also declared that "The President shall be commander-in-chief of the Army and Navy of the United
States and of the militia of the several states when
called into the service of the United States." Congress created the War Department, headed by a
Secretary of War, in its first session in 1789. The
Secretary of War conducts the management of military affairs as an executive cabinet member under
the President. The first Secretary of War was a
soldier, but most of the later ones have been civilians.

MILITIA—In 1792, Congress laid down the law
concerning the militia. On paper, the militia was a
system of universal training. Every able-bodied citizen between eighteen and forty-five was to be enrolled, equipped, and occasionally trained for military service. All this was to be under State control
and State-appointed officers. The great mass of the
population, however, probably never even realized
that they were considered militiamen. The various
States did organize bodies of militia with an out-
ward military appearance, but they varied widely

in quality. Here and there were a few "crack" outfits. These maintained a high tradition, but most of
the others were sadly lacking in discipline and organization. With their elected or politically appointed officers and occasional drills, a large part
of the militia was good for little more than Fourth
of July parades. Congress had put on paper the
theory that every able-bodied male owed military
service to his country—that much was important.
But it had created numerous separate little armies,
lacking the essentials of discipline and organization.
That law of 1792 governed the militia until 1903.

The Regular Army

TINY ORIGINAL ARMY—This naturally left the
burden on the little regular Army. And it *was* a little army. When the Revolutionary forces were dis-
banded in 1784, the standing army of the United
States was reduced to eighty men. It might have
remained that small indefinitely had it not been for
serious Indian attacks on the frontiers. The militia
proved unequal to the situation. The country saw the
need of a dependable body of regulars, so about
700 were authorized in 1785. The Indians kept up
trouble for another whole century.

NEGLECT DURING PEACE—For that reason, if for
no other, the United States maintained a standing
army. But it grew very slowly. Its size has been
called a barometer of the nation's fears. During a
war-scare, it expands rapidly, but it shrinks again
as soon as the crisis passes. The country pays little attention to the regulars in time of peace. Kipling expresses this clearly in his poem on "Tommy
Atkins," the British enlisted man:

"For it's Tommy this, an' Tommy that, an' 'Tommy, wait
    outside';
But it's 'Special train for Atkins' when the trooper's on the
tide."

REAL AND PAPER STRENGTH—Regiments were
made and dissolved in the committee rooms
of the Senate and House. But, even when
new ones were authorized, the recruiting officers
were often unable to find men. The actual size of
the Army, consequently, was sometimes only a quarter of its "paper" strength. Its average actual size
in the early years of the Republic was about 3,000
men. It was only 5,300 in 1845, and was barely
16,000 when the Civil War broke out in 1861.

SCATTERING THE ARMY—Most of these men were
"line" troops—infantry, cavalry, and artillery. A
few were in the "staff" departments—ordnance,
quartermaster, commissary, and the like. The bulk
of the infantry and cavalry were stationed in little stockades along the frontier to guard against
Indian attacks. Seldom was there as much as a battalion in one place. Save for the occasional Indian
forays, which might come any minute, the life was
monotonous and hard. The artillery had a pleas-
anter task, manning the little granite forts which
defended our seaports all the way from Maine to
the Gulf of Mexico. We can get some idea of this
wide scattering of the army from the figures just
before the Civil War. Of the 198 companies in the
army, 183 were on the wild frontier west of the
Mississippi, in 79 separate posts. The remaining
fifteen companies had to guard the whole Atlantic
coast, twenty-three arsenals, and the Canadian border.

ENLISTED MEN—The quality of the Army was

good, even if it was small. Discipline, we recall, is the principal quality which makes troops dependable.[2] Even at those isolated little frontier posts, discipline was maintained. At least once a day, the garrison paraded in the gaudy full-dress uniform of the period. Terms of enlistment were generally long—five and even seven years. This gave plenty of time to make real soldiers out of the recruits. They were, for the most part, of German and Irish stock. The pay was low. In 1790, the private received three dollars a month, from which a dollar was deducted for clothing and hospital stores. Even after the Civil War, he received less than fifteen dollars a month. Men, however, were usually found willing to forgo money for the sake of food, shelter, and the joys of soldiering.

WEST POINT—Very early, the government recognized the need for trained officers for the regular Army. The United States Military Academy at West Point had a modest start in 1805 as a training-school for engineers. In 1812, its scope was widened to prepare men for commissions in the "line." Every part of the country was eventually entitled to send boys to the academy, most appointments being made by the members of Congress. The cadets received little in the way of advanced military science, as the course of studies resembled a regular college curriculum. Engineering, philosophy, mathematics, ethics, chemistry, French, and drawing were being taught in 1850. The Academy put its special stamp on its graduates by developing discipline and military character. Doubtless, many boys sought appointments in order to get a free college education. A large number of the graduates, discouraged by the slow prospects of promotion, left the army for

[2] See p. 93.

civil life. They formed a valuable sort of unofficial officers' reserve corps, however. "Stonewall" Jackson, Grant, Sherman, and McClellan were among such West Pointers when the Civil War began.[3] In recent times, less than half of the army officers have been graduates of the Military Academy.

NO ADVANCED TRAINING—The lack of advanced training for officers was one of the chief defects in the old army.[4] An officer's required education stopped when he left West Point. No examinations were necessary for the promotions, which came with painful slowness only when vacancies happened to occur in one's own regiment. A major was apt to know no more of theoretical science than a second lieutenant fresh from the Academy. The major, to be sure, had had plenty of experience, but it was principally gained in tedious garrison duty with a small body of troops with little opportunity or incentive for study. Some officers did dig into military science on their own, but they were few. The worst effects of this system were shown in the higher commands, with the generals ignorant of the main principles of strategy and administration. Nothing in the form of a general staff existed to prepare intelligent plans or to test men's abilities.[5] That left a tremendous amount to chance when responsible commands were given out.

CONTINUED NEGLECT—The Civil War did not change the old system to any extent. In 1866, only 38,500 were in the Army; by 1879, the number had dropped to 20,000. The Army was still scattered among scores of posts. A whole regiment was almost never assembled except for an inaugural pa-

[3] See p. 239.
[4] See p. 103.
[5] See p. 138.

rade. The years between 1865 and 1881 have been called the "dark ages" of the Army. Officers who had been generals in the Civil War fell back to majors and colonels, with little prospect of further promotion. After every war, the nation seems so thoroughly "fed up" with fighting that the Army is quite completely neglected. It actually had to go for a whole year without pay in 1877.

THE EARLY "RENAISSANCE"—The so-called "renaissance" of the Army started about 1881. The first step was to train officers in the theory of tactics and technical developments, even if they had nothing more than companies with which to drill. A "School of Application for Infantry and Cavalry" was established at Fort Leavenworth, Kansas. Officers were detailed to this school for a two-year course. It started with general education and finished with the study of several works on the science and art of war. This was the rudimentary beginning of the extensive system of army schools maintained at present.

GENERAL UPTON—Meanwhile, General Emory Upton made a study of the principal foreign armies and wrote an elaborate report of their workings. He next investigated the history of the military policy of the United States, analyzing the record of our military history in war and in peace. He came to the conclusion that we had had no real military policy, and therefore made numerous recommendations, based primarily on his study of foreign armies. Among other things, he advocated the creation of a general staff, the requiring of examinations for promotions, and more widespread military education. General Upton died in 1881 with his work but half completed. His recommendations did not bear fruit for twenty years.

1898 a Turning-Point

NEW DUTIES—The year 1898 was an important turning-point in our military history. It saw the last real fight with the Indians. The job was finished which had kept the regular Army busy since the very beginning of the Republic. At the very same time, a new task was created. Within a few months, the United States secured an overseas empire—including the Philippines, Hawaii, and Porto Rico. These new possessions had to be garrisoned. An insurrection in the Philippines, for instance, kept a large part of the army tied up in those distant islands.

HIGHER EDUCATION—Still more important, the Spanish-American War of 1898 revealed numerous shortcomings in the Army. In that brief conflict, it proved itself much less efficient than the Navy. Steps were taken to remedy one of the old Army's worst defects—the lack of higher training for officers. Strangely enough, reforms came after a war—usually a time of army neglect. Many new officers came into the regular service directly after the war, so that for a while the West Pointers numbered only one tenth of the whole number. "Garrison schools" were started at every post to train these new officers in the fundamentals. These led to the "service schools," which developed from the original 1881 experiment at Fort Leavenworth. Finally, in 1903, the Army War College was opened at Washington to direct and coördinate the work of the various schools. From this naturally resulted the requirement that an officer must pass an examination before he can be promoted.

GENERAL STAFF—In 1903, Congress authorized the creation of a General Staff. This had been one of the most urgent recommendations of General

Upton. As we have seen, most of the European armies had had general staffs for years.[6] The new body was to prepare plans for national defense and to make arrangements for mobilization in case of war. Hitherto, such work had been done under the stress of emergency, so that blunders were bound to occur. Now a permanent body of experts was to arrange everything beforehand. The first General Staff consisted of about forty-five officers, from captains to generals. They were to serve for four years and then return to duty with troops. The Chief of Staff became the ranking officer of the Army. This General Staff was an extremely significant forward step. We have already seen its present organization.

MANEUVERS—One more innovation was the holding of large-scale maneuvers. Hitherto, we recall, the Army had been so scattered that regiments were rarely assembled as units. Now dozens of the smaller forts were abandoned. Large bodies of both regulars and militia were brought together so that the officers and men could practise under conditions resembling those which they would have to meet in war.

NATIONAL GUARD—The question of the militia also came up during this 1903 wave of reform. It had gone for more than a century under the old law of 1792. Now, the Dick Bill transformed the organized militia into a National Guard, which remedied some of the old defects. Within five years, the National Guard was to have the "organization, armament and discipline" of the regular Army. The men were to be paid for their time at drill, for target practice, and for summer camp. Regular Army officers were detailed as instructors. The bill repeated the provision of 1792 that all able-bodied men be-

[6] See p. 139.

tween eighteen and forty-five were classed as militia
—a shadowy claim of universal liability for military
service. Those not in the National Guard, however,
were known as reserve militia and were not subject
to call. The federal government was unable to
mobilize the militia without the consent of the State
governors, but the Dick Bill made a valuable contribution in providing for a uniform militia under
federal supervision.

FIVE YEARS OF PROGRESS—To sum up, the five
years after the Spanish-American War contained
more constructive military reforms than the whole
preceding century. The lack of training for officers
had been met by the establishment of a system of
schools all the way from the garrison school to the
Army War College. A General Staff had been provided so that the Army might plan intelligently for
emergencies. The National Guard had become more
standardized. The Regular Army had been so concentrated that large-scale maneuvers were possible.
Yet the principal evil of the old Army remained in
the new one—it was still non-expansive.

FIRST PROVISIONS FOR WARTIME EXPANSION

1916 REFORMS—The first important steps in
providing for the intelligent expansion of the peace-
time army came in the National Defense Act of
1916. We need not study it in detail, for many new
temporary plans were necessary when the United
States entered the World War a year later. Also
still more improvements were made in the post-
war policy now in force. A few things, however,
are worth remembering in connection with that 1916
act. It provided for a peace-time standing army of
175,000 men instead of the existing 100,000. Then,

it created the higher peace-time units of divisions and corps with general staffs, so that large numbers of men could be handled efficiently.[7] It gave the President, when authorized by Congress, the power to draft the National Guard into federal service without depending on the state governors. Finally, it took initial steps toward a permanent means of expansion by establishing the Officers' Reserve Corps and the Enlisted Reserve Corps on an effective basis. Civilians might qualify for reserve commissions by satisfactorily completing courses at authorized training-camps, while enlisted men were to pass into a reserve after their three-year enlistments of active service. These 1916 measures contributed to the success of the remarkable expansion of our army during the next two years.

PRESENT POLICY—NATIONAL DEFENSE ACT OF 1920

STEPS TOWARD PREPAREDNESS—This was a start in the direction which has been followed out more completely since the World War. In that contest, the United States was able to spend a whole year in preparing its troops for battle, as the Allies were, in the meantime, holding back the enemy. That was unusual. Another time, this country might have to stand alone from the start and defend herself. Plans, therefore, have been perfected to train, while we are at peace, the greatest possible number of men without interfering unduly with their private occupations or their freedom. It is extremely unlikely that we shall ever adopt the European system of universal compulsory military training, which takes two or three years directly out of every man's

[7] See p. 14.

business life. Consequently, most of the rank and file of any future wartime American army would still be green. The Navy, the Marines and part of the regulars would have to hold off the enemy while these raw troops were trained. The new policy, as embodied in the National Defense Act of 1920, gives training to those who most need it—officers and non-commissioned officers.[8]

THE REGULAR ARMY—SIZE—The standing Army is still small. The original plans for 200,000 men have been whittled down to about 135,000, including officers, men, and Philippine Scouts. Congress will not pay the bills for a larger army than that. There are about 12,000 officers. About one-third of the total force is infantry and about one-fourth is artillery—field and coast. More men are now in the air service than in the cavalry.

THE REGULAR ARMY—DISTRIBUTION—The Army is no longer scattered in little frontier posts for defense against the Indians, but about a quarter of it is stationed outside the country. In 1928, out of a total of 134,000 officers and enlisted men, roughly 96,300 were in the United States; 14,000 in Hawaii; 11,300 in the Philippines; 8,600 in the Canal Zone; 300 in Alaska; and 1,000 in China. The Philippine figures include some 6,500 Philippine Scouts under American officers. The Marine Corps is omitted from these statistics, as it is a part of the Navy and under naval jurisdiction, unless attached for duty with the Army by order of the President.

LEARNING AND TEACHING—One of the big contrasts with the old Army is that scarcely half the officers are on duty with troops. Most of the remainder are either studying or instructing. The aver-

[8] See selections from the text of this act in Appendix, pp. 393-414.

age officer spends about ten years in advanced study. About thirty-one army schools are in operation at present. At the top are the Army War College at Washington and the Command and General Staff School at Fort Leavenworth, Kansas. The special service schools cover everything from infantry (Fort Benning, Georgia) and field artillery (Fort Sill, Oklahoma) to the dental, veterinary, and music schools. Special provisions are made for teaching useful trades to enlisted men while they are in the service.

THE NATIONAL GUARD—The National Guard is now linked up more closely than ever with the federal government. It has a three-year enlistment period. Regular officers are assigned for instruction. The recruit takes an oath to support the federal as well as the State government. The total strength of the National Guard in 1928 was 181,-000, ranging from about 20,000 men in New York State down to 3 in Nevada.

R. O. T. C.—One of the most valuable provisions of the new army policy is the Reserve Officers' Training Corps. This is a direct step toward intelligent expansion in time of war. The idea is not entirely new. As early as 1862, Congress passed the Morrill Act, which gave free grants of land to many State universities. In return, the States promised to install compulsory military training for the first two years of the college course. This principle has been continued to the present, but it has been greatly expanded beyond the original "squads right" and "squads left." R. O. T. C. units have been established in 325 colleges and schools. The 100 junior units are for the most part in military schools or high schools. The 225 senior units are in colleges and universities. The War Department supplies all necessary equipment except shelter. Regular Army officers are detailed for the instruction. In the two-year "basic course," the students are grounded in the fundamentals of infantry, artillery, cavalry, or some other branch of the service, and are generally qualified to become non-commissioned officers. About 40 per cent of that total number continue to the "advanced" course, in which they receive more intensive training and attend a summer camp for six weeks. They receive pay for this, and become reserve second lieutenants upon satisfactory completion of the course. Nearly 175,000 students are enrolled in R. O. T. C. units. About 5,000 of these receive reserve commissions each year. The value of such a system in the plan of national defense is evident. It takes time to train officers, and in this way it is done without withdrawing men from their normal life.

THE ORGANIZED RESERVE—This naturally leads to the Officers' Reserve Corps, an organization which holds the reserve officers together, continuing and coördinating their work. The Officers' Reserve Corps consists not only of R. O. T. C. graduates, but also of former regular army officers, veterans of the World War and officers of several other classifications. Enlisted men in the regular Army are sometimes reserve officers at the same time. The period of a reserve commission is five years. The reserve officers may qualify for promotion by taking correspondence courses and by going to summer camps. This gives the government an organized body of about 10,000 officers upon whom to call in an emergency. The remainder of the organized Reserve— the Enlisted Reserve Corps—numbers scarcely 6,000 men.

C. M. T. C.—Another step toward training soldiers

in time of peace was the creation of Citizens' Military Training Camps. These are established in all parts of the country. They provide a month's training in a particular arm of the service, at the government's expense, for boys or men between seventeen and twenty-four. About 35,000 are trained each summer. Some of the promising men in these camps may qualify for reserve commissions. The others will probably be qualified to serve as non-commissioned officers in a draft army. Since the new developments in warfare are throwing more and more responsibility on sergeants and corporals, such training is of vital importance. In the C. M. T. C., as in the other features, the new military policy is trying to make this voluntary training as attractive as possible, instead of compelling service as many European nations do.

CORPS AREAS AND WARTIME EXPANSION—The new military policy has combined the three elements of Regular Army, National Guard, and Reserve into a comprehensive scheme for rapid expansion in wartime. The country has been divided into nine corps areas. Each of them is a complete unit with its regulars, National Guard, and reserves organized and coördinated. The areas are based on population rather than geographical size. The Second Corps Area, for instance, comprising New York, New Jersey, and Delaware, looks much smaller on the map than the Ninth, which includes California, Washington, Utah, Nevada, Idaho and Montana. In time of peace, the regular Army forces in each area assist in the training of the National Guard and the reserves. Each area has its skeleton organization for expansion in the time of war, with staffs, concentration plans, and other essentials all worked out in advance. It is planned that in a major war each corps area would furnish six divisions—one of regulars, two of National Guard, and three of reserves. This makes a total of fifty-four divisions for the whole country, so that, with auxiliary units, about 1,500,000 men can, in an emergency, be ready in a few months. Of course that huge organization exists only on paper. Even the regular army with its 135,000 men would have to double in size to fill nine divisions and also furnish trained men to the National Guard and reserve organizations. The National Guard, now 181,000 strong, would also have to expand to reach its eighteen-division war strength of 480,000. The reserve divisions have only part of their officers ready. They are purely "paper" organizations, but at least officers know what their functions will be in a war and the mold is prepared into which men can be poured in time of war. The whole of the reserve divisions will be created by means of a draft made in accordance with a law passed by Congress regulating compulsory service.

CRITICISMS OF POLICY—From a purely military standpoint, this present system is far less efficient than the European compulsory universal training. Yet many people in this country object violently even to this minimum of efficient preparation. They visualize the General Staff as a group of scheming war-lords, who are striving to catch the young manhood of the country in the toils of militarism and are heading us toward bigger wars.

ANSWERS TO CRITICISMS—A brief analysis of our present military policy should be enough to answer these arguments. Our military policy is *defensive*. We could not mobilize millions of trained men in a few days for a speedy offensive as Europe did in 1914. Most of the enlisted men in the war army would still be green, and several months would be needed to train them. During that time, the Navy, the regulars, and the Marines would have to hold the invader in check. The compensating fact is that this skeleton system is purely voluntary, and that it does not take several straight years out of the regular life-work of every young man. Trained officers and a plan for increasing the army rapidly are at least provided. It seems to be an intelligent compromise between military efficiency on the one hand and personal liberty on the other. At all events it is a tremendous advance over our old system of a good little army which could not grow efficiently.

CHAPTER VIII

EMERGENCY EXPANSION

AMERICAN MILITARY POLICY IN WAR

Our present military policy is based on costly lessons learned in our past wars. Time and again, the government has committed the same blunders. As a result, most of our wars have been dragged out to needless length and have been unnecessarily costly in men and treasure. Only in this century has America begun to profit by those lessons of the past.

TWO FALLACIES—The history of the United States military policy in war is a delicate one to handle. Plenty of Americans believe that any questioning of our record in past wars is sacrilege and treason. Two widespread beliefs have kept the man in the street from realizing the actual facts. One is the idea that the American army has been highly successful in every one of its wars. The older school history texts may be blamed for that. The other misconception is that "a million men will spring to arms overnight" whenever the nation needs them. Those two views have given the country a false sense of security. A half-century ago, General Upton, as we saw, went behind the scenes of our military glory and exposed the repeated record of inefficiency and faulty policy. Yet the government did not publish his report or act upon it until twenty years after his death. At last, the nation has begun to profit by past errors. It has not been a question of the heroism of American soldiers. The trouble came from lack of training, organization, and intelligent policy. The surprise is that the country did not learn its lessons sooner.

SUMMARY OF OUR WARS

THE SIX MAJOR WARS—The United States Army has engaged in six major wars, not counting border troubles or fighting with Indians and Filipinos. We shall take up in later chapters the three most important contests: the American Revolution (1775–1783); the ·Civil War (1861–1865); and the World War (1914–1918; United States participation, 1917–1918).[1] The other three were the War of 1812 (1812–1815); the Mexican War (1846–1848); and the Spanish-American War (1898).

THE WAR OF 1812—The War of 1812 against England was our least successful war. It arose partly from England's seizure of our ships and sailors, partly from her stirring-up of Indians on our frontier, and partly from the desire of a group of young "War Hawks" in Congress to seize Canada. The country was rushed into a three-year war in spite of unpreparedness. One scarcely recognizes this contest as the same war from its descriptions in American, Canadian, and English school histories. The American books dwell on the frigate fights and the battle of Lake Erie, for our Navy far outshone the Army. The only clean-cut military victory was at New Orleans—*after* the peace treaty had been signed. The Canadian textbooks tell how large American armies invaded Canada only to be thrown out by a handful of British regulars backed by Canadian militia. The English school-books scarcely

[1] See Chaps. IX, XI, and XIII.

mention the war at all, regarding it as a side-show in contrast with the much more serious contest with Napoleon. America did not lose the war, but neither can it be said that she won. It simply stopped. The peace treaty decided nothing but that.

THE MEXICAN WAR—The Mexican War arose from a dispute over the Texas boundary and ended with a great deal of Mexican territory, including California, in our hands. From the standpoint of military policy it was the most successful of our first five wars. Mexico, to be sure, was a much smaller nation, but she had a larger army and was fighting on her own ground. A campaign under the able, energetic leadership of General Winfield Scott enabled the United States to dictate the peace in the Mexican capital.

THE SPANISH-AMERICAN WAR—The Spanish-American War was a brief colonial contest, with no fighting on the mainland of either belligerent. The United States won a sudden and easy victory, but this was due rather to the efficiency of our Navy and the disorganized condition of the Spaniards than to the Army. The war lasted but a few months. At its end, we secured Porto Rico, the Philippines, and some small Pacific islands. In addition, Cuba, the immediate cause of the trouble, was freed from Spanish rule.

FAULTS OF OUR WARTIME POLICY

THE EIGHT FAULTS—Several outstanding faults in our wartime policy persisted until very recent times. They must be thoroughly understood, for their results cropped out in war after war. Briefly, the major defects were these:

1. Dependence on volunteers for increase of army
2. Short-term enlistments
3. Bounties
4. State control of volunteers as militia
5. Faulty replacement policy
6. Faulty selection of officers
7. Lack of general staff
8. Civilian interference

The basic trouble was, as we have already seen, that the old standing Army was non-expansive, as it had no adequate provision for increasing its size in time of war. The Revolution set up plenty of bad examples in military policy. These mistakes were more excusable at their time than in any other war because there had been no real chance for preparedness, and no previous examples for guidance. But instead of profiting by these Revolutionary mistakes, the government copied them in later wars. It was easier to follow precedents than to think up new plans. We shall take up in turn these eight main faults, showing how in each case the government eventually rectified its worst errors.

1. DEPENDENCE ON VOLUNTEERS

VOLUNTEERING OR CONSCRIPTION?—In every war, we have lacked enough trained men. As a result, tens of thousands of green, raw amateurs have had to be brought into service to raise the army to war strength. The two ways of bringing them in are —voluntarily or by compulsion.[2] The United States has ordinarily relied on volunteers. The repeated failure of this system has finally led to a combination of universal compulsory service with volunteers.

EARLY EXPERIMENTS—In the American Revolu-

[2] See pp. 93, 94.

tion, the government had no choice. It was too weak to compel men to service, had it so wished. The same reliance was placed on volunteers in 1812 and in the Mexican War. Early in the Civil War, the South started general conscription of all able-bodied men. The law was opposed and often defied, but it helped to keep the Confederate ranks filled. In 1863, the North tried a similar "draft" or conscription, but any one paying three hundred dollars could send a substitute in his place. The poor felt that this was class discrimination. This Union draft was operated by military officials and was expensive. It led to a severe riot in New York City, where many lives were lost. Only 119,000 men were brought into the Army, of whom 73,000 were substitutes. These were just a drop in the bucket compared with the 2,000,000 Northern volunteers. The Spanish-American War was so short that only the volunteers, who came at the first call, were needed.

THE WORLD WAR DRAFT—The World War saw the starting innovation of an immediate universal draft. The Selective Service Act put it into operation soon after we entered the war in 1917. It gave the government the power to call to the colors any able-bodied man within the age-limits prescribed by law. Opposition was at first feared, but the act was applied without friction. Every man between twenty-one and thirty-one, except those already in service, was required to register with the local draft board. This board was composed of civilians instead of army officers and served without pay. The age-limits were later extended to include all men between eighteen and forty-five. Altogether, 24,000,000 men were thus registered. From this number, 2,800,000 were selected by lot and drafted into service. Exemptions were made in certain cases, such as men with dependents or those needed in essential industries. Any "conscientious objectors" to war on religious or other grounds were not forced to fight, but were generally kept at the camps for special work. A man could no longer buy his way out of the draft by hiring a substitute. It was still possible to volunteer in the regular Army, National Guard, Navy, or Marine Corps. There were altogether 4,800,000 men in the armed forces of the United States, and 4,000,000 of these were in the Army. Thus 70 per cent of the Army was drafted. No stigma was attached to drafted men. Another big war will in all probability cause the government to resort again to compulsory service. In a lesser war, Congress will probably simply authorize an increase in the size of the regular Army.

2. SHORT ENLISTMENTS

NINETY DAYS—The principal evil arising from the volunteer system was the short-term enlistment. Men did not care to bind themselves for more than a few weeks or months until they knew whether they were going to like army life or not. The government was generally optimistic and expected the war to be over soon. Consequently, through several wars, three months was the favorite term of enlistment. Sometimes it was shorter than that.

HEAVY TURNOVER—The great trouble was that such a system greatly increased the number of green troops. A lot of men would just about be whipped into shape when their terms would expire and most of them would go home. Then the same process would have to be gone through with a new raw group. More than once, commanders rushed into battle simply to use troops before their terms were up. In war after war; the total number of men serving with the colors was tremendous, yet there were never many at any one time.

REVOLUTIONARY DIFFICULTIES—This was one of the principal sources of Washington's anxiety in the Revolution. When he took command of the army, he found that men were constantly coming and going—commuting, as it were, from their farms to camp. He complained that he had to disband one whole army and organize another in the face of the enemy while besieging Boston.[3] On one occasion, he called for men for only two days' service in order to get some fortifications dug in a hurry. Even those men were rated afterwards as Revolutionary veterans. Some soldiers, of course, did serve throughout the Revolution, but more typical was the case of a certain Rhode Island youth. He served three short enlistments in the army and ended up with a year in the navy.

WASHINGTON'S REGULARS—Washington insisted upon something more reliable than these ever-shifting short-term troops. He finally secured a few thousand regulars with long-term enlistments. They got the thorough training and discipline that comes only with time. In almost every encounter they showed their high quality, often standing fast while the green militia ran.[4] These long-term men were not necessarily braver, but soldiers had to have seasoning before they could stand their ground against the well-disciplined lines of redcoats. Here, as in later wars, most of these wartime regulars had no previous military experience, but they served long enough to get some. This little regular "Continental" army was the principal thing that staved off Washington's defeat and kept the Revolution going.

3 See p. 200.
4 See pp. 211, 230.

TREMENDOUS TOTAL—FEW AT ONCE—There were more than 525,000 separate enlistments in the American forces. Making deductions for the men who reënlisted, it is estimated that more than 400,000 different men served in the army at one time or another. Yet Washington never had 20,000 under his command at once. Large numbers of green men were in every battle. The British used only 40,000 men in the whole war. No wonder Washington exclaimed "What we need is a good army, not a large one."

1812—A REPETITION—It was the same story over again in 1812. Some 450,000 men served in the American ranks, while England had only a tenth of that number. Once more the green troops ran, while the regulars stood fast. The most notorious routing of raw troops was at the "battle" of Bladensburg, where a small British force easily pushed aside a large body of American militia, who fled and left the way open to Washington. The British, almost unopposed and consequently with few casualties, proceeded to burn the public buildings of the capital. Of the 450,000 Americans engaged in this war, only 63,000 served more than one year, while 147,000 were in the army less than a month.

THE MEXICAN WAR WALK-OUT—The danger of short enlistments was quite evident in the Mexican War. The volunteers signed up for "one year or the duration of the war." At the end of the year, the soldier—and not the government—could decide whether he was through or not. As a result, the campaign which won the war very nearly ended in failure, if not disaster. General Scott, in March, 1847, started inland from Vera Cruz to Mexico City. A month later, the one-year term of the volunteers expired. Most of them decided to go home. In one unit of 3,700 men, less than a hundred stayed. Scott was left, out-numbered three to one, and with insecure communications, in the heart of the enemy country. The Mexicans failed to make the most of this chance for an offensive. New recruits arrived, and Scott was able, after a dangerous delay of weeks, to get them into shape for his final brilliant drive.

THE CIVIL WAR—A BAD START—The Civil War saw little improvement. In the first wave of excitement, when men would probably have signed up willingly for one year or even three, President Lincoln called for 75,000 volunteers for three months' service. Of course, every one expected the war to be short, but the terms of these ninety-day volunteers expired before they were half trained. Then in a frantic attempt to use them before they scattered, these green men were sent against the Confederates at Bull Run on July 21, 1861, in spite of their commander's protest. Some volunteers actually "marched to the rear to the sound of the guns" because their enlistment expired that day. The battle hung in the balance for a long time, as the Confederate troops were also green. A little body of Union regulars nearly carried the day by standing fast, but the rest of the Union Army raced back to Washington in a panic.[5]

GRADUAL LENGTHENING—Congress learned some-something of a lesson from that. In the next call for troops, the men were given their choice of six-month or three-year enlistments, while efforts were made to get long-term men for the regular Army. Naturally, most of the recruits chose the six-month alternative. Next, Congress raised this minimum term to three years. The Confederates, as we saw, had enacted compulsory military service for the

[5] See p. 243.

duration of the war. When the Union resorted to this, their draft brought in too few men to affect the situation to any extent. The three-year Union enlistments did eventually produce enough well-trained troops for the final victorious campaigns.

SPANISH-AMERICAN WAR AND FILIPINO INSURRECTION—The Spanish-American War itself was over in a few months, so that the length of enlistments did not matter. But a native insurrection in the Philippines directly followed the peace treaty. The volunteers had enlisted for two years or for the duration of the war, having their choice at the end of two years as to whether they would go or stay. In reverse of the Mexican War, this actual contest ended before the two-year enlistment period. The volunteers again chose the quickest way out of the service, although an urgent emergency still continued in the Philippines.

THE END OF SHORT ENLISTMENTS—The World War saw the end of the short-term enlistments. Every one, whether volunteer, regular, or draftee, was in for the duration of the war unless it should last more than seven years. It was the only one of our six contests in which commanders were not faced with the prospect of having their forces melt away before their work was done.

3. Bounties

BRIBES TO FIGHT—The "curse of the bounty" was the natural by-product of the system of volunteers and short-term enlistments. Men usually enlisted easily enough in the burst of enthusiasm at the outbreak of a war. But recruiting became constantly harder as a contest dragged on. As long as the government was unable or unwilling to compel military service, it had to tempt men into voluntary enlistments. This lure was frequently in the form of "bounties" of cash or free land. On the whole, it was better to induce men to sign up for long terms by means of bounties than to have short-term enlistments without bounties; but the system produced the serious evil of "bounty-jumping." Men enlisted just for the bounty, deserting immediately and later enlisting again to collect another bounty. One successful bounty-jumper was found to have gathered in fourteen of these rewards.

REVOLUTIONARY BOUNTIES—Before the Revolution had been going a year, the bounty system was in full force. The first bounty was ten dollars for three-year enlistment. The amounts soon rose as the war dragged on and paper money fell in value. By 1779, recruits were being tempted with bounties of $1,000 plus a suit of clothes and 100 acres of land. In those days, the government had plenty of free land but little ready cash.

CONTINUED IN THREE WARS—It was the same story in the next three wars. In the War of 1812, bounties rose in two years from sixteen dollars to $124 plus 320 acres of land. In the Mexican War, twelve dollars was offered volunteers to reënlist for a second year of service. As we saw, many of Scott's men were not sufficiently tempted by this small bounty to stay with him another year. Even in the Civil War, millions were spent in bounties. They ranged as high as four hundred dollars toward the end. One tenth or more of the one and one-half to two millons who enlisted for the Union deserted, and many of these were undoubtedly bounty-jumpers.

ABOLITION AND ECONOMY—That was the last of this evil. The Spanish-American War was so short that bounties were not necessary. In the World War inducements were unnecessary. If a man did not enlist of his own accord, the draft was bound to get him sooner or later, if the government needed him. This was the main reason why in 1917–1918 the government raised twice as many men as the North had had in the Civil War at one-twentieth of the total cost.

PENSIONS—We are not taking up the matter of pensions here, as they had little effect on the Army while wars were going on. They were rewards of service after wars were over, rather than bribes to serve. After most wars, the government has been very generous to the veterans or their widows. In the World War, provisions were made instead for the soldier's dependents during his service, and only a small sum was given upon his discharge. An addition to this has since been granted in the "bonus," from which a veteran may eventually obtain something. It differs from a pension in that the veteran himself gets nothing from it for many years except the chance to borrow money, while his widow has only a specified sum in small payments based on the length of his service, and not a yearly income for life.

4. STATE CONTROL OF VOLUNTEERS

TWO MASTERS—A far more fundamental evil than bounties was the fact that great numbers of new troops raised in war were classed as State militia rather than federal troops. The States had some excuse for controlling their standing pre-war militia, but not for controlling their wartime volunteers. This faulty policy had far-reaching effects. It underlay at least half the defects in our old military policy. It hampered the government in the free use of troops, for the old militia laws restricted the purposes for which militia might be employed. States distant from the scene of action were often lukewarm about raising and supporting their quotas. Governors sometimes even refused to supply any troops.

REVOLUTIONARY LACK OF CENTRAL POWER—The States had some excuse for this in the Revolution, as they had been so recently only thirteen British colonies with little in common. They were held together only by the Continental Congress, to which they sent representatives. This body lacked the executive power which it claimed. It could only advise or beg the States to do something. If they refused, it could not compel them. The States were fighting British "tyranny," and were suspicious of any central power. Naturally, they preferred to control their own troops. They did at least accept Washington as a common commander-in-chief, but he secured his little body of regulars under Continental rather than State control with the greatest difficulty. With this lack of central authority, the organization, discipline, equipment, and pay of the troops was without uniformity. It was usually hard to get any money at all. The States would gladly turn out their militia in large numbers for fighting in their own territory, but they rapidly lost interest in campaigns hundreds of miles away.[6] Also in this and in several other wars, the States outbid the central government in bounties for volunteers.

DEFIANCE IN 1812—There was trouble again in 1812. According to the Constitution, the militia could be called forth "to execute the laws of the Union, suppress insurrections, and repel invasions." [7] The governors of Massachusetts and Connecticut refused to furnish troops, since New England disapproved of the war. Some of the Ohio militia would not cross into Canada when they found the opening plan was

[6] See pp. 196, 199, 205, 212.
[7] See p. 148.

for such an invasion. Technically, they were within their rights. This was an offensive operation, and the function of the militia was essentially defensive according to the Constitution. We saw, however, that they did little better in trying to defend Washington from the British.

DIVIDED AUTHORITY CONTINUED—The trouble kept recurring until the World War. In the Mexican War, it was the State volunteers who almost ruined Scott's campaign with their short enlistments. In the Civil War, State control was a constant nuisance. At its outbreak, the governors of Missouri and Kentucky refused to furnish troops. They were border States and were inclined to support both sides, so they stayed in the Union but favored slavery. Governors played an important rôle in the military preparations of the Union, as the States raised, equipped, and officered their own volunteers. Other difficulties arose from this source, as we shall see. It was again the same story of State-controlled volunteers in the Spanish-American War.

FEDERAL GOVERNMENT FINALLY SUPREME—Congress ended the practice by the National Defense Act 1916. This gave to the President the power to draft the National Guard into federal service.[8] Thus in the World War, the United States, and not the individual States, had full control. In every other war, all volunteer regiments had carried the name of their States. Symbols of this victory of federal control over State control in wartime were the new designations given former State regiments. For instance, the First Maine Infantry became the One Hundred and Third Infantry. Nowhere in the Army did State names remain.

[8] See p. 157.

5. REPLACEMENT POLICY

THE WRONG CHOICE—Naturally, a military unit loses many men from battle casualties, sickness, expiration of enlistments, and (sometimes) from desertion. One of two things can then be done. The unit can be allowed to dwindle away, or it can be maintained at full strength by replacements. The latter is the more sensible course, as the unit thus preserves an *esprit de corps*. Above all, this way gives raw recruits the opportunity to learn warfare alongside experienced soldiers. The United States, however, has followed the former course in most of its wars. Veteran units have been allowed to melt away, while whole new ones with green officers and men have been put into the line.

APPEALING TO SELF-INTEREST—Definite reasons exist for this, bound up with short enlistments and State control. In forming a new regiment, prospective officers would eagerly act as recruiting agents, whereas in filling up a depleted unit, its officers would be at the front and would have no incentive to recruit anyway, as they had their commissions. Let us suppose that a New York regiment, of originally 1,000 men, had dwindled away to 200, but without much loss of officers. The obvious and best thing would be to fill the empty ranks with 800 new enlisted men. But New York State would have a hard time doing this by simply asking for men. It would be much simpler to raise an entirely new regiment. The men who hoped to be its officers would do the recruiting work, moved by self-interest. The man who raised a thousand recruits might be made colonel; his helpers would get lower commissions. Consequently the original regiment would be left with plenty of experienced officers but not enough

men to do much, while the new green outfit would
have to learn at heavy cost what hard knocks had
already taught the original one. In our early wars,
it meant nothing at all to say, for example, that a
particular army consisted of ten regiments. Its force
might range from 500 to 10,000 men.

SHRUNKEN UNITS—Any one who visits Valley
Forge will realize what this system meant in the
Revolution. Markers indicate the camping sites of
dozens of regiments, yet Washington's total force
during that bleak winter was scarcely equal to three
modern war-strength regiments. In the battle of
Princeton, brigadier generals were commanding
fewer men than present-day infantry captains.[9] The
privates had nearly all gone home, but the officers
and skeleton outfits remained.

NON-REFILLABLE REGIMENTS—The same evil continued in the next four wars. Complete new, green
regiments were sent into the field alongside the frag-
ments of veteran outfits. We can see this clearly
illustrated on the battle-field of Gettysburg, where
markers show the length of front occupied by each
regiment. One Minnesota regiment, for instance,
went into action with less than one sixth of its original numbers.

WORLD WAR REPLACEMENTS—That was all
changed in the World War. Every organization was kept at full strength by replacements sent
in as soon as possible. The government was at last
acting upon General Upton's advice and the example
of other armies.[10] It provided regular machinery for
a steady stream of replacements. A policy of "territorial recruiting" was established. The country was
divided into sixteen districts, each having a canton-

[9] See p. 233.
[10] See p. 153.

ment with a depot brigade to sort out and train recruits. Hereafter a certain district was to furnish, not a successive series of fresh regiments with new officers, but merely a few organizations at the start, and thereafter simply large numbers of men to be used to fill up gaps anywhere in the whole Army. With the new recruits joining organizations from other parts of the country, State and sectional lines were eradicated. Washington had complained, "Connecticut wants no Massachusetts men in her corps, Massachusetts thinks there is no need for a Rhode Islander in hers." But now, officers and men of a single organization are often from many different parts of the nation.

A TYPICAL DISTRICT—We can see how the system worked in the case of New England, the first district. Altogether, it furnished nearly 250,000 soldiers, almost equivalent to ten divisions of 27,000 men. Yet only two divisions were originally manned by New Englanders. These were the Twenty-sixth, a National Guard division, and the Seventy-sixth, made up of National Army men or draftees. The district cantonment, with its depot brigade, was at Camp Devens, near Boston. The first men to arrive at Devens went into the Seventy-sixth. As soon as this division was filled, the remaining New England drafted men passed through the depot brigade and then were usually sent overseas to fill any vacancies which might occur. Even the Seventy-sixth Division itself was broken up to be used as replacements for combat divisions which had suffered losses. The Twenty-sixth, on the other hand, was the first National Guard division to cross, and it saw continual active service. It received over 14,000 replacements, more than half its original strength. But these replacements came from various parts of the country.

The Army did not take time to sort out new men from Maine and Connecticut to fill the vacancies in this New England division. Such replacements were greatest in the First and Second Divisions of regulars, which sustained the heaviest casualties. They were sent 30,206 and 35,343 replacements respectively, although their strength at any one time was never more than 27,000 each. The result of this new policy was that a division could nearly always be counted upon to have its full strength of 27,000 men. This was, of course, a great help to the staff in making strategical and tactical dispositions.

POLICY NOT MADE INTERNATIONAL—Although the new replacement policy was followed to the limit within our own army, General Pershing refused to carry it beyond that. He stubbornly resisted the demands of the British and French who wanted to use the American troops simply as replacements for their own depleted organizations. He felt that trouble would arise from serving under foreign officers, and that America should have the morale and prestige which would come from an army of her own. It was one thing to have Illinois troops under officers from California, New Jersey, and Alabama; it would be quite another thing to expect them to sink their identity in British or French divisions. For a while during the emergency of the German 1918 drive, some American units were thus submerged, but the Americans had their own army for their big participation in the last ten weeks of the war.

6. SELECTION OF OFFICERS

COMMISSIONING GREENHORNS—Of all the faults of our old military policy, the haphazard method of selecting officers was the most ridiculous and one of the most costly. Untrained officers were a curse in war after war. Men totally ignorant of military affairs became captains, colonels, and even generals through political influence. "Pull" was apt to count for more than merit or experience. In many cases, their work soon revealed that it takes more than a scratch of the pen and a good tailor to make an officer. The States generally commissioned all officers up to colonels in their volunteer regiments. Of these, the company officers (lieutenants and captains) were frequently elected by their men, while the field-officers (majors to colonels) were appointed by the governors. The President commissioned the generals, but often the States dictated his choice in this matter, too.

REVOLUTIONARY OFFICERS—This trouble started at the very beginning of the Revolution. Massachusetts, for instance, offered a captaincy to any man who raised a company of fifty-nine men, and a colonel's commission to any one who recruited ten such companies. Strange things naturally resulted. One captain acted as barber for his company. Other companies would elect captains only on condition that they would share their pay. Discipline was quite out of the question under such circumstances. Washington felt strongly that only "gentlemen" made real commanders. Politics extended to the higher grades. Washington himself was chosen by the Continental Congress more to block the New Englanders than for his military ability. Congress was not always so lucky in its choices. It promoted intrigue and inefficiency by backing the worthless Gates and Charles Lee. It divided the generalships evenly among the States. Benedict Arnold was certainly one of the ablest officers in the whole army, but his promotion was blocked because the quota of generals from his State was already full.[11]

POLITICS AND COMMISSIONS—The situation in the next war was worse, for no Washington was picked. Generals had to belong to the right political party. President Polk made his law-partner a general in the Mexican War in spite of the latter's complete inexperience.

FAULTY USE OF REGULARS—The big armies of the Civil War were full of misfit officers. At first the South was wiser than the North. At the outbreak of the war, about a third of the regular Army officers "went South" to fight with the Confederacy. They were placed in command of volunteer troops and most of them rose to be generals. This sprinkling of experienced leaders among the green organizations helps to explain the early Southern victories. But most regular officers in the Union Army were "out of luck" for a long time. The little Regular Army was kept intact when its trained officers and men would have been invaluable, scattered about to drill the green volunteers into shape. They would have acted as leaven for the whole mass. West Pointers were continued as lieutenants and captains far into the war, while their classmates became Confederate generals. For example, Sheridan, an outstanding Union general, spent the whole first year of the war as a captain in the regular Army, with little prospect of promotion. Then he became a colonel of volunteers. After that the way was clear, and within eight months he was a major-general. Many of his fellow-officers, however, stayed in their low ranks in the regular Army.

POLITICIAN-STRATEGISTS—In   the   meantime,

[11] See p. 198.

strange choices were being made for high command. One of the most notorious was Nathaniel Banks, former Speaker of the House and Governor of Massachusetts, who received a major-general's commission as a political reward. Utterly inexperienced, he made a constant series of blunders.[12] Lincoln appointed scores of major-generals and hundreds of brigadiers—many of them utterly green. He realized the worthlessness of some of these men who were forced upon him by State politicians. He once expressed great regret that certain army mules were starving; "I can create a brigadier general with a scratch of the pen," he said, "but those mules cost $150 apiece."

MERIT BASIS IN WORLD WAR—In the World War, the United States made a thoroughgoing attempt to create and promote officers on *merit* alone. The great army required 200,000 officers. Less than 6,000 were in the Regular Army, and 3,200 were in the National Guard. The responsible high commands were given to Regular Army officers who had shown noticeable ability in service schools, the War College and the general staff, as well as in command of troops. Regular officers also were to supervise the instruction of the new men. These were generally given temporary promotions to several grades above their previous rank.

OFFICERS' TRAINING-CAMPS—Two thirds of the officers in infantry and field artillery were selected in a series of officers' training-camps where they received commissions after three months of strenuous training, stiff competition, and demonstration of leadership. It was out of the question to turn out fully trained officers in so brief a time, but many of the unfit were at least eliminated. The "ninety-day

12 See pp. 279–284.

wonders" left much to be desired, but as a whole they were a vast improvement over the elected and appointed officers of previous wars.

OTHER SOURCES OF OFFICERS—In addition to the officers from the regular Army, the National Guard, and the training-camps, 16,000 Regular Army enlisted men were given commissions. Also 70,000 became officers directly from civil life, but of these 42,000 were physicians, 2,000 clergymen (as chaplains), and the other 26,000 mostly men with special business of technical experiences. Very few "line" commissions were given to untrained men. The results were apparent in the increased efficiency of the Army. To sum up, "of every six officers, one had previous military training, three were graduates of officers' training-camps, and two came directly from civil life."

7. LACK OF GENERAL STAFF

NO COÖRDINATION—Until the World War, no adequate means of coördinating the high command and the organization of the Army existed. In this absence of system, plans had to be improved in a hurry and often went wrong. Too frequently, the Army lacked unity in its operations, and bungled its supply system as well as everything else. Too much was allowed to depend on the personality of the commander. The country gambled and frequently lost.

WASHINGTON'S HANDICAPS—In the Revolution, Washington himself did much to overcome this lack of coördination. He was a good strategist and tactician, but not a great one. His chief work was in holding the army together by the force of his personality. He did his best to improve the training system, but this was a gigantic task in the face of short-term enlistments and the general apathy. He tackled the supply system too, but this was also hopeless with almost no money or even supplies. He could have functioned much more efficiently and with less drain on his vitality had he had a competent general staff to relieve from the burden of having to supervise himself the execution of all the details of his decisions.

GLARING EXAMPLE IN 1812—The War of 1812, as we remarked, saw the same bad policy but no Washington. Plans were made in the most slipshod way. Any one who wants to see how a campaign should *not* be run ought to study the invasion of Canada in 1812. The only "general staff" preparation consisted of an informal meeting between the President, the Secretary of War, General Hull, and General Dearborn two months before the war began. The last two were elderly civilians who had served thirty years before in the Revolution. The "plan" was to invade Canada from Detroit and Niagara at the same time, but the conference broke up without coming to any decision as to details or even time. When war was declared, letters were sent to notify the two generals of the fact. Mails were slow, and Hull heard from another source that the war was on. He immediately crossed into Canada from Detroit without any clear idea of what to do. An energetic British officer with a few well-disciplined troops organized the defense of Canada so well that he not only drove Hull out, but even chased him back to Detroit and forced the larger American force to surrender. Meanwhile Dearborn's invasion had been delayed by the refusal of the militia to serve outside the country. The two commanders were made the scapegoats for the total lack of preparation. Later in the war, some order was brought out of the chaos of plans by a few clever younger officers. Among them was Winfield Scott, whose able leadership helped to compensate for the same lack of system in the Mexican War.

CIVIL WAR EXPERIMENTING—The Civil War was run without efficient military control until the last year. The only coördination was in the President and Secretary of War, who had no military experience, and a pedantic "military advisor" without authority. We shall see how the command was split up and several almost independent armies roamed around with woeful lack of coöperation.[13] No trained staff-officers were in either army. Men who had seldom seen more than a single regiment assembled in one place were called upon to command 100,000 men. The North had to try seven commanders in succession before it found the right man.[14] Its army had to rely on Pinkerton detectives for want of an intelligence service and of good maps. Grant eventually worked out a fairly good staff system after previous blundering had unnecessarily lengthened the contest.

MISMANAGEMENT IN 1898—The Spanish-American War revealed inefficiency in the Army high command and administration. No plans worthy of the name had been made for the work which the Army was called upon to perform. Supplies, transportation and particularly sanitation were badly bungled. The Navy, on the other hand, was better prepared. It was this experience which led to the creation of the General Staff in 1903, with its various functions of preparation.

GENERAL STAFF IN WORLD WAR—The General

[13] See pp. 243, 270–272.
[14] See pp. 257, 258.

Staff justified itself in the World War. The United States gathered, trained, and used a much larger army than ever before with much less friction or blundering. The functions of the subdivisions of the General Staff—G1, G2, and the rest—were extended down into the lower units. One reason why the Allies wanted to absorb the American troops as replacements in their own units was their skepticism as to the efficiency of the American staffs. Eventually, however, the Americans fought under their own command, first in divisions, then in corps and finally in armies.[15] Half of the 4,000,000 American soldiers were carried overseas as the American Expeditionary Force. The transportation and supply of that huge force was in itself a miracle of management. The performance of the A. E. F. was proof of the advance we had made in military policy.

8. CIVILIAN INTERFERENCE

STATESMEN VS. SOLDIERS—The final defect in our old military policy was the interference of civilians in purely military affairs. It is the business of the civil government to determine *policy,* deciding when, with whom, and for what purpose a war is to be fought. It is the business of the soldiers to manage the strictly military affairs of strategy and tactics.[16] Sometimes it is hard to draw the line between the two. Frequently one party has interfered in the other's function. Most of the greatest military leaders avoided this problem, for they headed the civil government as well as the army. Alexander, Cæsar, Gustavus Adolphus, Frederick the Great, and Napoleon all enjoyed a free hand in this respect. It is

[15] See pp. 331, 341.
[16] See p. 113.

contrary to the traditions of a democracy, however, to permit such a combination. Our history has shown that politicians and soldiers do their best work in their own special spheres.

CIVILIAN SECRETARIES OF WAR—One particular fault in our system was the military power given the Secretary of War. He is, of course, the executive official of the Commander-in-Chief of the Army—the President. Most of our Secretaries of War have come into office without previous military experience. Yet time and again they have assumed in war the authority which properly belongs to trained soldiers. The President and Congress have also been guilty of such interference.

THE CONTINENTAL CONGRESS—The Continental Congress did its full share of interfering in the Revolution. Nor was this confined solely to the matter of military appointments and promotions. It meddled in strategy in the fall of 1776, when it ordered Washington not to abandon Fort Washington and Fort Lee on the Hudson after the fall of New York. As Washington foresaw, the British soon took the forts anyway, and captured many soldiers who could ill be spared.[17] Congress neglected to give Washington proper supplies or moral support, but it found time to legislate on what color underwear generals should wear.

POLITICS IN 1812 AND 1846—By 1812, a Secretary of War—and a poor one—took a hand in matters of strategy, and failed to remedy some glaring defects in military policy. In the Mexican War, it is claimed that the Democratic administration took away most of General Taylor's men while he was invading Mexico from the north, because he was a Whig and it was feared he would become too popu-

[17] See p. 202.

lar. Taylor lost the men, but he became the next President.

CIVILIAN "STAFF" IN THE CIVIL WAR—The outstanding case of civilian interference came in the Civil War. Lincoln's first Secretary of War was principally interested in getting fat contracts for his friends, but his successor, Stanton, took a very active part in all military affairs, including strategy, in spite of his lack of military training. In later chapters, it will be seen how these two civilians actually tried to direct the movements of the Northern armies.[18]

EVIL REMOVED BY 1917—The World War saw a marked contrast in this as it did in many other questions. President Wilson picked Pershing as the best man available for the command of the A. E. F., and then backed him to the limit. Of course, Washington was a long way from the Western Front. Secretary of War Baker tells of visiting Pershing on the eve of the St. Mihiel action. He asked the general if there was anything that he (the Secretary) could do. Pershing replied that he might pray for a fog for the next morning. Baker did—and the fog came. That was a far cry from the Civil War days when another Secretary of War was trying to outwit the brilliant Confederate general, "Stonewall" Jackson.

THE EIGHT POINTS REMEDIED—After a century and a quarter of blundering, the United States has at last done much to correct the eight chief defects in its military policy. In the World War, the addition of universal conscription to the volunteer system did away with short enlistments and bounties. State control was eliminated. With the new replacement policy, units were kept at par value. An earnest

[18] See Chaps. XI and XII.

attempt was made to appoint and promote officers on the basis of merit alone. A General Staff at last made intelligent plans and carried them out efficiently and without civilian interference. There were still some shortcomings, but this World War record is proof that military history has been studied to great advantage.

PART III

AMERICAN WARS AND CAMPAIGNS

CHAPTER IX

THE AMERICAN REVOLUTION

The fighting of the American Revolution extended over considerable time and space. There were campaigns along the Atlantic coast from Maine to Georgia, and inland as far as the Great Lakes and the Mississippi. But important activities seldom occurred in more than one place at a time. The actual fighting lasted six years, from the battle of Lexington in 1775 to the fall of Yorktown in 1781. The first three years centered in the North, and the last three in the South. The Americans sustained numerous defeats, but their victories at Trenton-Princeton, Saratoga, and Yorktown were enough to secure independence.

AN ENDURANCE CONTEST—Each side had certain definite advantages and disadvantages. The British had the harder task. Like the North in the Civil War, they had to subdue a vast region before the rebellion could be crushed.[1] The Americans simply had to make the British so weary of the war that they would let the colonies have their own way. The war was really an endurance contest, depending on the perseverance of the two sides. At times, it looked as though the Americans would not hold together long enough to wear out the British. The Americans fought few purely offensive campaigns, as the nature

[1] See p. 238.

of the contest called for a defensive rôle on their part.

WEALTH AND SEA POWER—The Americans lacked money and supplies for even the small regular army which they managed to hold together. They could count on the militia or minute-men to turn out when their own immediate region was in danger. But these untrained men were not dependable in battle.[2]

The British, on the other hand, had organization and wealth. Their experienced redcoats were well-trained, well-equipped, and well-fed. They were assisted by thousands of professional soldiers hired from Germany at about thirty-six dollars a head. The British Navy, ordinarily the best in the world, was a great advantage at first. Toward the end of the war, rotten ships and masts plus bad management so weakened it that the French fleets were able to threaten England's control of the sea. At this same later period, the French aid to the American army in the form of money, supplies, and regulars was offsetting England's original superiority in resources.

GEOGRAPHY—Geography favored the Americans. The British had to transport their men and supplies 3,000 miles across the Atlantic. The British Navy, it is true, could move troops rapidly from one part of the coast to another, leaving the Americans in doubt as to where they would strike next. The principal seaports fell into the hands of the British one after another. They had Boston in 1775, and took New York in 1776, Philadelphia in 1777, Savannah in 1778, and Charleston in 1780. The British had more to do, however, than to occupy seaport towns. They had to subdue the *entire* region. The Americans would retire inland. Then the British followed, and found themselves in trouble. Distances were

[2] See p. 176.

great, communications were bad, and there was constant danger of being cut off by a rising of local American militia.

FALSE OBJECTIVES—The British thus made their big mistake by violating the principle of the objective. They should have crushed Washington's main army instead of scattering their efforts in capturing seaports and subduing towns. On the other hand, some experts think the British should have trusted everything to their Navy. In a purely naval war, the Americans would have been cut off from all outside communications and trade by a rigid blockade. The British chose, however, blundering land campaigns combined with naval support. That is what we are to study.

BOTH SIDES DIVIDED—Neither side was united in the contest. It was not a clean-cut struggle between a united patriotic America on one side and a united despotic Britain on the other, as the older schoolbooks imply. Many Americans, dubbed Tories, sided with the English. Even more Americans were indifferent to the contest, and sometimes carried certificates of loyalty to both sides. In England a powerful political party, the Whigs, opposed George III, arguing for the Americans in Parliament. Some of them even rejoiced in American victories. Many prominent British generals and admirals were Whigs and some refused to serve against the Americans. Others who did serve, were probably less active than usual because of their Whig sympathies. Because each side was so divided, the contest has sometimes been called a civil war instead of a war between England and America.

THE AMERICAN COMMANDERS—The American Revolution produced no Marlborough nor Frederick the Great. The highest honors go without question to George Washington. He was an able commander, but his greatest work lay in holding the army together in the face of constant discouragement. Next to him came Nathanael Greene. The Americans were hampered by the selfish political intrigues of two prominent generals, Horatio Gates and Charles Lee, both former British officers. These men worked for the supreme command for themselves, and hindered Washington in every possible way. Probably the most brilliant of all the commanders was Benedict Arnold. He received very unfair treatment from Congress, but that by no means justified his treason in accepting a commission in the British Army in 1780 and trying to hand over West Point.[3] Several foreign officers were of great assistance to the American cause, notably Lafayette, von Steuben, De Kalb, Pulaski and Kosciusko.

THE BRITISH COMMANDERS—King George is said to have declared that he feared the incapacity of his own generals more than he feared the Americans. The principal British commanders in America were Sir William Howe, Lord Cornwallis, John Burgoyne, and Sir Henry Clinton. Howe, a Whig, lost several opportunities to end the war quickly because of his failure to seize the offensive. Cornwallis later made a good governor-general of India. He showed ability at times in the Revolution, but he was outwitted by Washington at Trenton and got himself into a hole in Virginia. Burgoyne, who likewise surrendered an army, was more successful as a playwright. Clinton was the most active of the four, but he was not given a free hand by his government. The British operations were guided—or rather misguided—from England by Lord George Germain, who had been cashiered from the Army twenty years

[3] See p. 182.

THE AMERICAN REVOLUTION 199

before, but who now held an important post in the King's cabinet. He was a wretched substitute for a general staff. The British should have observed the principle of simplicity by giving more complete power to a single commander-in-chief in America. At times, complete lack of coöperation existed between different generals. Above all, the principle of the objective was flagrantly violated in the failure, many times repeated, to break up the main American army.

THE WAR IN 1775—BOSTON AND CANADA

LEXINGTON AND CONCORD—Only a brief account of the major operations of the war can be given here. The fighting started on April 19, 1775, at Lexington and Concord near Boston. Some British regiments under General Gage had been stationed in Boston for some time. On the night of April 18th, he sent 800 men to destroy some military stores collected by rebellious colonists at Concord. The colonists were warned of this move, and a group of them opposed the British at Lexington the next day. The first shots of the war were fired, eight minute-men fell, and the redcoats went to on Concord. There they were stopped by a larger group of farmers, and had to retire. The British were shot at from behind walls and trees, all the way back to Boston, and lost some 273 men.

BUNKER HILL—The news of this encounter brought 16,000 colonists to the vicinity of Boston to form an army. Gage could probably have nipped the revolt in the bud with an energetic offensive. Instead, he neglected to occupy the hills commanding the town. He also wasted his chance to break up the unorganized militia as they were gathering. In June the Americans occupied Breed's Hill across the harbor in Charlestown. The British might have captured the hill easily by merely taking the neck of the peninsula behind it and so isolating it. Instead, their contempt for the colonial farmers led them to make a frontal assault against the entrenchments on June 17, 1775. Twice they attacked it in the parade-ground formation patterned after Frederick the Great. The Americans held their fire until the thin red lines were but fifty yards away; then twice they repulsed the redcoats with heavy loss. A third attack carried the hill, for the American ammunition was gone. The British lost 1,054 men in this unnecessary action, misnamed Bunker Hill. It was a blundering attack, carried out with great bravery.

EVACUATION OF BOSTON—The siege of Boston lasted for exactly nine months after Bunker Hill. Washington assumed command of the American army at Cambridge. It was constantly changing its personnel as men came and went.[4] Gage was replaced in the British command by Howe, who passively allowed himself to be blockaded. The British thus lost another good chance for offensive action. All through the winter Howe neglected to seize the hills commanding Boston. In March, the Americans moved artillery to Dorchester Heights, where they could fire into the town. Howe thereupon sailed away on March 17th, leaving behind large quantities of supplies.

TICONDEROGA AND CANADA—In the meantime, the Americans had captured Fort Ticonderoga, a highly strategic position on Lake Champlain. Encouraged by that success, they launched a winter campaign against Canada under Montgomery and Benedict Arnold, one going through Vermont, and the other through Maine. This was one of the few

4 See p. 170.

American offensives. Montreal was taken in November, but the Americans were repulsed before Quebec by Sir Guy Carlton, the Governor of Canada, on December 31st. His clever work soon drove them out of Canada.

THE WAR IN 1776—NEW YORK AND NEW JERSEY

FAULTY BRITISH POLICY—It was now high time for the British to take the offensive. They had stupidly allowed the Americans to do this at Boston and also against Canada. But from now on, for five years, the British took and maintained the offensive most of the time. Their superior organization, their sea power, and especially their purpose in the war threw this task upon them. But they constantly forgot their main objective—the crushing of the principal American army. Instead, throughout the war, they could not resist the temptation for side-shows. As one of their generals exclaimed, this led their army to be defeated in "damned driblets."

THE NEXT STEP—THE HUDSON—When the British sailed away from Boston in March, 1776, there was no telling where they would land next. Howe himself did not know. He went to Halifax and waited nearly three months for orders. Washington rightly reckoned that the next British blow would be at New York. This was the obvious step. If the British could gain command of the Hudson, they could cut off the seat of the revolt—New England—from the rest of the colonies. The Hudson offered practically the only satisfactory line of communications for operations into the interior. For this reason, Howe at last, in June, received orders to strike at New York. But Clinton, who was with Howe at

Halifax, had already been sent South on a wild-goose chase to capture Charleston, South Carolina. This Southern side-show ended in a repulse.

LONG ISLAND—While Howe was waiting for orders, the Americans had had plenty of time to fortify New York. Howe finally landed his forces on Staten Island near New York on July 3, 1776, the day before the Declaration of Independence was proclaimed. Clinton soon joined him from Charleston. They had some 32,000 British and Hessian regulars with which to attack the 18,000 raw Americans defending the city. The western end of Long Island, the present Brooklyn, was the scene of an important action on August 27th. The Americans here were poorly disposed, communications were bad and their left flank was unguarded. Howe defeated them, but, violating the principle of movement, failed to follow up his victory.

FALL OF NEW YORK—HARLEM AND WHITE PLAINS —Washington withdrew his men from Brooklyn and was slowly pushed out of New York by the British, who occupied it on September 15th. Once in New York, they stayed until the end of the war. Washington again fought the British at Harlem and White Plains, just above the city, but had to retreat into New Jersey. The Hudson had been fortified by the Americans to stop the British from seizing the whole line of the river to cut off New England. The forts up the river in the Highlands were secure, but Washington wanted to abandon Fort Washington and Fort Lee just above New York on opposite sides of the river. The Continental Congress, which was trying to control military affairs, would not agree to this. Consequently, the Fort Washington garrison was captured by the British on November 17th, while Fort Lee was given up a week later. By these mistakes, men—sorely needed—were lost to the American army.[5]

THE JERSEY CAMPAIGN—TRENTON-PRINCETON— Then followed Washington's retreat across New Jersey. The whole State fell into the hands of the British, who kept close behind him. His 18,000 men at New York melted to a scant 3,000. This slow retreat won Washington the title of the "American Fabius." He was too weak to offer battle, but he accomplished the march across the State without further loss of men. Once again, Howe had and lost the opportunity to crush the rebellion with a rapid blow. We shall pass over this episode, as it will be taken up in the next chapter in the more detailed study of the battles of Trenton and Princeton on December 26, 1776 and January 3, 1777, respectively. Washington was at his best in those battles. In ten days he changed the American situation from one of almost hopeless despair to one of hope. He outwitted the British, defeated them in two actions, and recovered most of New Jersey. He took up winter quarters about thirty miles from New York, at Morristown, where he threatened the British lines of communication into Jersey or up the Hudson.

THE WAR IN 1777—UPPER HUDSON AND PHILADELPHIA

BRITISH PLANS—The British, meanwhile, still wanted to secure the line of the Hudson and so cut off New England. General Burgoyne was to come down from Canada through Lake Champlain and upper New York to Albany. A side expedition under General St. Leger was to march to Oswego on Lake Ontario and down the Mohawk Valley. It

[5] See p. 189.

might have been more effective if Burgoyne and Howe had joined for a combined action. This would have been in keeping with the principle of mass, but the British wanted to ward off a possible second attack on Canada.

AN OLD ERROR—Many historians state that the British planned a threefold campaign in which Howe was to come up the Hudson, joining Burgoyne and St. Leger at Albany, with the colonies thus cut in two. The story was that Germain was in such a hurry for a week-end party that he neglected to send Howe's orders. Recently discovered military correspondence shows that no such triple plan was ever adopted—so a good story is spoiled.

BURGOYNE'S START—Burgoyne set out from Canada June 1, 1777. Fort Ticonderoga, which covered the approach, was recaptured on July 6th. Burgoyne proceeded southward. Six weeks later a force of Hessians, which he sent over to Bennington, Vermont, was badly whipped by a large militia force. In the meantime, St. Leger's expedition from the west had failed. He had advanced from Oswego and was besieging Fort Stanwix, later renamed Fort Schuyler. St. Leger's English and Indians drove off a relieving force in the woods at Oriskany near-by. Benedict Arnold next went to the relief of the fort. By a clever ruse, he sent ahead an exaggerated account of his strength, which caused the desertions of St. Leger's Indians and forced the British to retire. That settled Burgoyne's fate. A relief expedition did eventually start from New York, but it was too slow.

BURGOYNE'S SURRENDER—SARATOGA—The Americans under Schuyler fell back to Stillwater on the Hudson, about thirty-five miles above Albany. Schuyler was replaced by the incompetent Gates,

whose success was due in large part to the work of
his subordinates and the nature of the campaign.
Burgoyne might have retreated in safety, but he
determined to fight his way through the American
force, although it was more than twice as big as his.
Arnold attacked him with a small number of men
on September 19th, in a battle variously known as
Stillwater, Bemis Heights, or Freeman's Farm.
Gates, meanwhile, remained stupidly inactive with
the main body of his army. A second battle was
fought on October 7th in practically the same place.
Burgoyne was defeated and finally decided to attempt a retreat. It was now too late, for thousands
more of the American militia had swarmed to the
scene and were surrounding his 6,000 men. On October 17th, he surrendered his entire force to Gates at
Saratoga.

ITS IMPORTANCE—This surrender of Burgoyne's
was the real turning-point of the war. The moral
effect of the surrender of a British army was more
important than the actual loss of Burgoyne's 6,000
men. Its principal result was that it brought France
into the war on the side of the Americans. A treaty
was made by Benjamin Franklin early in 1778, in
which France agreed to help with money, ships, and
men. She, of course, was eager to revenge her previous defeats by England. This French aid was an
invaluable element in the American success.

HOWE AT PHILADELPHIA—BRANDYWINE, GER-
MANTOWN—While the Americans were defeating
Burgoyne in the North, Washington had been meeting with reverses. Howe had decided to take Philadelphia, as it was the seat of the Continental Congress. He started out with 18,000 men in June, 1777,
just as Burgoyne was leaving Canada, while Clinton was left with 7,000 men in New York. It was

this force of Clinton's which failed to relieve Burgoyne. Howe made several feints to deceive Washington, who expected him to go up the Hudson. At
last, Howe sailed away and Washington moved
south to oppose any attack on Philadelphia. The
British ships first tried the Delaware; then foolishly
made a long trip around to the head of Chesapeake
Bay. Washington tried to block their approach to
Philadelphia on September 11th at Brandywine
Creek. His left flank was turned and the British
entered Philadelphia on the 27th. A week later,
Washington attacked them at Germantown on the
north side of the city. His plan was good, but something went wrong in the fog and he was defeated.

THE WINTER OF 1777–1778—The occupation of
Philadelphia was of no great military value to the
British, but Howe had a delightful winter there. The
Continental Congress had fled far into the back coun-
try. Clinton, as we saw, tried to join Burgoyne as
Howe should have known enough to do. Washing-
ton moved his defeated army into winter quarters
at Valley Forge, not far from Philadelphia.

VALLEY FORGE—The rigors of that winter are
well known, though it was only one of the six win-
ters during which the ill-equipped Americans shiv-
ered. Washington had to face a plot of Gates and
other officers to oust him from command. Luckily,
Congress showed sense enough to retain him. During
the winter, Baron von Steuben, who had served under
Frederick the Great, gave some thorough training to
the little force at Valley Forge.

THE WAR IN 1778–1779—NORTH, WEST, AND
SOUTH

THE BRITISH SPLIT THEIR FORCES—The British
had no real plans for 1778. The policy of scattered

effort was evident in the orders sent to Clinton, who now replaced Howe in chief command. The principles of objective and mass were almost entirely disregarded. Clinton was ordered to detach several thousand men for various missions and to evacuate Philadelphia. No thorough plan for a decisive attack was given. Clinton disapproved of these plans of Germain's and wanted to resign. But he finally acepted them and started back to New York with his army. Adequate sea transportation was not available, so he marched across New Jersey.

MONMOUTH—Washington had been waiting for such an opportunity. At last he could take the offensive. He fell upon Clinton on June 28th, 1778, at Monmouth Court-House (or Freehold) near Princeton and Trenton. The battle was nearly lost by General Charles Lee, who ordered the Americans to retreat when all was going well. He wanted the supreme command and has been accused of doing this deliberately to discredit Washington. The latter, however, checked the retreat and turned the battle into a victory, though a less complete one than he had hoped. Clinton's force had many casualties, but was able to get to New York.

END OF NORTHERN FIGHTING—The battle of Monmouth really ended the important fighting in the North. It was a queer war, in which the main rival armies simply settled down near each other for three years. A real offensive on either side might have ended the struggle at any time. The British stayed in New York, holding only a small strip of land outside of the city. Clinton had to send so many men on remote "side-shows" in the South and the West Indies, that he could do no more than make occasional raids.

WATCHFUL WAITING—In the West Indies the

British and the French were trying to capture each other's valuable sugar islands. Washington, with about as many men as Clinton, remained in the vicinity of New York to watch the British. Though he took part in no major action for the next three years, he was doing some of his most valuable work. The people were tired of the war. It took all of Washington's patience, courage, and determination to hold his forces together and to keep the support of Congress and the States. The scene of action was transferred to the South by the British after Monmouth. It is in the Carolinas that most of the remaining fighting, before the final surrender at Yorktown, took place.

CLARK IN THE NORTHWEST TERRITORY—Before turning to the Southern campaigns, we must take notice of what George Rogers Clark was doing in the West. England hoped to retain the great Northwest Territory between the Alleghenies, the Great Lakes, and the Mississippi, even if she should lose the Thirteen Colonies. A few British posts were scattered through the wilderness. From these the Indians were incited to raid the frontier settlements. Clark's purpose was to stop these raids and possibly get control of the territory. In 1778, he made a brilliant expedition into the Northwest Territory with only a handful of Virginia militiamen. He surprised and took Kaskaskia on the Mississippi in July. This was followed by a daring midwinter march through half-frozen swamps and flooded rivers. It resulted in the surprise capture of the British garrison at Vincennes. He was unable to take Detroit, but his daring campaign helped secure the Northwest Territory for the United States at the final peace conference. This was naturally a tremendous factor in the westward expansion of the United States.

THE SHIFT TO THE SOUTH—The last three years of fighting centered in the South. Except for the final siege of Yorktown, it was on a much smaller scale than the earlier campaigning in the North. The British violated the principle of the objective when they carried the war into the South. They should have struck at the main American army that was settled down near New York. Clinton realized this, but he was not allowed enough men to do it. He did the only two things he could under the circumstances. He held on to New York and used it as a base for destructive raids along the coast to discourage the Americans. He also tried to gain control of the Southern States, trusting that the pro-British Loyalists or Tories would rise to help the redcoats. The South had hitherto seen no fighting except Clinton's unsuccessful attack on Charleston in 1776. The British were now campaigning not so much against American armies as against American endurance.

GEORGIA OVERRUN—The Southern fighting started in Georgia and worked northward through the two Carolinas to Virginia. The first step was the British capture of Savannah in the last week of 1778. Before long, the whole State was under British control. The royal governor was restored to office. The Americans tried to recapture Savannah in October, 1779, but the attack failed despite the assistance of a French fleet, leaving the British masters of Georgia.

THE WAR IN 1780—SOUTH CAROLINA

OCCUPATION OF SOUTH CAROLINA—Then the British tried to do the same thing to South Carolina.

Clinton came down from New York with nearly 8,000 men and some warships. He captured Charleston and its 2,500 defenders on May 12, 1780, and soon broke all effective American resistance. Early in June, Clinton returned to New York with part of the troops, feeling that he had done a good job. Cornwallis was left with a force of 4,000 men, which he scattered about the region. Four ports were garrisoned to ensure sea communications. Six inland posts were established to keep the State in order. Cornwallis hoped that the Loyalists would flock to the British standard. It proved to be poor policy to base military operations on such uncertain elements.

BROTHER AGAINST BROTHER—The inhabitants of South Carolina were divided about equally between pro-British Loyalists and pro-American "patriots" or Whigs. These two groups carried on a good part of the Carolina fighting. A bitter and sometimes savage "brother against brother" struggle between these two groups of Americans resulted. The South Carolinians were organized in rival irregular bands of "partisan" cavalry and backwoods riflemen. Both sides had exceptionally clever leaders for this sort of guerilla warfare: Tarleton and Ferguson on the British side, Sumter and Marion on the American. Sometimes they coöperated with the "regular" troops of their respective armies. More often, they were engaged in a private "all-Carolina" fight among themselves.

PARTISAN RAIDS—Exposed lines of communications were the weak points of the British forces throughout the Carolina campaigns. They tried to control the whole region with a few thousand men, consequently, there could never be many in one place. Communications were bound to be vulnerable. This was the chance for the "partisans" of Marion and of Sumter, "the Swamp Fox." Their trump cards were speed and surprise. They would suddenly swoop down, do their damage, and vanish. Tarleton might sometimes catch them napping, but he could not be everywhere at once.

CAMDEN—An American force of 3,000 men was soon sent to dislodge the British. The command was given to Gates, the accidental hero of Saratoga. But this time, he had no brilliant subordinates to win a victory for him. He wrecked his undeserved reputation almost at once. His first objective was Camden, the principal British inland post about 125 miles from Charleston. He picked the wrong road for a favorable approach and threw away several opportunities for victory. Cornwallis came to meet him just outside Camden. The British had 1,500 regulars and 500 militia. Gates had about 1,500 regulars and 1,500 militia. The British attacked the American militia who broke and ran. This exposed the flank of the American regulars, who had stood fast and were doing well. Tarleton completed the victory when he struck the unprotected regulars from the rear. The rest of the day was spent in chasing fugitives. The American casualties in killed, wounded, and prisoners totaled 2,000—equivalent to the whole British force. A few days later, Tarleton caught Sumter's little partisan band off guard and routed it also.

KING'S MOUNTAIN—Cornwallis now started for North Carolina. His hold on South Carolina seemed secure after this steady series of victories. Early in September, 1780, he crossed the border with two of his three columns, while Colonel Ferguson, the best rifleman in the British Army, swung far to the westward toward the mountains with the third, con-

taining 1,200 Carolina Loyalists. This third column
came to grief and spoiled the invasion for a time.
Ferguson was pursuing a partisan band and also
hoped to gather more recruits. Instead, he found a
swarm of hostile backwoodsmen menacing his advance. On October 6, 1780, he turned at bay on
King's Mountain near the border of the two Carolinas. The next day saw a unique battle for that
period of "thin-line" attacks and "Brown Bess" muskets. King's Mountain was a fierce struggle between
two bands of American frontiersmen, armed with
the deadly Kentucky rifle and stalking each other
from behind trees and rocks.[6] Ferguson and 400 of
his men were killed; the rest surrendered.

GREENE SENT TO THE CAROLINAS—This postponed Cornwallis's invasion of North Carolina. He
went back across the border and settled down at
Winnesborough, thirty miles from Camden. His outlook at the end of 1780 was not as rosy as it had
been four months earlier. King's Mountain had encouraged the partisans to renewed activity against
the exposed British communications. To make matters worse for Cornwallis, the Americans now sent
a *real* general against him. Nathanael Greene was no
Gates. Next to Washington, he was the best general
in the Continental army, and he brought several able
subordinates with him. Greene's strategy in the Carolinas during the next few months was brilliant.

THE WAR IN 1781—THE CAROLINAS AND YORKTOWN

GREENE'S STRATEGY—Cornwallis invaded North
Carolina a second time early in January, 1781. He
had received reinforcements, which brought his force
up to about 3,000. Greene had only about 2,000. His

[6] See pp. 17, 58.

objective was the wearing-out of the British force and the prevention of an effective occupation of the Carolinas. He knew that it would be folly to attack the British in their full strength. So he decided upon the risky expedient of dividing his little force. This was a well-considered violation of the principle of mass. He himself retired back into North Carolina with half of his army, hoping this would lure Cornwallis farther and farther from his base. The other half he gave to Morgan for a drive to the westward around the British left wing. Cornwallis was thus compelled to divide his own force too. Had Cornwallis kept his army together and attacked Greene's half of the force, Morgan could have made a clean sweep of the British posts toward Georgia with the other half. Had Cornwallis turned his full force against Morgan, on the other hand, Greene could have walked into Charleston. Greene saw that the chances were probably better against a divided British army.

COWPENS—He was right. Cornwallis sent Tarleton to handle Morgan with 1,100 of his 3,000 men. They met on January 17, 1780, at a place called Cowpens, a few miles from King's Mountain. Morgan arranged his men with a deep river in their rear so that the militia would have less temptation to run. A final lucky maneuver, in which the Americans feigned retreat, resulted in the complete defeat of Tarleton. He lost 800 men. For the second time in four months, Cornwallis was struck a crushing blow on his left flank.

GUILFORD COURT-HOUSE—But Cowpens left the two halves of Greene's army seventy miles apart. Between them was Cornwallis—twice as strong as either of them. While Greene's main army was retiring through North Carolina as a decoy, Cornwallis was in hot pursuit of Morgan's men, who were racing to rejoin Greene. Flooded rivers enabled Morgan to make a narrow escape. On February 9th, he joined Greene at Guilford Court-House in North Carolina, only thirty-five miles from the Virginia border. Here Greene expected reinforcements, but they had not arrived. He continued to retire northward, and crossed the River Dan into Virginia. Cornwallis could not cross the river because Greene had taken all the boats, so he headed south again. Greene did not want that. He had lured the British more than 100 miles from their base and wanted to keep them on this futile chase. So he recrossed the Dan into North Carolina to play hide and seek with Cornwallis until reinforcements should arrive. They came at last, and he had 4,500 men to face the 2,200 British. But Cornwallis had regulars, while Greene's men were largely militia. Greene at last allowed Cornwallis to overtake him at Guilford Court-House on March 15, 1781. The ensuing battle was hard fought, and ended somewhat in favor of the British.

CORNWALLIS ABANDONS THE CAROLINAS—It was a barren victory for Cornwallis. He had failed to crush Greene as he had done Gates. The battle casualties had so reduced his force that he could not continue his cherished plan of conquering North Carolina. He retired down the Cape Fear River to the sea at Wilmington, North Carolina. There he made a surprising decision. It was expected that he would return by sea to Charleston. He had been sent to the Carolinas to hold them in British control. Instead, he defied Clinton and surprised Greene by abandoning the remaining Carolina garrisons to their fate and starting overland for Virginia. That was the beginning of the end.

GREENE REGAINS SOUTH CAROLINA—Greene

spent the spring and summer dealing with the remaining 1,400 British in South Carolina. They put up a spirited defense. Greene was beaten in April at Hobkirk's Hill outside Camden, and in September at Eutaw Springs outside Charleston. But these tactical defeats did not prevent Greene's strategic success. He lost all his battles, but he broke the British hold on the Carolinas by wearing out their force. They had nothing but Charleston left by the middle of September, 1781.

MANEUVERS IN VIRGINIA—Meanwhile, Cornwallis had marched overland to Virginia. At Petersburg, near Richmond, he took over some regiments which had been raiding the State under Benedict Arnold, now a British general. This raised his total numbers to 5,000 regulars. As in the Carolinas, the British were able to march along almost wherever they pleased, but their hold on a district lasted only as long as their redcoats were in sight. Lafayette was trying to defend the region with 3,000 Americans. For ten weeks, the two forces maneuvered around the peninsula between the York and James Rivers. We shall hear more of this same peninsula when we study McClellan's campaign in 1862.[7] The Americans and British both received reinforcements. Early in August, Cornwallis placed his 7,000 men in Yorktown, where he expected to have sea communications.

PLANS FOR COÖPERATION—Now we can see the rival forces lining up for the final campaign. Cornwallis was in Yorktown with Lafayette near-by. Clinton was in New York, watched by Washington and some French regulars under Rochambeau. The total numbers on each side were about equal. If either side could concentrate its forces while the

[7] See Chap. XII.

other remained separated, victory would be easy.
The navies were to settle that question. Up to this
time, British warships had been able to assist troop
movements almost at will. But now a powerful
French fleet under De Grasse was on its way from
the West Indies to face the British fleet under Admiral Graves.

THE YORKTOWN CAMPAIGN—The Americans and
French debated whether to attack New York or
Yorktown. They decided on the latter. De Grasse
agreed to sail for Chesapeake Bay. Washington
created the impression that he was about to attack
New York, in order to keep Clinton's forces there.
Then, with remarkable speed and secrecy, he and
Rochambeau set out on August 17, 1781, for Yorktown. The army hurried along the familiar road past
Princeton and Trenton to Philadelphia before the
men suspected that they were going to Virginia.
Naturally this move took Clinton by surprise. Washington arrived at the head of Chesapeake Bay early
in September; then vessels transported the army to
the vicinity of Yorktown.

FAILURE OF BRITISH FLEET—This approach, with
its mobility and surprise, was one of the master-
strokes of the war. The army and navy, moreover,
coöperated to a high degree. De Grasse was blockad-
ing the mouth of Chesapeake Bay by the beginning
of September, to prevent any assistance from reaching Yorktown. On September 5th, Admiral Graves
tried to break the blockade. After a bungling attack,
he went back to New York with his ships badly
mauled. For once, England did not control the seas.
That naval action sealed the fate of Cornwallis.

SIEGE OF YORKTOWN—The allied armies now
settled down for a formal siege of Yorktown. It was
conducted more or less according to the Vauban

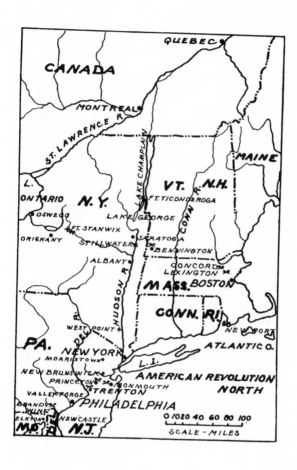

QUEBEC

CANADA

MONTREAL

ST. LAWRENCE R.

MAINE

L. ONTARIO

N.Y.

LAKE CHAMPLAIN

VT.

N.H.

CONN. R.

OSWEGO

FT. TICONDEROGA

LAKE GEORGE

FT. STANWIX

SARATOGA

ORISKANY

STILLWATER

BENNINGTON

ALBANY

CONCORD

LEXINGTON

HUDSON R.

MASS. BOSTON

CONN. R.I.

WEST POINT

NEW PORT

DEL. R.

PA.

NEW YORK

ATLANTIC O.

MORRISTOWN

L. I.

NEW BRUNSWICK

AMERICAN REVOLUTION

PRINCETON

MONMOUTH

NORTH

VALLEY FORGE

TRENTON

BRANDY-

PHILADELPHIA

WINE

ELKTON

NEWCASTLE

0 10 20 40 60 80 100

MD.

N.J.

SCALE - MILES

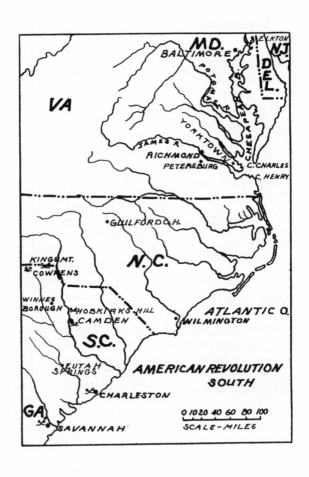

MD.

BALTIMORE

N.J.

ELKTON

DEL.

VA

POTOMAC R.

CHESAPEAKE

YORKTOWN

JAMES R.

RICHMOND

PETERSBURG

C. CHARLES

C. HENRY

GUILFORD C.H.

N.C.

KING'S MT.

COWPENS

WINNES BOROUGH

HOBKIRKS HILL

CAMDEN

ATLANTIC O.

WILMINGTON

S.C.

EUTAH SPRINGS

AMERICAN REVOLUTION

SOUTH

CHARLESTON

GA

SAVANNAH

0 10 20 40 60 80 100

SCALE-MILES

formula for the approach by parallel lines.[8] There were about 9,000 Americans and 7,000 French regulars against 7,000 British. Cornwallis foolishly abandoned his outer defenses without a fight. The allies rushed the second line of defenses.

RELIEF DELAYED—In the meantime Clinton, with another 7,000 redcoats, was waiting for Graves's fleet to convey him and his men to the relief of Yorktown. The plan was for this fleet to try to force its way up the Chesapeake, but it had been much damaged in its first fight with De Grasse. Repairs were essential, and no spare masts were on hand for the repairs. When the troops finally sailed, it was too late.

SURRENDER—On October 15th, the British had made an unsuccessful sortie; then they tried to escape across the river, but the wind came up. On October 19, 1781, four years and two days after Burgoyne's men had laid down their arms, Cornwallis surrendered his army. That practically ended the fighting of the Revolution. A few spasmodic skirmishes occurred afterward. The British kept their garrisons in New York, Charleston, and Savannah until after the final peace was signed in 1783.

REASONS FOR VICTORY—The American victory was due to several causes. In the first place, the strategy of the British was bungling. They scattered their efforts instead of crushing the main American army. Then the invaluable aid of the French army and navy made possible the final victory at Yorktown. But the Revolution would not have lasted long if Washington had not kept American resistance alive with his courage and determination. That, more than the occasional flashes of his strategic genius, carried the war through to its successful close.

[8] See pp. 80, 90.

CHAPTER X

TRENTON AND PRINCETON

Washington's strategy was at its best in the operations which included the twin battles of Trenton and Princeton. They were small encounters, from the standpoint of numbers. Altogether, not 8,000 men took part in either engagement. Yet they have strategical and historical importance far beyond many other battles where ten times that number were engaged.

A TURNING-POINT—Washington's little command was practically all that America had left in the shape of an army. On Christmas Day, 1776, it looked as though the game was up for the Americans. Ten days later, Washington had recovered most of New Jersey from the British. He had outwitted the enemy in two clever strokes. Although outnumbered in the region as a whole, he had twice secured the local superiority of numbers, which brought victory. The work of Washington and his little army during those ten days formed a "turning-point" of the Revolution, second in importance only to Saratoga.

THE RETREAT THROUGH NEW JERSEY

LOSS OF NEW YORK—The five months following the signing of the Declaration of Independence were black ones for the revolutionary cause.[1] The rout

1 See pp. 202, 203.

of the Americans at the Battle of Long Island on August 27th had been followed by the British occupation of New York. Then had come the actions at Harlem and White Plains. Washington retired into New Jersey. Forts Washington and Lee, on the Hudson above New York, soon fell to the redcoats.

PURSUIT ACROSS NEW JERSEY—Late in November, General Howe had started to chase Washington across New Jersey. The route of the two armies was the old Post Road, the main artery between New York and Philadelphia. (This retains its importance to-day as the Lincoln Highway.) The superior forces of the British occupied town after town just a few hours after Washington's rapidly melting army had left. On November 28th, the British were at Newark. Three days later, the Americans had just time to break down the bridge over the Raritan at Brunswick (now New Brunswick). Even as Washington retreated, a battery in his rear-guard was firing on the redcoats. The Americans went through Princeton, sixteen miles farther, on December 2d. Howe was inexcusably slow in following. A rapid pursuit would have meant an easy victory. As a Virginia colonel remarked, "General Howe had a mortgage on the rebel army for some time, but has not yet foreclosed it." The British did not reach Princeton until December 7th. By that time, Washington was ten miles away at Trenton and was taking his army over the Delaware River into Pennsylvania. The last boatloads were barely across when the British advance-guard arrived—to be greeted with grapeshot from across the river.

A HOPELESS OUTLOOK—Washington was temporarily safe. Every boat for miles up and down the Delaware had been carried over to the Pennsylvania shore. There were no bridges. Washington had conducted an able retreat through New Jersey without losing a single man. But that State was now abandoned to the British, on top of the loss of New York City. The American army, 18,000 strong three months before at Long Island, had melted away to a scant 3,000. That handful of men was all that lay in the way of British victory. A steady series of defeats and retreats had been their portion. It was expected that Pennsylvania would fall next. The Continental Congress, on December 14th, abandoned Philadelphia for safer quarters at Baltimore.

SCATTERED BRITISH GARRISONS—But the British were conducting the war in a leisurely manner. They felt that they could "foreclose their mortgage" at any time. Winter fighting was not in style in that day's comfortable methods of warfare. Howe, therefore, decided to distribute his army in small cantonments throughout New Jersey. He thought that spring would be time enough to get the Americans, if they still had any army left. Headquarters were established at Brunswick, where great quantities of stores were gathered. A garrison was left at Princeton, but more important for us at the moment was the one at Trenton. This post was intrusted to three regiments of Hessians, with a handful of British horse, under Colonel Gottlieb Rall. The total guard numbered about 1,500. Six miles down the river at Bordentown, a similar force of Hessians, with some Scotch troops, were settled for the winter. Howe has been criticized for scattering his army among small posts too separated for mutual support. The winter months, as we said, were considered as "time out." Lord Cornwallis, the second in command, planned to spend the winter in England, returning in time for the spring season. He had already sent his bags aboard a ship at New York.

EXPIRING AMERICAN ENLISTMENTS—Cornwallis was going to have to unload those bags again. Washington knew that a decisive stroke was necessary while he still *had* an army.[2] Most of the militia had left. The enlistments of many of the regulars expired on the last day of the year. Energetic recruiting in Pennsylvania supplemented his numbers with some 2,500 new militia.

HESSIAN CARELESSNESS AT TRENTON—The isolated post of Hessians at Trenton was a tempting target for Washington's stroke. Howe had played into his hands by establishing it. Rall still further helped by failing to guard the town properly. His officers urged him to throw up redoubts[3] and to have adequate pickets at the various ferries. Rall refused, expressing unbounded contempt for American military prowess. He felt perfectly competent to handle any Yankees who might come. Rall was a good man for the offensive under a superior officer, but he neglected the principle of security.

The Surprise Attack at Trenton

TRIPLE ATTACK PLANNED—Washington was informed of the weakness of the Hessian position by John Honeyman, an American spy, who had been selling cattle to the Hessians, under the guise of a Tory butcher. Washington planned his surprise for Christmas night, foreseeing that the German Christmas revels would leave the Trenton garrison more befogged than usual.[4] He gave orders for a triple

[2] See 170.
[3] See p. 87.
[4] See p. 343.

attack from the Pennsylvania side. The Pennsylvania militia were to cross far down the river at Bristol to capture the post at Bordentown. A second force was to go across just below Trenton in order to cut off any Hessian retreat. Washington himself, with the main body of 2,500 men, was to cross at McConkey's ferry eight miles up the river from Trenton and surprise the Hessian garrison.

CROSSING THE DELAWARE—The weather was bad on Christmas night. A heavy wind churned up the ice-cakes sweeping down the Delaware in the strong current. These conditions prevented the two auxiliary forces from crossing. Washington luckily had some Massachusetts fishermen among his regulars. They were able to force the boats across the ice-choked river. The crossing started about sunset on Christmas Day. By four the next morning, December 26th, even the artillery had been carried across.

APPROACHING TRENTON—Washington's march on Trenton was by two parallel roads. Washington, with one body of the troops, went along the old river road on a route about eight miles in length. Greene took the rest of the men a somewhat longer way by the Pennington road. Snow and rain commenced to fall intermittently, so that the priming powder of some of the flintlocks was wet. Many of the men kept their muskets dry by covering them with blankets. Washington remarked that the affair could be settled with only the bayonet anyway.

THE BATTLE OF TRENTON—The surprise was quite complete. The Americans drove in the outposts, a quarter of a mile from the town, at eight o'clock. The drunken Hessian regiments formed with difficulty in the crowded streets. The sleet prevented effective use of their muskets or artillery. American artillery commanded the principal streets before the garrison could get in shape for action. Washington threw a brigade across the main road to Princeton to cut off any retreat that way. The only other way of escape lay southeast down the river toward Bordentown, where the American auxiliary force had been unable to cross the churning river. Several hundred Hessians headed by the British horse did escape before the Americans could close in on that unguarded side. The remaining Hessians attempted a brief resistance, but quickly saw the futility of holding out against the superior numbers surrounding the town. One after another, the three regiments surrendered.

A ONE-SIDED AFFAIR—The affair at Trenton was more a surprise than a battle. The fighting in the town lasted scarcely three quarters of an hour. The casualty returns show how one-sided it was. The Hessians lost about 100 killed and wounded, and nearly 900 prisoners. Washington reported that the Americans had only four wounded.

WIDESPREAD EFFECT—This unexpected and clean-cut victory thrilled America and dumbfounded the British. The ragged little force, which had just retreated across New Jersey, had turned and whipped professional soldiers. The string of disheartening defeats was ended at last. The prestige of the enemy regulars was lessened. The feat threw great credit upon Washington's leadership and upon the determined courage of his men.

CRITICAL SITUATION AFTER TRENTON

WASHINGTON'S POSITION RISKY—Yet the American position was by no means secure. Thousands of enemy troops were in the region. An action would be risky for the Americans because of the ice-choked

Delaware in their rear. So they trudged back to Mc-Conkey's ferry that same day and recrossed the river to Pennsylvania.

ACROSS THE DELAWARE AND BACK—Then a complication arose. It will be recalled that the original plan for the Christmas attack had not been carried out by the Pennsylvania militia down the river at Bristol. But on the 27th, without consulting Washington, they finally got over to the Jersey side, whereupon the Bordentown garrison of Hessians and Scotch fled in haste. Washington did not want to leave these militia troops alone in Jersey exposed to a counter-attack. Once more he took his main force back over the Delaware. This time it was a slow process, lasting several days. He was able to persuade more than half the regulars to stay in the service after the 31st [5] for at least a few weeks until the crisis was over. His troops, about 5,000 strong, were encamped by January 2d just outside of Trenton between Assunpink Creek and the Delaware.

CORNWALLIS APPROACHES IN FORCE—The British were busy in the meantime. Cornwallis unpacked his baggage and hurried into New Jersey. He gathered the scattered garrisons on his way and reached Princeton January 2d. He had about 10,000 men, "the flower of the British Army."

THE BRITISH REACH TRENTON—Cornwallis left the Fourth Brigade, consisting of three regiments under Colonel Charles Mawhood, as rear-guard at Princeton. This brigade of about 2,500 was to join the main body the next day. This was the force which Washington was to fight in the battle of Princeton. Cornwallis proceeded along the Post Road toward Trenton, leaving on the way another brigade at Maidenhead, the present Lawrenceville. He was op-

[5] See p. 170.

posed during the remaining six miles of his march by skirmishers sent out by Washington. These were finally driven back, but they had delayed the British progress. It was nearly dark when Cornwallis appeared on the north bank of Assunpink Creek opposite the American camp.

CORNWALLIS'S PROCRASTINATION—Washington's situation was grave. If Cornwallis had pushed an immediate attack, he could probably have captured most of Washington's force. Some of his staff urged this, but Cornwallis decided that there would be plenty of time to "bag the fox in the morning." After a little skirmishing at the creek, the British settled down for the night. That delay saved the Americans.

ESCAPE TO PRINCETON

THREE WAYS OUT—Three courses were open to Washington. He might stand and fight, but any prospect of success against the powerful regiments of British regulars was slight. He might retreat down the river into South Jersey, but the British could coop him up there. The third course seemed to offer the only chance of escape, so he acted upon it. If he could slip out of his position during the night, he could fall upon Mawhood's rear-guard at Princeton with superior numbers. He might even be able to go to Brunswick and capture the rich British stores there. He could at any rate save his army. It was a chance for a clever stroke and a second victory. There is some question as to whether this plan was Washington's own or General St. Clair's. Washington generally receives the full credit for it. This flanking maneuver is considered the most brilliant in the war.

WASHINGTON SLIPS AWAY—Washington at once ordered an appearance of unusual activity on his side of the creek to deceive the British. Large camp-fires were lighted. Earthworks began to be thrown up as though in preparation for the morning's attack. In the meantime, the wheels of the gun-carriages were wrapped in cloth so they would not rumble. Then the army slipped away for Princeton by an occasionally used road. This route was a rough one, but they had to avoid the Post Road because of the reserve brigade at Maidenhead. A sudden turn in the weather favored them. A mild thaw for the past few days had turned all roads into almost impassable mud, but freezing temperature that night made it possible to move the guns and stores more easily over the improvised route.

TRENTON VS. PRINCETON—The action at Princeton deserves a more detailed study than the fighting at Trenton. The significant feature at Trenton was the surprise approach. The battle itself consisted merely in surrounding the town. The approach to Princeton was an even more brilliant surprise, though the ice-cakes of the Delaware have appealed more strongly to the popular imagination. In getting to Princeton, Washington literally escaped the jaws of a superior force and was able to throw his army on a smaller portion of the enemy. Even then, the outcome of the battle hung in the balance for a while, and is worth studying "play by play."

THE BATTLE OF PRINCETON

FIVE PARTS OF BATTLE—The battle of Princeton can be best understood if we divide it into five "acts," or to use a more correct term, phases. Of these the most important were the second and the third, which took place on rising land just east of Stony Brook, a small stream which the Post Road crossed about two miles west of the town. The principal landmarks on the battle-field were the residences of William and Thomas Clark. The former, with its square orchard, was on a crest some eighty feet higher than the brook and not far from the Post Road. It was the scene of "Act II." The Thomas Clark house was about 500 yards to the southwest on a somewhat lower rise at the edge of a grove. The climax of the battle, in "Act III," occurred in the field between these crests. Washington approached Princeton from the southwest, not by the west as he would have done on the Post Road. He entered the town by a "Back Road" which has since disappeared. This ran parallel to and about three quarters of a mile to the south of the Post Road. The Quaker Road, running along Stony Brook, joined this "Back Road" to the Post Road.

We should keep in mind several distinct units on each side, for each unit played a separate part. These units are designated on the map by letters.[6] The advance-guard of the Americans was made up of regulars under Sullivan (A). After these were about 350 Maryland, Delaware, and Virginia troops under Mercer (B). The main body of the army was composed of a large body of green Pennsylvania militia under Cadwallader (C), followed by a rear-guard of regulars under Hitchcock (D). The British had three regiments of infantry, plus about fifty dragoons and some stragglers who were joining their regiments. The brunt of the fighting fell upon the Seventeenth Regiment, together with a detachment from the Fifty-fifth and the dragoons (X). Behind them, in an intermediate reserve was the bulk of the Fifty-

[6] See Map II, plate 4.

fifth (Y). The Fortieth Regiment had been left behind in Princeton, and came into action only at the end of the fight (Z). Altogether at Princeton there were about 2,500 British against 5,000 Americans.

"ACT I"—RECOGNITION

THE AMERICANS DIVIDE—The "first act" of the battle was one of mutual recognition. It occurred just about sunrise on January 3d. The Americans on their way from Trenton had reached the junction of the Back Road and the Quaker Road. Sullivan, with his advance-guard (A), turned to the right along the Back Road. Mercer (B), who followed, was sent up the Quaker Road to break down the bridge at Worth's Mill, where the Post Road crossed Stony Brook. This was to be done in the expectation of cutting off Mawhood's retreat toward Trenton and also to slow up any pursuit by the main British force. The principal American force (C) had not yet reached the road fork near the Quaker Meeting-House.

MAWHOOD TURNS BACK—In the meantime, Mawhood's column (XY) was already in motion. He had left the Fortieth in Princeton before dawn and had started along the Post Road with the other two regiments for Maidenhead and Trenton. By the time the two American advance groups had split, as just indicated, the British regiments (XY) had already crossed the bridge at Worth's Mill, and had reached the top of the hill beyond (cf. I, XY). It was then that the British looked back and saw Sullivan's advance-guard on the Back Road (cf. I, A). It is unlikely that they saw Mercer advancing along the Quaker Road or that Mercer saw them (cf. I, B). Mawhood may have thought that Sullivan's men were merely a group of stragglers retreating from Cornwallis's force at Trenton. At any rate, he could not leave the Fortieth alone in Princeton to bear the attack, nor leave the supplies at Brunswick unguarded. He hastily retraced his steps back along the Post Road, across the bridge, and up the hill on the eastern side. His purpose was to cut across country to get between Sullivan (A) and Princeton. Mercer (B), advancing up the Quaker Road, had by that time sighted the British and realized the futility of trying to break down the bridge, as he was outnumbered. He therefore went up the sharp slope to his right in order to rejoin Sullivan (A).

"Act II"—Mawhood vs. Mercer

THE RACE FOR THE ORCHARD—The "second act" occurred when Mawhood (X) and Mercer (B) met in the William Clark orchard. Mawhood was already past the orchard on the Post Road when he saw Mercer's men ascending the slope from Quaker Road. Mawhood sent most of the Fifty-fifth (Y) on toward Princeton. He himself with the Seventeenth and the remainder of the Fifty-fifth (X), headed for the orchard by turning south from the Post Road. His fifty dragoons were in advance of this body.

MERCER ROUTED—These dragoons fired upon Mercer's force as they passed the southeast side of the orchard. With this fire on their flank, the Americans changed their front, hurried through the orchard and took a position on its northeast side behind a hedge (II, B). The dragoons, outnumbered, had a hard time to hold their own until the rest of

Mawhood's force came up. Then the situation was reversed, for the Americans were now the outnumbered ones. Mercer's infantry fired three volleys, whereupon the British charged them with the bayonet. The Americans were poorly supplied with bayonets. At any rate they broke and ran back toward Cadwallader's militia. Their officers tried in vain to rally them, and in so doing suffered severe casualties. General Mercer was bayoneted and mortally wounded. One of the surprising features is that each side had two field-pieces in action at a range of scarcely forty yards, yet only about thirty men were killed. The "second act" was a victory for the British.

"ACT III"—MAWHOOD VS. MAIN AMERICAN ARMY

PROFESSIONALS VS. AMATEURS—The crisis of the battle followed immediately in the next act, the third. Mercer's men ran toward the ridge where the Thomas Clark house stood. Mawhood's men followed. This time they were decidedly outnumbered, as they now came into contact with the main body of Washington's army. But the question rested on the quality of the rival troops.[7] The redcoats were well-trained professional regulars. The militia had been in military service less than a month. They came into the battle under trying circumstances. It is difficult enough for green troops to deploy from a marching column into a battle front on a drill-field. It would have been, therefore, hard for these men to form their line even behind the shelter of the

[7] See pp. 93, 170.

small hill on which the Thomas Clark house stood. To make matters worse, they had to be brought onto the battle-field in column, and deployed under fire. More than that, no sooner had they started to deploy than the panic-stricken men from Mercer's broken force (B) came running through their ranks. It was small wonder that the green militia wavered, mixed up their deployment, and started to follow Mercer's men back over the hill. One battery of Pennsylvania artillery was all that held up the British advance at this crisis.

THE AMERICANS RALLY AND WIN—Washington exposed himself recklessly to rally the wavering troops. He ordinarily kept in a more sheltered position, for his officers made him realize that his leadership was indispensable to the American cause. But in this encounter, if his army should be beaten by inferior numbers, it would be all up for that cause. Everything hung in the balance for a few minutes. The British fired a volley. When the smoke cleared away, the Americans saw to their joy that Washington was unharmed. One bullet could have changed American history. Gradually the unwieldy body of the militia formed their line, stiffened by Hitchcock's regulars (D), who had been behind them and now took their position on the right. Still farther to the right was a body of riflemen. The superior numbers of the Americans now enabled them to form a semicircle so that their right practically flanked Mawhood's force. The Americans then returned the British fire. The outnumbered redcoats broke and fled. The crisis of the battle was over.

THE "FOX-HUNT"—The American troops had been under such an intense strain so long that for several hours they celebrated the victory with a regu-

lar "fox-hunt" after the fleeing British. Some redcoats escaped to Maidenhead by the Post Road.
Some others headed for Brunswick in the opposite
direction. Large numbers, however, were captured.

"Act IV"—Frog Hollow; Sullivan and the British Reserve

BRITISH RESERVE ROUTED—In the meantime the
"fourth act" was taking place nearly a mile to the
eastward of the main battle-field. It will be remembered that Mawhood had sent the Fifty-fifth Regiment (Y) back to the high land toward Princeton
(II, III, Y). At the same time, Sullivan's advance-
guard (A) had advanced along the Back Road
to a position nearly due south of this (II,
III, A). These two forces neutralized each other
while the main fighting was going on. Neither
dared to return to help its own side for fear
of being taken in flank by the other. After Mawhood's men (X) had been routed in the third phase,
the Fifty-fifth (Y) retired toward Princeton. It was
joined by the Fortieth (Z), which had started out
of town at the sound of the guns. These two regiments (Y, Z) took up a position on the northeastern
side of Frog Hollow, a ravine formed by a little
stream (IV, Y, Z). Their position seemed secure,
as they were sheltered at the top of a steep bank.
Sullivan (A) advanced to dislodge them. The British
suddenly abandoned the position and fled toward
the town. They made almost no resistance against
practically even numbers. Perhaps the rout of the
Seventeenth (X) made them think that the whole
American army was after them.

"Act V"—Nassau Hall—Surrender

THE LAST ACT—The fifth and final phase occurred at Nassau Hall in the center of the town. This large stone building was the seat of the College of New Jersey (now Princeton University) and was being used by the British as a hospital. A considerable number of redcoats took shelter inside it, and broke out the windows to use musketry against the Americans. The latter brought up a battery and fired three rounds through the southwest windows of the building. Then an American major pounded at the door. At that, this last remnant of the British surrendered.

CASUALTIES—The battle of Princeton was over. Washington had shattered Mawhood's Fourth Brigade. Accounts vary as to the casualties. Howe reported that the British lost eighteen killed, fifty-eight wounded and 200 missing (prisoners). Washington estimated the British losses at double that number. The Americans lost relatively few. It was generally agreed that not more than thirty were killed. The proportion of officers was high. General Mercer, two colonels, a major, and three captains fell. This high proportion of officers is not surprising, considering that in Washington's "army" of 5,000 —less than a modern wartime brigade—there were some eight generals and thirty colonels. The inflated American military rank was not backed by enlisted men, just as the inflated paper money was not backed by gold.

BRITISH PURSUIT—The main British army at Trenton was under way by this time. Cornwallis had awakened that morning to find the Americans gone. He started back toward Princeton. Several miles ahead of him, the brigade he had posted at Maidenhead was also on its way to Princeton, "in a most infernal sweat, running and puffing and blowing and swearing at being so outwitted." They had learned of Washington's successful stroke from fugitives of Mawhood's brigade.

THE TRIPLE CHASE—Washington realized that this Maidenhead brigade would be on his trail before long. He assembled his men from their "fox-hunt" and started eastward toward Kingston and Brunswick. There were thus four bodies of troops on the Post Road at once, all headed eastward in a sort of double pursuit. First, the group of British fleeing from the battle hurried toward Brunswick. After them came the Americans, followed by the British brigade from Maidenhead and finally the main force of the outwitted Cornwallis.

THE BRITISH DELAYED—Washington left Princeton not a bit too soon. His rear-guard, which stopped to chop down the bridge at Worth's Mill, had a skirmish with the advance-guard of the Maidenhead brigade. This delayed the pursuit somewhat. Then some stragglers further held up the British by firing a single gun from the abandoned redoubt which covered the approach to Princeton. The Americans were thus enabled to make good their retirement.

DILEMMA AT KINGSTON—Washington had a difficult decision to make when he reached Kingston three miles east of Princeton. His original plan had been to go on to Brunswick to capture the stores there. These contained more than $250,000 in gold in addition to great quantities of supplies, which would have been a godsend to the hungry, ragged, unshod American army. Washington could still have captured the stores, as they were lightly guarded. The British were so close behind him, however, that he feared that they would come upon his men before

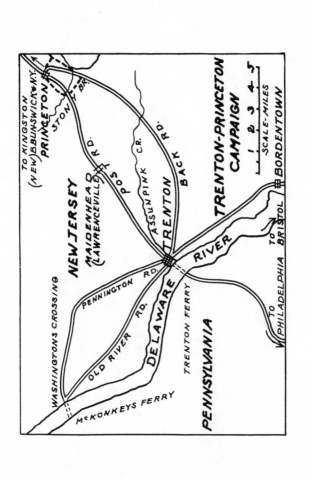

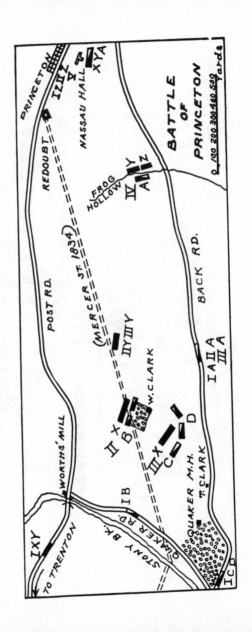

BATTLE
OF
PRINCETON

0 100 200 300 400 500 yards

they could appropriate the stores. He was strongly tempted. If he had not violated the principle of movement, wasting time with the pursuit of the British after the battle, he could probably have accomplished his purpose. Now, it seemed too late. Reluctantly he left the Post Road after breaking the Kingston bridge. He retired into the hills to the northward and finally made his winter headquarters at Morristown.

EFFECT OF OPERATIONS—The combined effect of the battles of Trenton and Princeton revived the confidence and determination of the Americans. Their cause had seemed lost two weeks before. Now Washington with his poorly equipped army had twice turned on the British. He had regained all of New Jersey, except the small strip near New York. He had beaten both the Hessian mercenaries and the regiments of British regulars. His men had shown that the redcoats were not invincible. He himself had completely outwitted their leaders. The stroke at Trenton was the more dramatic of the two, but the escape from Cornwallis and the routing of his rear-guard at Princeton was probably the cleverest piece of generalship in the war. Cornwallis said after his surrender at Yorktown four years later that Washington would probably be remembered in history more for his brilliant work at Trenton and Princeton than for the final victory in Virginia.

CHAPTER XI

THE CIVIL WAR

The American Civil War was a four-year struggle (1861–1865) in which the North finally prevented the South from leaving the Union to set up an independent nation. It was hard-fought, for the two sides were fairly evenly matched. The first two years went in favor of the South. After that, the superior numbers and resources of the North gradually wore down the Confederacy until its final surrender in 1865.

SECESSION—The question of slavery and of the continued political domination of the nation by the South formed the background of the struggle, but the war itself was fought for the preservation of the Union. The election of Abraham Lincoln in November, 1860, was a victory for the new Republican party, which definitely opposed the extension of slavery. A month later, South Carolina seceded, or withdrew from the Union. The other States in the far South soon followed her. Delegates from these seceded States gathered in February, 1861, at Montgomery, Alabama, where they formed a government known as the Confederate States of America. When Virginia seceded in April, Richmond became the capital of the Confederacy.

FORT SUMTER—The seceded States took over most of the national property within their borders, but the forts at Pensacola, Florida, and Charleston,

South Carolina, were held by loyal commanders. At Charleston, Major Anderson moved his men into the more easily defended although uncompleted Fort Sumter in the middle of the harbor. A steamer with supplies for him was driven off by the fire of the other Charleston forts in January. Finally on April 12, 1861, the other forts opened fire on Fort Sumter itself. Two days later, the Stars and Stripes were hauled down in surrender. The four-year contest had begun.

CALL FOR VOLUNTEERS—President Lincoln the next day called for 75,000 volunteers to serve for three months. It was felt that the South could be brought to terms quickly and easily. Less than three weeks later, he called for 42,000 regulars to serve for three years or the duration of the war. The South had already commenced raising troops on a large scale. It resorted to conscription long before the North made any attempts toward compulsory service.[1]

RESEMBLANCE TO THE REVOLUTION—There are several points of similarity between the Revolution and the Civil War.[2] The North, in many ways, was in the position of England. It had the larger population,—about 22,000,000 people, with very few slaves in its twenty-two states. The eleven seceding States had a population of about 9,000,000, more than a third of whom were slaves. The North, therefore, had about four times the white population of the South. Like England, the North was a wealthy manufacturing region. Its factories could provide the munitions and other materials necessary for war. It was able to trade freely with other countries, and actually prospered during the war. Having control

[1] See pp. 168, 172.
[2] See pp. 195, 196.

of the sea, the northern warships assisted the troop movements, coöperated with the armies and tightly blockaded the Southern ports. This was an opportunity which the English Navy had neglected in the Revolution. This blockade kept from the South the European military supplies, which it needed badly because of its own meager factory system. Finally, like England, the North had "law and order" on its side. It regarded the Southerners as "rebels" against the legitimate government of the United States.

SOUTHERN ADVANTAGES—All these advantages would seem to make the Civil War a one-sided contest. But that was not the whole story. The South had fewer men, but they were better prepared for military service. Living an outdoor life the average Southerner was better acquainted with horses and guns than the average Northerner from office or factory. Of course, there were some hardy farmers —especially from the West—in the Union armies, also. The South, like the colonies in the Revolution, was fighting in its own country. It had the strategic advantage of "interior lines." It could move its troops from one scene of action to another more easily than the Northerners, who were attacking from the outside. The North had to use more men, because it was generally taking the offensive and had to guard its long lines of communication. Military experts have reckoned this a five-to-two advantage for the South.[3] The North, like England in the Revolution, had the more difficult task in the war. In order to achieve its purpose, it had to crush the whole South—a vast region with very poor communications. The South merely had to make the North so tired of the war that it would give up the contest and let the Confederates have their own

[3] See pp. 116, 197, 298.

government in peace. This seemed all the easier because the North was not altogether united. Many
opposed the idea of keeping the Southerners in the
Union by force. Lastly, we recall that the Americans in the Revolution received invaluable assistance
from France. The South, likewise, counted strongly
on the active help from England and France.

SOUTH HAD BETTER GENERALS AT START—Above
all, the South was particularly fortunate in its generals. Many of the best officers in the regular Army
"went South" in 1861. Jefferson Davis, the Confederate President, was a graduate of West Point, had
served in the regular army and had been Secretary
of War. He was thus in a better position than Lincoln to select the best officers for command. Though
he played favorites, he wisely scattered the regular
officers throughout his army in high commands, instead of keeping them together as a unit.[4] Foremost
among these was Robert E. Lee, a military genius.
Rarely does one man have the choice of commanding
either of the rival armies in a war. Lee was offered
the command of the Union armies in the field, but
he would not fight against his own state. Instead,
within a year, he was commanding the principal
Southern army. His decision for the South probably lengthened the war by three years. The two
Johnstons, Joseph E. and Albert Sidney, were also
rated among the very best of the regular army officers. Only "Stonewall" Jackson, of the outstanding
Southern generals, was not a well-known officer. He
was a West Pointer, to be sure, but in 1861 he was
teaching. On the other hand, the leading Union
generals were nearly all in the "dark horse" class,
like Jackson. They were West Pointers, but had left
the service. For instance, Sherman was teaching and

[4] See p. 183.

Grant was practically a down-and-out failure.[5] The North had to experiment with a long series of commanders before it found the right man.

CIVIL WAR STRATEGY—Many of the Civil War generals had served as lieutenants or captains in the Mexican War fifteen years before. Scarcely one of them had ever commanded as many as 500 men in action. Von Moltke, the great Prussian general of that day, said that he was not bothering to follow the campaigns of the Civil War because the movements of "armed mobs" did not interest him. Many of the campaigns were little better than that, but some generals showed real strategical genius. The English in later years have made a special study in their military schools of the campaigns of Lee and Jackson. Von Moltke himself could scarcely have taken exception to the strategy of the Confederate defense of Richmond in 1862, but his general staff system would have carried it out more efficiently.[6]

WASHINGTON AND RICHMOND—The major operations of the Civil War fall into two great divisions. Some of the Union armies went after Richmond. The others tried to cut off the outlying portions of the Confederacy. The most prominent theater of operations was the dreary wilderness between Washington and Richmond, where each side was trying to capture the enemy's capital. Both knew how great the moral effect of such a capture would be, especially on foreign nations which might recognize the South. The main objective should be, of course, the enemy's principal army. In this case, the capitals as objectives were really the same thing. The situation resembled a football game, in which each team has the enemy's goal-line as its objective, for it was

[5] See pp. 138, 139.
[6] See p. 152.

almost certain that the main hostile army would be at such an objective to defend it to the limit.[7] The two capitals were only about 100 miles apart as the crow flies, but the intervening country was a God-forsaken waste of swamps and underbrush crossed by many rivers. In that region, so unpromising for brilliant maneuvers, the blue Army of the Potomac fought the gray Army of Northern Virginia throughout the war, making it the center of the greatest interest.

MISSISSIPPI AND SOUTHEASTWARD DRIVE—Meanwhile, far-flung operations of almost equal importance took place in remote parts of the South. These can be divided into two principal movements. One was the opening of the Mississippi by the Union armies with the help of the Navy. It was accomplished in two years, and cut off the states beyond the great river. The other movement is more difficult to follow. It was the cutting in two of the remaining part of the Confederacy east of the Mississippi. It followed a general southeastward direction. The start was near the junction of the Mississippi and Ohio Rivers. The fighting gradually worked southeast through Kentucky and Tennessee and ended with Sherman's march through Georgia to the sea. These western campaigns have been described as a "constriction" movement in which the Union forces gradually strangled the South by cutting off its sources of support and supplies.

TWO DISTINCT THEATERS—We shall keep these eastern and western theaters of war entirely distinct for the sake of clearness. Each will be taken up separately before, and then again after, the turning-point of the war in 1863. We lack space to describe minor campaigns or operations, such as the

[7] See p. 117.

Union effort to capture the Southern ports in order to tighten the blockade.

The War in the East to Gettysburg

EARLY SOUTHERN SUCCESS—The principal events of the first two years of the war in the east consisted of five unsuccessful Union attempts to capture Richmond and two unsuccessful Confederate attempts to invade the North. The Southerners, Lee and Jackson, proved more than a match for a succession of Union commanders—McDowell, McClellan, Pope, Burnside, and Hooker.

CONFEDERATES NEAR WASHINGTON—Both sides, at the outbreak of hostilities, quickly assembled armies in many different regions. Here we shall deal only with the particularly important concentration of forces around Washington. While Lincoln's ninety-day volunteers were assembling at Washington, the Confederates under General Beauregard posted themselves in strength about thirty miles away at Manassas Junction. It was a strategic point, being a railroad center, and covering a most obvious route toward Richmond. The place is sometimes referred to as Centreville (an adjacent town), but it is better known in history by the name of a small nearby stream, Bull Run.

DEMAND FOR ACTION—The North demanded action early in the summer of 1861. The newspapers clamored "On to Richmond!" The terms of the ninety-day volunteers were about to expire. General McDowell, in command of the Union forces around Washington, wanted more time to whip the raw recruits into shape. The agitation for action forced a premature move.[8]

[8] See p. 172.

FIRST BULL RUN—FIRST DRIVE FOR RICHMOND—
McDowell attacked Beauregard's position at Bull
Run on July 21st. The armies were about alike in
size and inexperience. The struggle lasted all day.
About noon the North seemed to be ahead, but the
Southern "Stonewall" Jackson won his nickname and
the battle by his stubborn stand. The South received
fresh reinforcements late in the afternoon. By six
o'clock the Union Army was in full retreat—a dis-
ordered rout—along the road to Washington. This
tactical victory could have secured decisive strategical results if it had been immediately followed up
according to the principle of movement.[9] The Confederates, however, were themselves too disorganized by the battle to turn this rout into a real disaster for the North. As it was, the North was dumbfounded by the news of the defeat; the South was
elated. The country settled down for a real war.

MCCLELLAN ORGANIZES THE ARMY—It was eight
months after Bull Run before the North started out
in force to attack Richmond a second time. During
the fall and winter, the new volunteers were drilled
by General McClellan. He succeeded to the command after a clever minor victory in West Virginia.
"Little Mac" was thirty-four, an excellent organizer, and extremely popular with the army. He was
impatient with the attempts of Lincoln and Stanton,
the Secretary of War, to guide affairs with their lack
of military experience,[10] and he treated Lincoln with
insolence.

CONFEDERATES ABANDON CENTREVILLE—Meanwhile the Confederates spent the winter near Bull
Run at Centreville. They might have made a successful attack on Washington before McClellan had

9 See p. 122.
10 See pp. 187. 190.

organized his huge new force, but they let the opportunity slip. "Stonewall" Jackson did urge such an energetic offensive before the North was ready, but his superiors decided to rest on the defensive. In February, 1862, they abandoned their position at Centreville as McClellan marched out to occupy it.

PENINSULA AND SHENANDOAH CAMPAIGNS—SECOND DRIVE ON RICHMOND—McClellan determined to go down the Potomac and attack Richmond from the sea while other Union forces would converge by land from the north and the west, as on the spokes of a wheel. Altogether the North had about 200,000 men in the region, while the South had only half that number for the defense. The ensuing campaign was perhaps the most brilliant of the war. It will be passed over here, as the next chapter takes it up in detail. In brief, McClellan with about 105,000 men approached Richmond up the Peninsula between the York and James Rivers and was finally able to post picket-lines within four miles of the Confederate capital. Unfortunately for the North, "Stonewall" Jackson was in the meantime doing wonders with a little force in the Shenandoah Valley. This river-valley, between the Blue Ridge and the Allegheny Mountains, was west of the main theater of war and was a sheltered "back door" to Washington and the North. Here Jackson darted about and administered a series of defeats to much larger Union armies. These defeats so scared the North that large numbers of troops were kept from coöperating with McClellan for fear Jackson would threaten the safety of Washington.

THE SEVEN DAYS: MCCLELLAN WITHDRAWS—Finally Jackson joined Lee in Richmond. In the "Seven Days' Battles" from June 25 to July 1, 1862, they forced McClellan to abandon the siege of Richmond.

Lee, as he did so often, used the tactical offensive while on the strategical defensive.[11] McClellan had been overcautious, and so missed the chance to use his superior numbers. Yet he pulled his army out of a tight place with ability and sailed back to the Potomac.

SECOND BULL RUN; THIRD DRIVE—While McClellan and his forces were returning, General Pope was placed in command of about 47,000 men for a third attack on Richmond. This time it was to be overland. Lee continued to act on the principle that the "offense is the best defensive." Pope was coming after Lee. Lee decided to get him instead. He took the long chance of dividing his force in the face of superior enemy numbers. This did not violate the principle of security, for Lee knew that Pope was not able enough to take advantage of the situation.[12] Jackson went ahead with a portion of the force. He slipped around to the rear of Pope's forces and destroyed or looted the Union supplies at Manassas Junction, which had been in Northern hands since McClellan occupied it in February. When Pope turned to punish him, the rest of the Confederates came through the mountain passes and caught his army in flank. A sharp fight took place on the old battle-field of Bull Run, in the last days of August, 1862. Pope's army, beaten in this Second Bull Run encounter, retired to Washington. The third Union attempt on Richmond had failed.

ANTIETAM—FIRST CONFEDERATE INVASION—Lee now felt the time was ripe for an invasion of the North. He realized that the Union army was demoralized after the Second Battle of Bull Run, so he carried his policy of the strategical offensive further.

[11] See p. 119.
[12] See p. 126.

Observing the principles of movement, he "kept things moving" in hopes of making big gains before the Union Army could recuperate. He immediately started for Maryland. This State was partly Southern in its sympathies, and might rise to join his forces. He might even be able to threaten Washington, Baltimore, or Philadelphia. McClellan was once again placed in command of the Union forces. He pursued Lee into Maryland with more active energy than he had shown on the Peninsula. The armies met on September 17, 1862, on Antietam Creek, where it enters the Potomac. Lee was caught in a cramped position with little room to maneuver.

UNION VICTORY NOT FOLLOWED UP—This battle of Antietam or Sharpsburg was fiercely fought. It counted as a Northern victory, for it forced Lee to abandon his invasion.[13] Had McClellan followed up his victory with repeated blows, according to the principle of movement, he might have put Lee's army definitely out of commission. "Little Mac," after "saving the country," allowed the Southerners to escape, in spite of constant prodding from Washington. As a result, he was replaced on November 7th by General Burnside, who had already conducted an able operation on the Carolina coast. McClellan did not appear in the field again. He has been bitterly criticized for his excessive caution, but Lee later called him the ablest Northern general against whom he had fought.

FREDERICKSBURG—FOURTH DRIVE ON RICHMOND —The North seemed to go from one extreme to another. The premature attack at Bull Run had been followed by McClellan's slow and cautious operations. These were condemned. Burnside now sinned through over-rashness. In undertaking the fourth of-

[13] See p. 120.

fensive against Richmond, he made Fredericksburg his first objective. Like Manassas Junction, this town figured strongly in the strategy of the region, as the other railroad to Richmond crossed the Rappahannock River there. On December 13, 1862, Burnside threw his Army of the Potomac in a frontal attack upon the strongly fortified Confederate positions at Fredericksburg. Six times the blue lines made heroic charges. Southern batteries and riflemen, securely hidden in a sunken road, mowed them down. The Union casualties amounted to some 10,000, while the Confederates lost less than 5,000. Thus, Lee and Jackson once more stopped a drive against Richmond.

CHANCELLORSVILLE—FIFTH DRIVE—Five months later, the Army of the Potomac returned for still more punishment on the same site. It had been again reorganized. The command was now in the hands of "Fighting Joe" Hooker. Hooker had a splendidly equipped army of about 130,000 when he crossed the Rappahannock for the fifth drive. As usual, Lee and Jackson were waiting with barely half as many men. This time the battle was fought over a range of nine miles, from Fredericksburg to Chancellorsville.

SOUTH WINS BATTLE, LOSES JACKSON—It lasted for five days, May 1–5, 1863. The Northern Army seemed to have gotten beyond Hooker's control. He started action with a movement which would have caught the small Confederate force between two fires. Naturally, having the larger force and every favorable circumstance, it was up to him to maintain a constant offensive. With every promise of success, he stopped the advance for some unaccountable reason, violating the principles of the offensive and of movement. Again Lee and Jackson took a chance and divided their force in the face of overwhelming numbers. Jackson made a surprise attack upon the unsuspecting Union right flank, routed it, and completely upset Hooker's plans. The result was a sweeping Confederate victory, but its cost was heavy. Jackson was mortally wounded by his own men while returning from a reconnaissance. Hooker's great army retreated across the Rappahannock, but Lee no longer had his "right arm." The South later claimed that as long as Lee and Jackson worked together, it meant success. Within two months after "Stonewall's" death, the tide had turned against the South.

THE SECOND CONFEDERATE INVASION—Lee followed up the victory with an invasion of the North —the principles of movement and of the offensive again. He knew that the North was discouraged by the defeats of Fredericksburg and Chancellorsville. He felt that the Union might be ready to make peace if he could now capture some important Northern city. The South had available nearly 200,000 men east of the Mississippi, but President Davis, contrary to the principles of mass and of economy of force allowed Lee less than 80,000 for his invasion. Lee crossed the Potomac into Maryland on June 17, 1863, just as he had done nine months earlier. Hooker thought this was the chance for a successful drive against defenseless Richmond, but, as always, Washington was more interested in its own security. After a dispute over this with Stanton, Hooker was replaced late in June by General Meade, a corps commander of fair ability. Advanced units of the Confederate invaders penetrated far into Pennsylvania, but Meade approached Lee's army, keeping between it and Washington.

GETTYSBURG—The armies met quite by chance in the little Pennsylvania town of Gettysburg, a few miles from the Maryland border. Lee and Meade had each picked a different site, as each wanted the tactical defensive, but a clash between advance detachments fixed the decisive battle upon the hills of Gettysburg. The fighting started on July 1, 1863, and lasted three days. On the first day, the Union forces, badly outnumbered, were pushed back with heavy losses to a strong defensive position on Cemetery Ridge. Their line curved backward at one end, like a fishhook so that the Union forces were in a compact position and could relieve the different parts of their line easily. On this small scale, they had the advantage of "interior lines." Reinforcements finally gave the Union forces a total of about 90,000 against about 75,000 Confederates. The battle hung in the balance on the second day. A spirited Confederate offensive might have carried the field before the Union position was thoroughly organized, but this opportunity was allowed to slip away.

PICKETT'S CHARGE; TURN OF THE TIDE—The climax came on the afternoon of the third day, July 3d. Three Confederate divisions under Pickett charged the Union center after a long artillery duel. A few Confederates reached the crest of Cemetery Ridge, but the rest were blasted to pieces by the Union artillery and rifle-fire.[14] That was the "high water mark of the Confederacy." The tide of the war turned that afternoon, as the shattered remnants of Pickett's forces retreated.

Lee generously took full responsibility for the defeat, but some of the blame seems due to the stubbornness of Longstreet, the second in command, who did not coöperate as Jackson usually had. On the Northern side, the victory seemed to have been the result of good judgment and energy on the part

[14] See p. 61.

of several Union generals rather than of any guiding
genius of Meade's. Like McClellan after Antietam,
he violated the principle of movement by failing to
follow up his victory with a pursuit of Lee's beaten
forces.

Lee was in a tight place for several days, as the
flooded Potomac was at his back. By the time that
Lincoln's urgent prodding had stirred Meade into
pursuit, the Potomac had subsided. Lee escaped into
Virginia with an army which still had two years of
fight in it. But it was to be two years of losing fight.
Lee was to find the Union Army led by a more
stubborn and persistent commander, when he next
met it.

The War in the West to Vicksburg

GETTYSBURG AND VICKSBURG—The North had
good cause to celebrate the Fourth of July in 1863.
On the day after Pickett's charge at Gettysburg,
Grant captured the most important remaining stronghold on the Mississippi. Vicksburg marked the turning of the tide in the west, just as Gettysburg did in
the east.

TWO MOVEMENTS IN WEST—But we are ahead of
the story in the west. The operations there were
spread over a much wider area, and are not as simple
to follow. Once again, we must recall the two offensive movements on the part of the Union in this
region. One was the clearing of the Mississippi to
isolate the western Confederate regions. The other
was the attempt to cut in two the Confederate territory east of the Mississippi by a southeasterly
movement from Kentucky to Georgia.[15]

RIVAL LEADERS—No major action occurred in the

[15] See p. 241.

west in 1861. Missouri, a "doubtful State," was
saved for the Union through the quick and able work
of a General Lyon. He was killed shortly afterward, and the command was given successively to
the inadequate General Frémont, who is better
known as a politician and explorer, and to General
Halleck, who knew the science of war thoroughly,
but could not apply it. Both in turn were sent East;
Frémont to help in the Shenandoah,[16] Halleck as
military adviser to Lincoln. The Union forces in the
west were finally formed into three armies, the Cumberland, the Tennessee, and the Ohio. Their most
prominent commanders were Buell, who apparently
was unfairly treated, Rosecrans, a man of moderate
ability, and Grant, whose luck was better. The Confederates were at first under Albert Sidney Johnston,
one of the most promising officers in the regular
Army before the war. After his death, the command
fell to Braxton Bragg, a "dyspeptic martinet," who
was much better liked by President Davis than by
his subordinates. Later Joseph E. Johnston, who
ranks close to Lee and Jackson in ability, was commander there.

QUALITY OF TROOPS—The Union armies in the
west were made up of husky, corn-fed farmers. On
the whole, they made better fighters than the soldiers
in the east. The Confederates in the west, on the
other hand, lacked the fine discipline and morale of
the forces in Virginia.

RIVER WAR; RAIDS—River warfare was an important feature of the western fighting. Unless the
North had the rivers, it would have the very difficult task of defending long lines of land communications in enemy territory. Confederate raiders with
"partisan cavalry," like Forrest, Morgan, and

[16] See p. 272.

Mosby, were particularly apt at destroying railroads. The Union wanted, therefore, to get control of the rivers so it could transport supplies more easily and with comparative safety. We have seen how Mc-Clellan utilized water transportation in the Peninsula Campaign. It played an even more vital rôle in the west. Most important of the rivers was the Mississippi. Next came the Cumberland and Tennessee both of which join the Ohio just before it enters into the Mississippi. These flowed through the heart of the Confederacy. The North realized how invaluable they would be as lines of communication if it could seize them. A number of crudely armored gunboats were quickly constructed at St. Louis by the North for this river warfare. These were manned by western rivermen and deep-water sailors under Commodores Porter and Foote. They helped the Union armies tremendously.

CONFEDERATE LINE OF DEFENSE—The Southerners, seeing the danger of this type of warfare, proceeded to defend the strategic points along their rivers. On the Mississippi, the fortifications stretched at intervals from below New Orleans nearly up to the junction with the Ohio. Forts Henry and Donelson guarded the Tennessee and Cumberland Rivers respectively. These were a part of the first line of Confederate defense in the west, stretching along the Kentucky-Tennessee border from Columbus on the Mississippi eastward to Bowling Green, Kentucky.

FORTS HENRY AND DONELSON—The first important Northern victories in the war came in February, 1862, when Grant launched a combined military and naval attack on Forts Henry and Donelson. It was his first prominent appearance and showed the kind of energetic offensive of which he was capable. Fort

Henry fell to the gunboats on February 6th. Most of the garrison escaped to Donelson, twelve miles away. Ten days later, Grant and the gunboats forced the "immediate and unconditional surrender" of Fort Donelson. The Confederate first line of defense had fallen. Union gunboats could now penetrate far into Tennessee. This was the first step in the Southeastward movement through the heart of the South.

SECOND LINE OF DEFENSE—SHILOH—Albert Sidney Johnston now fell back to the Confederate second line of defense, a hundred miles south. The key position on this new line was Corinth, Mississippi, an important junction on the Memphis and Charleston Railroad. Grant was finally sent up the Tennessee River to Pittsburg Landing, twenty-three miles above Corinth. Before moving against Corinth with his 42,000 men, Grant was to await General Buell, who was coming with 21,000 more. Grant was caught napping, in a flagrant disregard of the most elementary teachings of security. He had selected a position with his back to the Tennessee River, which flowed between high bluffs at that point. He did not throw up intrenchments or provide proper outposts. Johnston, with 40,000 men, completely surprised him on April 6th. A few of Grant's units made a stubborn stand and prevented a complete rout, but thousands of stragglers in their rear were cowering under the river bluffs. Buell's arrival on the next day changed this battle of Shiloh, or Pittsburg Landing, into a Union victory, but it was an expensive one. Grant lost 13,000 men, nearly a third of his own force. The Confederate loss was 10,000, but it included Johnston.

EXCESSIVE CAUTION—The overcautious Halleck, who was soon to go to Washington as military advisor, now assumed command of the large combined

Union Army. Grant had failed to follow the principle of security, but he had at least gone energetically at his objective with a proper appreciation of the offensive. When his dismissal was urged, Lincoln declared, "I can't spare that man; he fights." Halleck went to the opposite extreme. He overemphasized security, ignoring the objective and the offensive. After Shiloh, the Confederates were beaten and badly outnumbered. Corinth was only twenty-three miles away. "Stonewall" Jackson with his rapidly moving infantry could have covered twice that distance in a day, but Halleck, as deliberate as McClellan, wasted a month in a careful approach.[17] By that time, the Confederates had abandoned Corinth. Halleck did not pursue them. Satisfied with the occupation of that railroad junction, he paid no attention to his proper objective—the destruction of the enemy army.

NEW ORLEANS—In the meantime, Union ships and Union troops had been clearing the upper and lower reaches of the Mississippi. A Union flotilla of wooden warships under the command of Farragut fought its way past the forts and Confederate ships below New Orleans before sunrise on April 24th. The next day that great commercial city surrendered and Farragut proceeded up the river.

POPE CLEARS THE UPPER MISSISSIPPI—At the same time General Pope, with the aid of gunboats, was clearing the upper river by working down from St. Louis. This was the achievement which gave him the appointment as head of the Union Army in the east before Second Bull Run.

Most of the Mississippi was now in Union hands, but the South could still draw men and supplies from beyond the river as long as they held the hundred-

[17] See p, 274.

odd miles between Vicksburg and Port Hudson. Vicksburg was the main river stronghold. Securely perched on high bluffs 200 feet above the river, it held out for another year.

BUELL AND BRAGG—The summer of 1862 saw in Kentucky and Tennessee the rival campaigns of the Union forces under Buell and the Confederates under Bragg. Lincoln wanted aid to go to the inhabitants of eastern Tennessee, who were still loyal to the Union, so Buell was sent toward Chattanooga. Meantime, the Confederates wanted to recover Kentucky with its strong slave-holding sentiment. The two campaigns merged into a mutual chase around Kentucky with no decisive results. Both commanders threw away opportunities and neglected their main objective—the crushing of the rival force. Buell was replaced in the fall by General Rosecrans, who chased Bragg into Tennessee, occupied Nashville, beat Bragg just south of Nashville at Murfreesboro on the last day of the year, and strengthened the Union hold on Tennessee. The Confederates retired to Chattanooga in the southeastern corner of the State. It is around there that we shall see the next acts in the southeastward movement during the latter half of 1863.

VICKSBURG CAMPAIGN—In November, 1862, while Rosecrans's campaign was going on in Tennessee, Grant began his operations against Vicksburg. Six times he tried to take this "Gibraltar of the Mississippi." His attempted overland movement from Corinth failed, because the Confederates destroyed his lines of communication. He and Sherman, who was just coming into prominence, tried to approach from the swamps just north of the city and again failed. Grant kept his men busy digging canals to divert the river from its course. This was done successfully in the flood of 1927, but in 1862 the river would not change. Finally he started from a new and different angle. The following brilliant campaign showed his energy, originality, and resourcefulness at its best.

He marched his army down the west bank of the river until opposite Bruinsburg, some forty miles below. Union ships, which had boldly run past the guns of Vicksburg, ferried his troops across on April 30, 1863. Grant then struck out in a northeasterly direction. He lived off the country so that he would not have to bother any longer with lines of communication. His first objective was Jackson, the Mississippi state capital, about forty-five miles east of Vicksburg. He reached there just ahead of the Confederate Joseph E. Johnston, who was on his way to the relief of Vicksburg. After defeating Johnston and leaving a force to detain him at Jackson, Grant headed west for Vicksburg. Pemberton, the comander of Vicksburg, came out to meet him with the garrison, but Grant pushed him back into the town. In less than three weeks, Grant had marched 200 miles and won five battles, taking 8,000 prisoners and eighty guns. He had scattered one army larger than his own and had shut up another army in Vicksburg itself.

FALL OF VICKSBURG—After all that, the fall of Vicksburg was simply a matter of time. Grant's original army of 20,000 was reinforced to 50,000 and maintained a close siege.[18] Each side built elaborate field fortifications. Vicksburg was under constant shell-fire. Food was so scarce within the town that rats sold at a premium. On July 4th, the day after Pickett's charge at Gettysburg, Pemberton surrendered Vicksburg. Five days later, Port Hudson also

[18] See p. 90.

surrendered to another Union army. It was 120 miles below Vicksburg, and was the last remaining Confederate river stronghold. As Lincoln remarked, the "Father of Waters" once more flowed unvexed to the sea.

THE WAR IN THE EAST—1864

A NORTHERN LEADER AT LAST—The North felt that at last it had found the leader it needed. McDowell, McClellan, Pope, Burnside, Hooker, and Meade had all been tried and found wanting. Grant had shown a high quality of strategy in his Vicksburg campaign. Above all, he had a persistent driving force. He could appreciate the real objective and would pursue it with all possible energy. He often neglected the principle of security, but what the North needed most was a man who could utilize its great advantages in numbers and material.

NORTHERN WEALTH AND NUMBERS—By the second half of the war, the superior population and resources of the North were beginning to tell. It had enough guns and ammunition. Its troops were well-fed, well-clothed, and well-armed. Above all, there were plenty of them.

THE SOUTH FEELS THE PINCH—The Confederacy was nearing the end of its rope. Its paper money was rapidly becoming worthless. The pinch of the blockade was beginning to tell. So was the loss of the Trans-Mississippi region. The Southern regiments were frequently on half-rations. Many lacked shoes and adequate clothing. Battle casualties could not be replaced. The North was refusing to exchange prisoners. It meant terrible hardship for the Union soldiers in Confederate prisons, but it kept down the man-power of the Southern armies. The extra men still left in the South were avoiding service in spite of conscription. Desertions were on the increase. The main hope of the South was the peace sentiment in the North. Every one was growing weary of the war. Anxiety increased at Washington as the presidential election of 1864 approached. Lee no longer had hopes of dictating a peace in Baltimore or Philadelphia, but he still had a chance to hang on long enough to wear out Northern patience. The last half of the war, therefore, was a trial between Northern persistence and the Southern supply of food and available men.

GRANT COMMANDER-IN-CHIEF—The Union at last realized the necessity of providing for unity of command. Grant was called north to become Commander-in-Chief of the Union armies in March, 1864. No longer were Lincoln, Stanton, and Halleck to attempt to run the armies from Washington. Lincoln, once he found his general, gave him full support, though Stanton still occasionally tried to interfere.

GRANT VS. LEE—Grant crossed the Rapidan on May 4, 1864, for the bloodiest campaign of the war. He was determined to push his way through to Richmond, whatever the cost. He was not the equal of Lee in strategy, but he had superior numbers. He could afford to lose men as Lee could not. "I determined," Grant wrote later, "to hammer continuously against the armed force of the enemy and his resources, until by mere attrition, if in no other way, there should be nothing left of him but . . . submission." It was a brutal policy, but the North had no Lee and had to pay a terrific price for that lack.[19] Grant at least brought the war to an end.

[19] See p. 316.

Grant and Lee have been compared to a man with a club fighting a man with a rapier.

THE WILDERNESS—Grant set out with 102,000 men for a direct overland attack. Union flanking movements in the Shenandoah and up the James River failed to distract Lee's attention from Grant's main army. Quite properly, he concentrated his efforts on that huge invading force. The fighting commenced on May 5th, in the tangled underbrush of the Wilderness, the scene of Hooker's defeat at Chancellorsville exactly a year before. The unwieldy Union Army could not be maneuvered properly in the thickets. Two days of steady fighting resulted in more than 17,000 Northern casualties; that was only a beginning.

SPOTTSYLVANIA—Grant then tried to slip around Lee's left flank, but Lee was waiting for him at Spottsylvania Court-House, where they fought for five more days, May 6th to 12th. This was about the first appearance of modern trench warfare. Both sides "dug in." The capturing and recapturing of trenches was very similar to the fighting on the Western Front in the World War.[20] The fierce struggle here raised Grant's total casualties to nearly 50,000. The Confederate losses were very much less. The North clamored against "Butcher Grant," but he retorted that he proposed "to fight it out along this line if it takes all summer."

COLD HARBOR—Once more he tried to move around Lee's left, hoping to get between him and Richmond. But Lee cleverly anticipated every move, and was always there to meet him. By the end of the month Grant had reached the scene of some of the Seven Days' Battles on the outskirts of Richmond.

[20] See pp. 90, 91, 304.

The first three days of June saw the battle of Cold Harbor, "the costliest and most futile in the entire war." Lee was well intrenched. Again and again, Grant attempted frontal attacks all along the line. They were repulsed with terrific loss. Within three hours Grant lost nearly 12,000. The Confederates retained their position practically intact.

"ATTRITION"—Grant had used up more than half his original force in hammering his way to the place where McClellan had stood in 1862. But losses had been replaced with fresh troops, while Lee's 30,000 casualties could scarcely be made good. This campaign played its part in the final Union victory, but it decidedly diminished Grant's fame as a strategist because of its terrific cost in human life.

SIEGE OF PETERSBURG—Grant moved his base on June 12th, to the James River, just as McClellan had done during the Seven Days.[21] His next offensive was against Petersburg, twenty miles due south of Richmond. Its capture would threaten the capital's communications with the rest of the Confederacy. Lee beat Grant to Petersburg. The next nine months were spent in besieging it. The Union forces blew up part of the fortifications by exploding a great mine of gunpowder under them, but the advantage of this surprise was not followed up before the defenders rallied. This fighting in fixed positions was quite different from maneuvers in the open field. Generals in the World War might have gained some useful lessons from the siege of the Petersburg earthworks.

RAID AGAINST WASHINGTON—Grant had worn down the Confederate man-power at tremendous cost. The next step was to cut down the Confederate food-supply. The Shenandoah Valley, in addition to

21 See pp. 290, 293.

its strategic importance as a sheltered approach to the North, was also valuable as the granary of Virginia. Lee, after Cold Harbor, sent General Early with 15,000 men to drive the Union forces out of the valley. Early succeeded. He then made the final raid into Maryland. On July 11th, he was five miles from Washington. The Washington forts had been stripped of garrisons for Grant's great drive. Union reinforcements arrived, however, before Early attacked, so he returned to the Valley.

DEVASTATION OF SHENANDOAH—In October, Sheridan, the youthful subordinate of Grant, went into the valley to end its prosperity. He defeated Early at Cedar Creek. Then, with the Confederates out of his way, he proceeded to destroy all the barns and mills stored with the rich harvest of the fertile Shenandoah. Sheridan's work was so complete that he said, "A crow flying over it would have to carry its own provisions." Virginia had lost her granary, and consequently the defenders of Richmond and Petersburg had to tighten their belts.

The War in the West and Far South
after Vicksburg

REMAINING TASK IN WEST—The fall of Vicksburg had been the turning-point in the west, but much remained to be done. The Mississippi was in Union hands, and the far Western States were cut off from the Confederacy. But the Confederacy east of the Mississippi still had to be cut in two. The southeastward movement, starting with the capture of Forts Henry and Donelson, had gone only halfway.[22] It had brought Kentucky and most of Tennessee under Union control, but the Confederates

[22] See p. 241.

still held Chattanooga in the southeastern corner of Tennessee. Beyond that lay Georgia, a rich region which furnished the Confederacy with much-needed supplies. We shall now see how the southeastward drive was pushed past Chattanooga to Savannah, entirely cutting off the far South from the main theater of operations in Virginia.

MARKING TIME—At first the going was slow. We will recall that on the last day of 1862, the Union Army under Rosecrans had defeated Bragg at Murfreesboro below Nashville. Bragg had retired up the Tennessee River to a position not far from Chattanooga. For the next six months both generals remained almost stationary. Each wanted to prevent the other from sending reinforcements for the Vicksburg campaign. There were merely minor skirmishes.

APPROACH TO CHATTANOOGA—At last, Rosecrans moved against Bragg in June, 1863. He maneuvered Bragg out of his position the week before Vicksburg fell. The Confederates fell back on Chattanooga. Rosecrans proceeded carefully, putting his communications in good condition as he advanced. His objective was Bragg's army. He wanted to put that out of the fight so as to secure Chattanooga.

IMPORTANCE OF CHATTANOOGA—Chattanooga was one of the most vital strategic points in the whole Confederacy. It is located at the point where the Tennessee River breaks through the southern end of the Appalachian Mountains. Northward, those high mountains effectively separated the eastern and the western theaters of war, for armies could cross them only with the greatest difficulty. The Cumberland Gap, far to the northward, had similar importance. The gap at Chattanooga naturally made it an important railroad center. Once the Union secured it, not only would the way be open for an advance into Georgia and the Carolinas, but it would even open a back-door route to Virginia.

CHICKAMAUGA—Bragg was forced to abandon Chattanooga on September 9th by a clever maneuver of Rosecrans, who approached from an unexpected direction. The Confederates disappeared behind the rough, steep parallel ridges which come up to the river on the south side at Chattanooga. Rosecrans pursued them into this difficult region with his army badly strung out. Bragg fell upon him at Chickamauga Creek on September 19th. He cut the Union Army in two. Part of it retreated to Chattanooga. The left, under Thomas, stood firm and prevented a disaster. After this battle of Chickamauga, Bragg was able to occupy the heights called Lookout Mountain and Missionary Ridge that overlooked Rosecrans's army in Chattanooga. Here he threatened the Union lines of communication. Rosecrans, caught with his back to the river, was faced with starvation. It did him no good to hold Chattanooga as long as the main enemy army of the region was undefeated and threatening.

LOOKOUT MOUNTAIN—MISSIONARY RIDGE—Grant came to take charge of this grave situation a month later. This was three months after his capture of Vicksburg and four months before he became Union Commander-in-Chief. Clever engineer work opened up a new line of communication for him. Reinforcements began to arrive. Grant decided that he had force enough to drive Bragg from the heights overlooking the town. On November 24 and 25, 1863, vigorous attacks under Sherman, Thomas, and Hooker drove the Confederates from Lookout Mountain and from Missionary Ridge. Some of the fighting was "above the clouds." The Union lines swept up the steep ridges without even waiting for orders. Bragg's defeated army withdrew from the region. In the meantime, Burnside, who had gone on an expedition into northeastern Tennessee, had been surrounded at Knoxville. So some of the Union troops from Chattanooga were immediately rushed to his relief. They drove off the Confederates. Tennessee was completely cleared of Southern troops. More important, with Bragg's army removed, the way was now open for the Union forces to advance into Georgia. Sherman was given the command of the final stage of this southeastward drive when Grant became commander of all the forces.

SHERMAN ENTERS GEORGIA—On May 4, 1864, the same day that Grant was crossing the Rapidan for his costly Virginia campaign, Sherman set out from Chattanooga for Atlanta, 100 miles distant. Like Grant, Sherman had an army of about 100,000. "Joe" Johnston had replaced Bragg. Like Lee, Johnston had only 60,000 men to oppose the Union offensive. In those respects, the two campaigns were very similar. But Atlanta was not as vital a stake as Richmond, so Johnston did not engage in the type of desperate battle which was being fought during these same weeks in the Virginia wilderness. It was a time when it was best not to take the offensive. He used Fabian strategy and tactics, tearing up railways and doing whatever he could to delay Sherman's progress without fighting a pitched battle. He realized that he had one of the last remaining Confederate armies and that the South could not spare the men for a probably costly battle. Like Lee, he hoped that a long enough delay would make the North weary of the war. But Sherman kept steadily on, rebuilding the railways and constantly lengthening his lines of communication. He laid siege to Atlanta on July 17th.

BATTLE OF ATLANTA; HOOD RETIRES—Johnston was then replaced by Hood, who had the reputation of being a hard fighter. Discarding Fabian strategy, he attacked both wings of Sherman's army within a week and lost 10,000 men. He abandoned Atlanta on September 2d to move back against Sherman's long line of communications and the Union positions in Tennessee. This did not dislodge Sherman, who simply detached Thomas to watch Hood. We shall hear of these two later, at Nashville.

THE "MARCH TO THE SEA"—Sherman himself left Atlanta on October 17th for his famous "March to the Sea." Like Sheridan's in the devastation of the Shenandoah Valley which started that same week, his purpose was purely destructive. Georgia was one of the richest parts of the whole South. Hitherto it had escaped the ravages of war. The Confederacy was depending on Georgia's agriculture and industry. Sherman entirely cut off this source of supply. His army cut a swath more than 200 miles long and sixty miles wide through the heart of the state. As in' the Shenandoah, it was fall, and harvests had just been stored. Sherman's army looted or destroyed everything in sight. Practically no Confederate armed force was on hand to oppose their progress. The South to-day is still bitter over that "wanton destruction." Sherman finally reached Savannah on December 10th. The southeastward movement, starting at Forts Henry and Donelson, had reached the sea. The Confederacy was cut in two from west to east.

NASHVILLE—Shortly before Sherman emerged at Savannah, Hood created consternation in the North. He defeated a Union corps at Franklin, Tennessee. Nashville was held by Thomas, the "Rock of Chickamauga." Yet Hood seemed to have a clear field to do almost anything he pleased in that region. The North waited in frantic impatience for Thomas to do something. At last, on December 27th, he inflicted upon Hood "the most smashing defeat of the war," just outside Nashville.

SOUTHERN ENDURANCE FAILING—The Confederacy had not long to live. It had lost hope. Lee and Johnston had played their waiting game hoping that the North would finally grow weary of the attempt to maintain the Union. But the North had reëlected Lincoln in November, 1864. Hunger and desertions increased among the Confederates. Yet in spite of their defeats, the South still had corn, cattle, munitions and men.

SHERMAN IN THE CAROLINAS—Sherman started north from Savannah through the Carolinas to complete the "constriction" movement. United with Thomas again, he had 90,000 men. The South called "Joe" Johnston back to command the shattered remnants of Hood's army, but with his scant 25,000, he could do little to delay Sherman. Charleston was captured. Columbia, the capital of South Carolina, was "pretty much all burned," as Sherman put it. The capture of Wilmington closed the last possible port to the blockade-runners.

LEE ABANDONS PETERSBURG—In the meantime, Grant's siege of Petersburg lasted nine months. Lee, inside the Petersburg lines, had some 54,000 men, who steadily melted away by desertion. Outside, Grant had more than twice as many. On April 1, 1865, some of Lee's men were defeated by Sheridan at Five Forks, ten miles from Petersburg. The victorious Union forces gained control of one of the two remaining railroads running into Petersburg.

Lee finally saw that his only chance was to break away and join Johnston's force in Carolina. The next

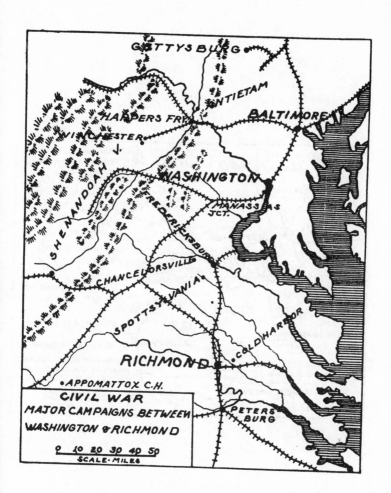

GETTYSBURG

ANTIETAM

HARPERS FRY

BALTIMORE

WINCHESTER

SHENANDOAH

WASHINGTON

FREDERICKSBURG

MANASSAS JCT.

CHANCELLORSVILLE

SPOTTSYLVANIA

COLD HARBOR

RICHMOND

APPOMATTOX C.H.

PETERSBURG

CIVIL WAR
MAJOR CAMPAIGNS BETWEEN
WASHINGTON & RICHMOND

0 10 20 30 40 50
SCALE-MILES

CIVIL WAR

SHOWING PARTICULARLY
MAJOR CAMPAIGNS
OUTSIDE VIRGINIA.

0 50 100   200
SCALE - MILES

night he abandoned Petersburg. Grant at once was able to occupy Richmond.

APPOMATTOX—Lee was at large, but his liberty was short. He planned to strike southwest for Danville, Virginia, but the non-arrival of expected rations delayed him. Poor staff work thus dogged him to the end. Sheridan cut off his avenue of escape at Appomattox Court-House, seventy miles west of Richmond. So Lee surrendered his remaining 28,000 men to Grant there on April 9, 1865. President Davis urged Johnston to keep up the fight, but Johnston saw the futility of further resistance. He surrendered his army to Sherman at Greensboro, North Carolina, on April 26th. The Civil War had lasted just four years.

OUTCOME LONG DOUBTFUL—The North had kept the South in the Union, but this success had not been a foregone conclusion until the end of 1864. Lee and Jackson maintained superiority in the field for two years. Then for another year, it looked as though the Northern morale might weaken. The re-election of Lincoln showed that the North was still in the fight. It was then that the Southern morale broke.

QUALITY OF CIVIL WAR LEADERSHIP—To the student of military history, the Civil War shows only a few cases of strategy at its best among numerous examples of inferior leadership. Much depended on the individual ability of the commander. In those days before the United States Army had thorough staff training, this dependence was too often a gamble. Lee and Jackson were at their best in the defense of Richmond and the Second Bull Run campaign of 1862. They applied all the principles of strategy brilliantly. Some claim that Thomas, another Virginian, fighting for the North, would have equaled them if he had had the opportunity. His leadership at Nashville was particularly able. Grant and Sherman stand on a somewhat lower scale. Grant's Vicksburg campaign is offset by Shiloh and Cold Harbor. He neglected security just as McClellan overemphasized it.

TACTICAL DEVELOPMENTS—Aside from strategy, the Civil War is interesting as a period of new tactical developments, due largely to the introduction of the rifle and rifled artillery, which were just coming into general use.[23]

We saw other lessons of the war in connection with military policy.[24] This short study has outlined only the major campaigns. The history of the four years has much else of interest—in foreign relations, naval warfare, and political and economic features—which cannot be discussed in this brief scope. The outcome of the war did not depend entirely upon the few great commanders or even upon the 3,000,000 men who fought under them.

[23] See pp. 18, 36, 61.
[24] See pp. 172, 177, 179, 183, 184, 187, 190.

CHAPTER XII

THE PENINSULA AND SHENANDOAH CAMPAIGNS OF 1862

Civil War strategy was its best in the spring and summer of 1862, when Lee and Jackson saved Richmond from Union armies more than twice as large as their own combined force. The two great Confederate leaders worked in perfect harmony. As long as Jackson lived, the South seemed almost invincible in Virginia.

RELATION OF THE TWO CAMPAIGNS—The Peninsula and Shenandoah Campaigns were closely related. The Peninsula Campaign was McClellan's effort to reach Richmond from the sea, which was controlled by the North. He advanced from the coast up the ninety-mile peninsula between the James and York Rivers. Several other Union armies were at the same time threatening Richmond from other directions as if on the spokes of half a wheel. The Shenandoah or "Valley" Campaign of "Stonewall" Jackson was a successful effort to keep these other armies so busy that they could not join McClellan to close in on Richmond. With 17,000 men, Jackson baffled the Union troops, and defeated them in detail by a brilliant use of surprise, mobility, and interior lines. After doing all this, he joined Lee outside Richmond for the Seven Days' Battles, which forced McClellan to abandon his campaign.

The situation in Washington in 1862 helps to explain these campaigns. Lincoln and his Secretary of War, Stanton, took an active part in managing the Union strategy. Neither of them had had any scientific military experience.[1] Both were insistent on one point. Washington must be defended at all costs. Its fall might mean foreign recognition of the Confederacy. The cordon of forts around the capital had a regular garrison of about 40,000 men. Even that did not prevent an occasional panic. Consideration of the security of Washington was one of the main things which influenced the movements of both sides.

MCCLELLAN'S "MUD MARCH"—Late in February, 1862, General McClellan, then commander of the Union armies, went out to attack Centreville, occupied by Confederates since the First Bull Run the summer before.[2] His horses, guns, and men floundered in the miry roads. He found the position abandoned by the Confederates, who had retired toward Richmond. On his return to Washington after this fruitless "mud march," he urged that the next attack against Richmond be from the sea so as to avoid the overland difficulties of bad roads.

HIS PLAN OF CAMPAIGN—He finally persuaded the authorities to agree to this. His so-called Peninsula Campaign was the only one of the six main Union drives against Richmond that went by sea. Lincoln hesitated in fear that the Confederates might attack Washington while the Army was on the water. McClellan, however, arranged an adequate garrison for Washington's defense. He counted on having about 150,000 men for his campaign. The first transports sailed for the Peninsula on March 17, 1862.

[1] See p. 187.
[2] See p. 242.

DISLOCATION OF UNION PLANS

THE EFFECT OF KERNSTOWN—Six days later, "Stonewall" Jackson dislocated the movements of all the Union troops in the region. We shall see later how at Kernstown in the Shenandoah Valley he fell upon retiring Union troops under Banks.[3] These had been recalled from the Valley to join McClellan's expedition. Instantly, Washington was in a panic. Lincoln and Stanton in their alarm did several foolish things, which undermined McClellan's campaign just as it was starting.

MCDOWELL'S 37,000—In the first place, they violated the principle of mass by detaching from his forces 37,000 men under General McDowell to keep them near-by as additional protection to Washington. This was naturally a severe blow to McClellan. It might be said that the Peninsula and Shenandoah campaigns hinged on that corps of McDowell's. Ten weeks later, Lincoln decided that Washington was safe again, so he ordered this corps to start overland for Richmond. In this way, these troops would be kept between the Confederates and Washington as long as possible. McClellan was forced to weaken his position on the Peninsula in order to coöperate with this overland project. But McDowell's men never reached Richmond. Again the work of Jackson in the Shenandoah frightened Lincoln and Stanton so that they held McDowell back a second time, but McClellan did not know this. We must keep those 37,000 men of McDowell's constantly in mind. They influenced every move, though they scarcely pulled a trigger all that spring.

SIX SEPARATE ARMIES—The second grave error of Lincoln and Stanton was a direct violation of the

[3] See p. 280.

principle of simplicity.[4] McClellan had hitherto been in supreme command of all the Union troops in the theater of operations. Now the amateur strategists split the forces into six separate, independent armies in place of one. McClellan was left with only 105,-000 men for the Peninsula attack. Another 100,000 Union troops were badly scattered. McDowell was given a separate command with his important 37,-000. So was Banks, who was kept in the Shenandoah with 20,000 to watch Jackson. Frémont, on his way from the west through the Alleghenies with 25,000 to join in the attack, had still a third separate command. Even the 10,000 at Fortress Monroe, near the top of the Peninsula, were removed from McClellan's command and set up by themselves, while the Washington garrison formed the sixth separate army. The only coördination for these 200,000 men lay in the two civilians, Lincoln and Stanton. This division of command, combined with the fear for the safety of Washington, gave Lee and Jackson their opportunity.

THE PENINSULA CAMPAIGN

THE "MONITOR" AND THE "MERRIMAC"—When McClellan landed at Fortress Monroe with his diminished force, he took stock of the situation. The most natural line of approach was by the James River on which Richmond is situated. But the James was not safe in March, 1862. The Confederates had converted the warship *Merrimac* into an ironclad. She had just destroyed two helpless wooden Union frigates in Hampton Roads. The Union ironclad *Monitor* had checked this mad career the next day, but the *Merrimac* was still intact at Norfolk. Until

4 See p. 126.

she was destroyed, Union transports could not safely ascend the James.

THE BASE AT WHITE HOUSE—The only alternative was to go up the York River and its tributary, the Pamunkey. McClellan, therefore, made his base on the Pamunkey at White House, as a railroad ran from there to Richmond. The destruction of the *Merrimac* in April cleared the James River, but by that time McClellan had been ordered to keep his White House base, in order to coöperate more easily with McDowell's projected overland march.

THE RIVAL COMMANDERS—The 105,000 men of McClellan's Army of the Potomac were subdivided into five corps, commanded by Franklin, Sumner, Keyes, Heintzelman, and Porter. He also had, as we know, possible reinforcements of more than 70,000 under Banks, Frémont, and McDowell. The Washington garrison was not reckoned as part of this offensive force. Richmond was defended by a Confederate force of about 65,000 under General Joseph E. Johnston. It was called the Army of Northern Virginia. Its principal "divisions" were commanded by Longstreet, A. P. Hill, D. H. Hill, Huger, and Magruder. Its cavalry was under J. E. B. Stuart. Lee was serving as military advisor to President Davis at Richmond.

ADVANCE UP THE PENINSULA

THE DELAY AT YORKTOWN—The first obstacle met by McClellan, as he came up the Peninsula, was the Confederate position at Yorktown. Johnston had stationed General Magruder here with about 20,000 men. They defended the town with earthworks, even using some of the old trenches dug by the British in 1781. McClellan wasted a whole month in a formal siege of these lines, while the Confederates had a chance to strengthen the defenses of Richmond.

LACK OF INFORMATION—We must remember that McClellan was handicapped by lack of information. Instead of having an official intelligence service or active cavalry, the North depended upon the reports of Pinkerton detectives, who invariably overestimated the Confederate strength. They were a poor substitute for the modern G-2.[5] McClellan thought that the Confederates had 180,000 men for the defense of Richmond, whereas they had at most 65,000. Also, no maps were available, so both armies were surprisingly ignorant of the terrain. The Northerners finally secured the better maps, but at this time they were badly hampered by not knowing the country.

MCCLELLAN'S CAUTION—Also we must not forget that McClellan was instinctively cautious. He had seen McDowell's unseasoned regiments routed at the First Bull Run the previous summer. He wanted to do the job properly. He desired a well-trained, well-equipped army, large enough to give him an overwhelming advantage. Such a force could dictate an unquestioned peace in Richmond. He was constantly clamoring for reinforcements, even when he outnumbered the Confederates two to one. He neglected the advantages of the offensive in overemphasizing security.

YORKTOWN ABANDONED—On May 3d, McClellan was at last ready for a final assault on the Yorktown lines. A month before, he could have carried them easily, but he did everything too deliberately. Dozens of great mortars were laboriously placed in position for the attack. Then, with everything ready, he found that Magruder's little force had slipped out!

[5] See p. 141.

The Yorktown trenches had delayed McClellan while Richmond was being better fortified.

THE CHICKAHOMINY—Then McClellan faced the problem of the Chickahominy River. Like McDowell's army, it was an extremely important passive factor in the campaign. As long as McClellan was under orders to be ready for McDowell's junction with his right flank, he had to divide his army by the Chickahominy. This stream is of moderate size, running fairly parallel to the James, which it joins at some distance below Richmond. As Richmond is south of the Chickahominy, it was necessary to cross the river before attacking. At the same time, part of the army had to be kept on the north bank to meet McDowell. The Confederates were enabled to catch McClellan twice with his army thus divided by the river. In each case, they secured local numerical superiority by falling on the weaker isolated flank.

FAIR OAKS (SEVEN PINES)—McClellan sent the two corps of Keyes and Heintzelman to the south bank on the last day of May. The other three corps were still on the north bank, stretched out to meet the McDowell reinforcements—which never came. Heavy rains had suddenly turned the Chickahominy into a freshet. Its weakened wooden bridges were liable to go at any minute. Johnston seized this opportunity to fall on the two isolated corps on the south bank. This stroke started the two-day battle known as Fair Oaks, or Seven Pines. Part of it was fought within five miles of the capital.

Johnston's plan was excellent. But here we see the first example of the inadequate staff work which so often marred the clever strategy of the Confederate leaders. They badly needed a good G-3.[6] Johnston or Lee would conceive brilliant plans for sepa-

[6] See p. 141.

rate units to approach by different routes and fall simultaneously on the enemy. But they would then neglect to translate those ideas into fool-proof orders. Their directions to the division commanders were frequently verbal. The concerted attack, instead of being fixed for a definite "H" or "zero" hour, depended upon some stupid signal such as a shot or a yell. Few of the officers knew the first elements of staff work, and the troops were green.

Johnston's plan for Fair Oaks was to have the divisions of Longstreet, Huger, and D. H. Hill approach by separate roads. Then, coming together, they would pinch in the flanks of Keyes's exposed corps with their superior numbers. Longstreet picked the wrong road, already jammed with Huger's men. They were delayed, and the force of the simultaneous attack was lost. Even at that, the Union forces were in a tight place on the first day of the battle. Finally, Sumner brought a division across the swollen stream on a shaky bridge just in time to bolster up their weakening line. The fighting was sharp, but the two corps were not annihilated as the Confederates had planned. The battle was renewed on June 1st, but the Confederates finally withdrew to Richmond at noon. They lost about 6,000 men and the North about 5,000.

MCCLELLAN SETTLES DOWN—The Northerners won Fair Oaks because the Confederates retired after their attack. But it was not a decisive victory. McClellan's advance was slowed up, and practically stopped. He spent some time repairing the weakened bridges, and then settled down in a strongly intrenched position before Richmond. All the corps were now on the south bank of the Chickahominy except Porter's, which stayed to guard the line of communications to White House and to be ready to join McDowell. The advanced Union pickets were only four miles from Richmond, and could even hear the clocks in the city striking the hour.

LEE IN COMMAND—Fair Oaks had another result. Johnston was wounded during the action. It is said that he was riding out to an exposed position to avoid President Davis, who, like Lincoln, too often meddled with strategy and even tactics.[7] After Johnston was wounded, Lee became commander of the Army of Northern Virginia.[8]

THE SITUATION AROUND RICHMOND—The situation was grave for Richmond. It was guarded, as we know, by only about 60,000 men, while McClellan was just outside with 100,000 (after the losses at Fair Oaks). While McClellan was awaiting McDowell's extra 37,000 men before attacking, still other Union armies, as we shall see, were advancing toward the city. Johnston had favored calling in all the Confederate troops in Virginia to risk everything in a great pitched battle before McClellan's reinforcements arrived. Lee had a more subtle plan.

THE SHENANDOAH CAMPAIGN

We must turn to the Shenandoah Valley to understand this plan, which "Stonewall" Jackson so ably carried out. We shall learn why McDowell never came overland to join the right wing which McClellan left exposed, and also what happened to the two armies of Banks and Frémont. Jackson, with a handful of men, was holding back not only McDowell's 37,000 but at least an equal number under the other two generals. His campaign, which had started just as McClellan was leaving the Potomac,

[7] See pp. 187, 190, 239.
[8] See p. 239.

is one of the masterpieces of modern military history.

THE VALLEY—The Shenandoah Valley, it will be recalled, lies between the Blue Ridge and the Allegheny Mountains, and was important as a "back door" to Washington from the South. The valley runs for about 140 miles from the Potomac at Harper's Ferry southward to below Staunton. On one side, it is separated by the Blue Ridge from eastern Virginia, where the main armies were fighting about Richmond. On the other side rise the Alleghenies, tier after tier. The valley averages twenty miles in width. Down its center runs the Shenandoah River, which is divided for fifty miles of its course into two branches by the Massanutton Mountains, 2,500 feet high. The main artery was the Valley Turnpike, stretching from the Potomac south through Winchester, the main town; past Strasburg and Harrisonburg and Staunton to the head of the valley.

Three railroads served the valley. Along the Potomac was the Baltimore & Ohio, very important for Union communications. A branch from this ran up the Valley to Winchester. In the center, the Manassas Gap Railway enabled the Union to bring reinforcements from Bull Run, only sixty miles from Strasburg. In the south, Staunton was connected with Gordonsville and Richmond by the Virginia Central, which was the only road in Confederate hands. The valley, with its fertile farms—which Sheridan was later to ravage [9]—afforded a much better terrain for maneuvers than the tangled wilderness of eastern Virginia. The Massanuttons could shelter flanking movements against the enemy in the other half of the valley. The numerous gaps through the

[9] See p. 261.

Blue Ridge offered rare possibilities for a genius like Jackson.

"STONEWALL" JACKSON—Jackson himself, a West Virginian, was no smooth and polished aristocrat like Lee. He was somber, silent, and stern, with an underlying fierceness. He was a Presbyterian of the grimmest type. He never marched or fought on Sunday if he could possibly help it, but he studied Napoleon's *Maxims of War* almost as thoroughly as his Bible.[10] Small wonder that he was generally considered "queer." Big things were expected of Lee, from the beginning, but Jackson was a "dark horse" like Grant. He had finished at West Point just before the Mexican War, in which his gallantry won him the rank of major of artillery. Then, bored with garrison life, he left the Army, and was teaching when the Civil War broke out. At Bull Run, his stubborn stand helped to turn the day. After that, men forgot his first name—he was "Stonewall." He had spent the winter in the valley, and was at Winchester with about 4,600 men when activities started in 1862.

THREE PHASES OF THE CAMPAIGN—His operations in the Shenandoah fall into three parts. First came his action at Kernstown in March. Then followed six weeks of comparative inactivity. The real Shenandoah campaign, with its constant, rapid movements, lasted from May 4 to June 9, 1862.

BANKS INVADES THE VALLEY—The first part started on February 27th, when Banks entered the valley with 38,000 men. Every one expected Jackson, outnumbered more than seven to one, to fall back. Banks was a "political" general with no previous military training. His services as Speaker of the

10 See p. 115.

House and governor of Massachusetts had won him a major-general's commission.[11] Such a man naturally made a foil for Jackson's brilliant strategy. Banks advanced slowly up the valley and finally occupied Winchester. Then, as we recall, McClellan prepared to launch his Peninsula Campaign. It was planned to withdraw all of Banks's men from the valley except a division under Shields. This was to be left to guard the Baltimore & Ohio and keep an eye on Jackson. By the middle of March, the other divisions were on their way back to the Potomac to join McClellan.

KERNSTOWN—Then Jackson struck. On March 23d, he dislocated the Union plans by falling on Shields's division, three miles south of Winchester. Misinformed, Jackson thought he was attacking only a small rear-guard. Instead, he was engaging Shields's whole force, twice the size of his own. In three hours of sharp fighting, Jackson lost a quarter of his infantry and had to retire.

IMPORTANCE OF KERNSTOWN—Kernstown was a tactical defeat, but a surprising strategical success. Washington, as we have seen, was thrown into panic. Jackson's little force had hitherto been scorned as a mere body of observation. Now, it was felt that strong reinforcements must be near him or he would not have dared attack. McClellan's forces were already partly at sea. Lincoln and Stanton imagined large armies of Confederates sweeping down on the capital from Harper's Ferry. That little battle ruined the Union plans. Banks was left in the valley with 20,000 men. McDowell and his 37,000 were kept near Bull Run, where he could quickly send reinforcements to the Shenandoah or to Washington, if needed. An extra division of 9,000 men

[11] See p. 184.

was sent to Frémont, who was on his way through the Alleghenies toward the valley. The Kernstown affair thus kept some 60,000 Union troops from the attack on Richmond. The forces, moreover, were now separated into several independent armies. All this happened because a handful of Virginians had taken a bold chance.[12]

SIX QUIET WEEKS—No real fighting took place in the valley for more than six weeks after Kernstown. Jackson retired to Mt. Jackson, thirty-five miles southward on the turnpike. Banks followed very slowly, and halted near-by. The superior Confederate cavalry under Ashby kept Jackson constantly informed of the Union movements, or rather, lack of movements.

By April 17, Banks was finally prodded into activity by his superiors. He started southward down the turnpike. Jackson, who by this time had 6,000 men, withdrew. In three days, he made a forty-mile march southeastward to Elk Run, near Swift Run Gap in the Blue Ridge. Banks moved only twenty-five miles in ten days, and reached Harrisonburg. Now he had a clear road to Staunton, the only important town left in Confederate hands —and barely twenty-five miles away. It was guarded by 2,800 troops. Frémont was within thirty miles of Staunton, coming from the west with his 25,000 men. It looked as though Staunton and the valley were doomed unless the 9,000 Confederates could defeat the two Union Armies before they united.

LEE'S COÖPERATION—The real Shenandoah campaign, as we said, lasted from May 4th to June 9th. Lee, then military advisor, deserves part of the credit for its success. Jackson immediately grasped

12 See pp. 271, 272.

his bold idea that an energetic campaign in the valley might keep the superior Union armies from joining McClellan before Richmond. The average general would have massed his troops around the threatened capital. Instead, Lee sent 8,500 additional men, under Ewell, to help Jackson in the valley.

"LEAVING THE VALLEY"—Then things started. Leaving Ewell at Elk Run, Jackson crossed eastward over the Blue Ridge by the first of May. That looked as if he were on his way to defend Richmond. His men were downhearted at the idea of abandoning their valley to the Northern armies. On May 4th, they came to the railroad station at Meechum's River, where they boarded a train. The train started —not eastward toward Richmond—but, to their intense joy, westward back into the valley to Staunton. With Jackson's own men so completely in the dark, the surprise of the Union generals can be imagined.

THE BATTLE OF McDOWELL—Jackson's idea was to march out westward into the Alleghenies and to hold up Frémont by defeating his small advance-guard. Collecting the 2,800 men at Staunton, he met this advance-guard on May 8th about thirty miles west of Staunton near the town of McDowell (not to be confused with the Union general).

Jackson assumed the tactical defensive on so steep a mountainside that the Union artillery could not reach him. The outnumbered Northerners delivered an unsuccessful attack. Jackson wired this simple message to Richmond: "God blessed our arms with victory at McDowell yesterday." For the next four days, Jackson pursued this little beaten force back toward Frémont's main body near Franklin. Then, Jackson returned to the valley, but his men held the mountain passes. Frémont was temporarily checked.

BANKS RETIRES TO STRASBURG—Now, free from attack from the west, Jackson was ready to turn on the army of Banks, his main objective. Banks had missed his great chance. At the end of April, he had had 20,000 men and a clear road to Staunton. But he lacked the offensive spirit. Since then, orders from Washington had cut his force in half, so that he had had to retire to Strasburg. There, he had "dug in." His strong intrenchments covered the approach up the turnpike.

JACKSON'S FORCE INCREASED—Jackson had no intention of storming intrenchments of that sort, but he did plan to crush Banks somehow. Jackson's force now numbered 17,000, since he had been joined by Ewell and the Staunton defenders. He marched up the turnpike as far as New Market, so that Banks would expect to have his earthworks stormed.

A SCREENED APPROACH—But the attack came from quite a different direction. Jackson used the Massanutton Mountains to surprise Banks. As we said, this range really cuts the Shenandoah into two valleys for about fifty miles. Between the Blue Ridge and the Massanuttons lies the Luray Valley, narrow, heavily wooded, and sparsely settled. It was up this valley that Jackson went, instead of continuing on the turnpike.

FRONT ROYAL—Banks had foolishly stationed 1,000 men at Front Royal, at the northern end of Luray Valley, to guard the Manassas Gap Railroad. They were nine miles from his main force at Strasburg. This little garrison, like the rest of Banks's men, was basking in the sun on May 23d, completely bored with the war. Suddenly, from the wooded valley, Jackson's men fell on them with full force and completely routed them.

"MR. COMMISSARY BANKS"—Banks was in a bad fix. Jackson had taken him in flank. The Union communications were threatened both toward the Potomac and Manassas Gap. If Banks had retired as soon as the first fugitives arrived from Front Royal, he might have saved his vast accumulation of rich stores. But, politician that he was, he was "afraid of appearing afraid." He wasted a whole day. At last, on the morning of May 24th, he started for Winchester. His main body of infantry got away safely, but his long wagon-train was seized by the Confederates. Jackson's men spent the entire day looting the rich stores while they fought the stubborn rear-guards. The Union general was called "Mr. Commissary Banks" by his grateful enemies, who had badly needed his supplies.

WINCHESTER—At Winchester, Banks made a stand on the next day. Outnumbered, his men broke at the first Confederate charge and fled through the town. Jackson urged his men on after them, crying, "Press forward to the Potomac!" He wanted to keep after the routed Northerners to wipe them out. But he could not keep up the pursuit dictated by the principle of movement. His cavalry was unfortunately not at hand. Banks was able to keep a safe distance ahead and to get across the Potomac at Williamsport at noon on the 26th. He felt himself lucky to escape, but he left the valley cleared of Union troops.

SECOND PANIC IN WASHINGTON—Jackson had a bigger purpose than simply routing Banks and ridding the valley of Northerners. The strategical effects of Kernstown were repeated. Washington was once more terrified. Frenzied imaginations again pictured Jackson swooping down on the capital. Frantic appeals were sent to the Northern governors for more militia.[13] Most important, McDowell's 37,-000 men were again kept from the Richmond attack. They had this time gone from Manassas Junction as far as Fredericksburg, and were all ready to join that exposed right wing of McClellan's. Lincoln was to have reviewed them on May 26th before they left. Instead, that was the day of terror in Washington, when Banks's fleeing army arrived. So, five days later McClellan was fighting at Fair Oaks without the needed reinforcements on his right flank. McDowell never did arrive, as a result of this second scare.

JACKSON'S PREDICAMENT—In spite of all this success, Jackson was in a tight place. His loot from Banks, so sorely needed by the South, meant a long, clumsy wagon-train. And the situation called for the utmost speed.

ALMOST TRAPPED—Lincoln and Stanton, with maps and telegrams, laid a trap to cut off his retreat. Superior Northern forces were to close in immediately from opposite sides of the valley. Frémont, at last, was approaching through the Alleghenies from the west. From the east were coming 21,000 men under Shields, followed by the rest of McDowell's force. Other smaller Union forces were not far distant, bringing the total to about 60,000 men against Jackson's 17,000. But numbers never worried Jackson. He held interior lines. The Union armies were not only under several leaders, but they were also too widely separated for good coöperation.

THE RACE FOR STRASBURG—The trap was to be sprung at Strasburg. On May 29th, Jackson was

[13] See p. 177.

fifty miles north of there, near Harper's Ferry. Frémont was twenty miles from Strasburg, to the westward, and Shields about half that distance to the
eastward, at Front Royal. The race was close. The
little Confederate force, with its delaying baggage,
did escape the trap, but it was by a very narrow margin. On June 1st, Jackson's rear-guard had to fight
off Frémont's advance-guard in Strasburg.

NUMBERS NOT EVERYTHING—In the fourteen
days from May 19th to June 1st, Jackson's 17,000
men marched 170 miles; routed Union forces totaling 12,500; threw the North into panic; dislocated
the plans of 170,000 Union troops; captured vast
stores; and still escaped, although surrounded on
three sides by 60,000 enemies. Brilliant strategy
like this is not necessarily bloody. The Confederates lost only 400 men in accomplishing these wonders.

THE CHASE CONTINUES—The disappointed Union
generals at Strasburg gave chase, but the Massanuttons separated them, and prevented concerted action. Shields hoped to catch Jackson in the rear by
coming through the Luray Valley, while Frémont
hurried after Jackson down the turnpike. The Confederate cavalry under Ashby had to keep fighting a
constant rear-guard action. The Confederates succeeded in gaining a day on their pursuers by burning the bridge near Mt. Jackson, where the turnpike
crossed the river.

INTERIOR LINES—Jackson knew that he would be
lost if the two Union armies joined—and they
could do so at the southern end of the Massanuttons. He was ready to prevent this by the night of
June 7th. Frémont was at Harrisonburg, so Jackson posted Ewell's divisions at Cross Keys to hold
him off. Jackson himself, three miles away at Port

Republic, prepared to meet Shields, whose force was strung out over twenty-five miles in the Luray Valley.

CROSS KEYS AND PORT REPUBLIC—On June 8th, Ewell beat back Frémont at Cross Keys. It was a hard-fought battle. Ewell's men were outnumbered nearly two to one. The next day at Port Republic, Jackson was also successful against Shields, when he emerged from the Luray Valley.

Then the two Confederate forces reunited and burned the only bridge over the river at that point so that Frémont could not pursue them. With his interior lines, Jackson thus defeated the enemy in detail. Not content with this, his cavalry chased Frémont through Harrisonburg all the way back to Strasburg. In the whole campaign from Kernstown to Port Republic, North and South had each lost about 2,300 men in killed and wounded. But the North had also lost an equal number in missing, chiefly captured, against only 300 for Jackson.

"HOLDING THE BAG"—These twin battles ended the Shenandoah Campaign. Jackson gave every indication of continuing the fight there in the valley. The Union forces did not dare to move away, and were left "holding the bag." They did not know what might happen next, but Lee and Jackson were through with the Shenandoah.

THE SEVEN DAYS—JUNE 26–JULY 2, 1862

RICHMOND AGAIN—The scene of action now returned to Richmond. Jackson's work in the valley was finished. He left the baffled Union generals there, in momentary expectation of a surprise attack. That was the purpose of his campaign. But he went to Richmond—they did not.

McCLELLAN'S ARMY STILL SPLIT—McClellan, as
we remember, had been settled down before Richmond since June 1st after the battle of Fair Oaks.
His army was again divided by the troublesome
Chickahominy. At Fair Oaks, his weak left flank on
the *south* side of the river had been attacked. Now
two thirds of his 105,000 were at last south of the
river behind powerful intrenchments and only a
few miles from the city. But on the north side Porter was at Mechanicsville with about 35,000 men.
He was guarding the railroad line to their base at
White House and still waiting vainly for McDowell.

STUART'S RAID—Once again, the Confederates
were ready to take advantage of the divided army.
As before, they determined to fall upon the weaker
portion, which this time was *north* of the river. In
preparation, the Confederate cavalry under J. E. B.
Stuart made a spectacular raid around the whole
Union Army. They found that Porter's right flank
was unprotected and that the railroad to White
House was lightly guarded.

LEE'S PLAN—Lee, thereupon, perfected his plans
to drive McClellan away from Richmond. Jackson was to hurry down from the Shenandoah, so
that the Confederates would have about 88,000 men
to oppose McClellan's 105,000. Of these Confederates, 28,000 would hold the main Union forces
of 70,000 south of the Chickahominy. The main
body of the Southerners, on the other hand, were to
crush Porter's 35,000 north of the river, and thus
cut the Union lines of retreat to their base at White
House. This plan gave the outnumbered Confederates local tactical superiority, north of the river.
The plan was clever, but it was risky, too. McClellan had the chance to reinforce Porter, as there were
several bridges across the river, or even to capture

Richmond by pushing aside the small defending force. But Lee thought he could safely gamble upon McClellan's supercaution.[14]

MECHANICSVILLE (BEAVER DAM CREEK)—The plan was put into operation in what are known as the Seven Days' Battles, between June 26th and July 2d. First, the Confederates were to direct their opening attack against Porter at Mechanicsville. He took up a strong defensive position on Beaver Dam Creek, which flows into the Chickahominy. Jackson, who was still en route from the Shenandoah, was expected to strike Porter in the rear. That would, it was hoped, cause Porter to relax his hold on the bridges so that Confederate divisions could cross from Richmond to join in the battle.

A PIECEMEAL ATTACK—But Jackson was late. At the time he was expected, he was still three miles away across a swamp. The divisions of Longstreet and A. P. Hill grew so restless that they crossed the river anyway—without the signal and under heavy fire. Lee, seeing that Jackson was not there yet, tried to stop them, but his orders arrived too late. Time and again Longstreet and Hill threw their men against Porter's strong position, but each time they were thrown reeling back. In a few hours, they had lost 2,000 men and Porter only 360.

GAINES'S MILL, JUNE 26TH—That night Porter retired down the north bank of the Chickahominy to Gaines's Mill. Here he had an even stronger defensive position on a high plateau, with the approach protected by woods and a sluggish creek. The next day, the 27th, saw a repetition of the Mechanicsville attack. Again Jackson was late. Once more Longstreet and Hill made costly frontal charges. They tried to scramble up the hill, but according

[14] See p. 126.

to Porter, "brigade after brigade seemed almost to melt away."

PORTER FINALLY BEATEN—Eventually Jackson's divisions arrived via Cold Harbor to strike Porter's right flank. But orders went wrong. Instead of a concerted attack from all directions, the divisions charged separately. Porter was able to concentrate on each in turn. His splendid resistance against superior numbers broke at sunset, when at last a Confederate charge succeeded in carrying the hill. Jackson was urged to turn Porter's retreat into a rout as he had Banks's. It could have been easily done, but Jackson's energy seemed to have left him. He let Porter retreat across the Chickahominy to the south bank, destroying the bridge behind him.

INACTIVITY ON THE SOUTH BANK—McClellan's right flank had been driven in and no more troops left north of the river. The amazing thing is that McClellan stayed idly south of the river with 70,-000 men when adequate reinforcements might have saved the situation for Porter. Nor did McClellan try to take Richmond while so many Confederates were engaged on the other side of the river. He still thought he was facing 100,000 men instead of the actual 28,000 defenders of the capital.

THE CHANGE OF BASE—But McClellan did one clever thing, even if he did let slip his wonderful chance for an offensive. Once again, he did not neglect security. The Southerners thought their attack on Porter would trap McClellan by cutting off his line of retreat to his White House base. He fooled them. Quickly and quietly, he shifted his base to Harrison's Landing behind him on the James River. By the time Porter retreated, McClellan no longer had any use for that railroad north of the Chickahominy.

MCCLELLAN'S WITHDRAWAL—The rest of the Seven Days' Battles were fought south of the river. McClellan determined to escape from his position after Porter's retreat. His supercaution made any other course seem impossible to him, especially as he still exaggerated the number of Southerners. Lee put all his efforts into trying to prevent this escape. McClellan found that a retreat from his position was a difficult operation. There was only one road by which he could withdraw his men, guns, and thousands of supply-wagons. To make matters worse, that road went through White Oak Swamp, which parallels the Chickahominy. If the single bridge across the swamp should be cut, he would be trapped.

THE ONLY QUIET DAY, JUNE 28TH—Little happened on the third day, the 28th. McClellan burned the rest of the lower bridges across the Chickahominy to hinder the pursuit. That night he started his retreat with great efficiency.

LEE'S PLAN OF PURSUIT—Lee naturally planned to trap McClellan before he reached the James. Jackson was to follow McClellan through the swamp. In the meantime, the rest of the Confederates were to hurry around the swamp by roads which met at its other side. But it was too complicated a plan to be carried out with inefficient staff work and little knowledge of the region.

SAVAGE STATION, JUNE 29TH—On the fourth day, the whole Union Army got successfully through the swamp. Also at Savage Station north of the swamp, the rear-guard beat off a Confederate division. Lee's divisions were maneuvering to close in on McClellan.

THE CONCENTRATION FAILS—The crisis of the Seven Days came on the fifth day—the 30th. If

Lee had been able to concentrate his entire force, McClellan probably could never have reached the James. As it was, only 20,000 Confederates got into action. Jackson did not arrive because he had to stop to rebuild the destroyed bridges across the Chicka-hominy and White Oak Swamp in the face of heavy fire from the Union rear-guard. For the third time in the Seven Days, Jackson was late. Huger was held up because the Northerners had blocked his road with felled trees. Magruder, after fighting at Savage Station, had crossed to the road south of the Darby-town Road and was late. Holmes, approaching by the turnpike along the James River, was held up by the shelling from Union gunboats and by the Union advance guard on Malvern Hill.

FRAYSER'S FARM (GLENDALE), JUNE 30TH—So, for the third time, the divisions of Longstreet and A. P. Hill, which had come by the Darbytown Road, had to bear the brunt of the fighting. They were outnumbered and beaten back at Frayser's Farm (Glendale). Yet within sound of their guns were the delayed Southern divisions, totaling more than 50,000 men.

MALVERN HILL, JULY 1ST—Still Lee kept on try-ing to stop the retreat. The last and largest battle occurred on the sixth day, July 1st, at Malvern Hill, near the James. McClellan was slowly slipping farther away, heading for the James and the Union gunboats. This battle was a repetition of Mechanics-ville and Frayser's Farm. The result of a strong Northern defensive position, backed by heavy artil-lery, and a piecemeal attack by the Confederates was another Union victory. For hours, the Southerners attacked by divisions one by one until they were cut to pieces. A simultaneous attack might have carried the day.

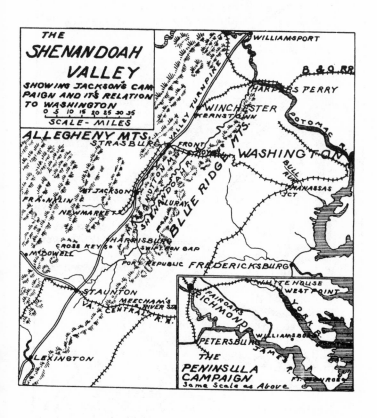

THE
SHENANDOAH
VALLEY
SHOWING JACKSON'S CAMPAIGN AND ITS RELATION TO WASHINGTON
0 5 10 15 20 25 30 35
SCALE- MILES

WILLIAMSPORT

B & O RR

HARPERS FERRY

WINCHESTER
KERNSTOWN
POTOMAC R.

ALLEGHENY MTS.
STRASBURG
FRONT
VALLEY TURNPIKE
WASHINGTON

BULL RUN

MANASSAS JCT

MT. JACKSON
LURAY
BLUE RIDGE MTS
SHENANDOAH R.
MASSANUTTON MTS.

FRANKLIN
NEWMARKET

HARRISBURG
CROSS KEYS
SWIFT RUN GAP
McDOWELL
PORT REPUBLIC   FREDERICKSBURG

STAUNTON
MEECHAM'S RIVER STA.
VA. CENTRAL R.R.

WHITE HOUSE
WEST POINT
FAIROAKS
RICHMOND
YORK
PETERSBURG
WILLIAMSBURG
JAMES

LEXINGTON

THE
PENINSULA
CAMPAIGN
Same Scale as Above
FT. MONROE

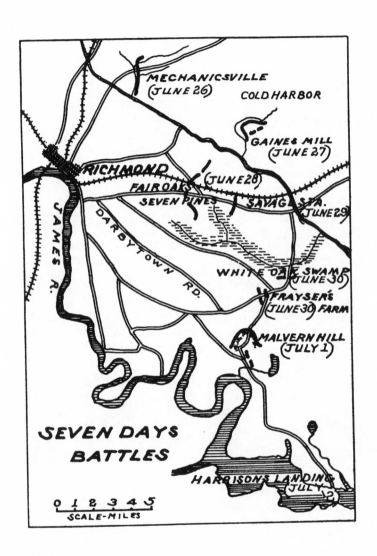

BOTH SIDES DEMORALIZED—The last encounter demoralized both sides. The Confederate divisions were shattered and weary. The Union Army was thinking only of retreat. A vigorous final charge by either side would probably have been victorious. But McClellan had no thought of a counter-offensive and Lee was discouraged. The Confederate losses had been heavy. The Seven Days cost the South more than 20,000 casualties out of some 88,000 men. Of these, more than 3,200 had been killed and nearly 16,000 wounded. Longstreet's division had lost half of its 9,000 men. Richmond was one vast hospital. The Union losses were less than 16,000 out of 105,000, including 6,000 captured. Most of these last were in the hospitals abandoned by McClellan in his retreat.

HARRISON'S LANDING, JULY 2D—The next day McClellan continued his retreat to Harrison's Landing. Here, between his strong position and the Union gunboats on the James, he was safe from Lee, who gave up the pursuit. McClellan planned next to move against Petersburg in order to get the "back door" to Richmond. Permission was refused from Washington. It should be said in McClellan's behalf that at Harrison's Landing, he was in as good a position to attack Petersburg as Grant was two years later after his failure at Cold Harbor. And McClellan had lost only a fraction of the men that Grant threw away in reaching Richmond's suburbs by the overland route. As it was, however, McClellan finally took his army back to the Potomac by water.

STRATEGICAL VICTORY FOR SOUTH—Except for Gaines's Mill, the Seven Days' Battles were a series of tactical victories for the Union. McClellan staged a most successful retreat. Yet the Seven Days must

be rated as a *strategic* victory for the South. Mc-
Clellan was dislodged by Lee from his intrenched
position in the outskirts of Richmond. True, Lee
did not destroy McClellan's army as he had hoped,
but he did definitely end the threat of invasion.

That threat had been very real three months
earlier with the huge Union armies concentrating
against Richmond. McClellan had been too cautious, and Jackson had so frightened Washington
that half the invading forces never arrived. Now,
early in July, the Army of the Potomac was taking
to its boats in acknowledged failure, while the other
Union armies were still hunting for the elusive Jackson in the Shenandoah. Jackson was not at his best
in the Seven Days, but he and Lee worked together
for ten more months in marvelous coöperation. This
strategy in the first half of 1862 is enough to show
why they are rated as two of the greatest American
soldiers.

CHAPTER XIII

THE WORLD WAR

The World War lasted from midsummer of 1914 to the late autumn of 1918. All the "great powers" were involved in the struggle. The victors were the Allies, of whom France, England, and Russia were the leaders, later being joined by Japan, Italy, and the United States. The losers were the Central Powers, headed by Germany and Austria. Among the lesser nations, Turkey and Bulgaria alone sided with the Central Powers. Serbia and Belgium were with the Allies from the start and numerous other small countries came in with them. The fighting centered in Europe, but it extended to Asia and Africa. Three empires were overthrown and several new nations were created. The struggle was different from any other in history because of its magnitude and its direct influence on the people of almost the entire world.

MAGNITUDE OF THE WAR—The war was fought on a far vaster scale than any previous contest. Armies were reckoned by millions instead of by tens or hundreds of thousands. Sixty-five million men were mobilized and ten million were killed. Ammunition and supplies of every sort were expended with unheard-of lavishness. The direct cost of the four years' fighting has been estimated at nearly two hundred billions of dollars.

THE "HOME FRONT"—The war affected more

than those vast armies alone. The whole populations of the principal belligerents were caught in its grip. It was literally a war of nations. Not simply did armies fight armies, but peoples opposed peoples, whether in front-line trenches or at home. The older men, the women, and the children remaining behind had to be taken into account in the conduct of the war. Their importance was twofold. In the 'first place, they took up the tasks hitherto performed by able-bodied men. The armies at the front depended upon them to "carry on." Women toiled even in munitions factories and on transportation systems. Second, the people's *morale* was of the utmost significance. More than one strategic move was made primarily for its moral effect, not only on the armies but especially on the people behind them. All the countries were flooded with ingenious propaganda to bolster up the morale of one's own side and to undermine the enemy's. In the final outcome, these people behind the lines played a tremendous part. The terrific stress of four years strained the morale of the leading belligerents almost to the breaking-point. When a country collapsed, as several did, the "home front" generally cracked first, and then the army went to pieces. Thus Russia went out, followed by Turkey, Bulgaria, Austria, and finally Germany herself.

THE ALLIANCE SYSTEM—Who was to blame for starting the war? That question is still bitterly disputed. Of course the Allies considered the German side guilty, while the Central Powers placed the blame on the Allies. We shall not take up this argument here. Latest authorities are inclined to divide the responsibility and place it rather on certain underlying circumstances than on any one country or individual. At any rate, Europe had long been divided into two great armed camps. Germany and Austria were allied as early as 1879. Italy joined them shortly afterward, as a rather uncertain ally. To offset this Triple Alliance, France and Russia came together about 1891. England later went in with them in the "Triple Entente"—a "friendly understanding." Between 1905 and 1913, several serious diplomatic crises occurred, notably in Morocco and the Balkans. Any one of them might easily have started war between the two hostile groups.

OUTBREAK OF THE WAR—The spark which ignited the magazine was the assassination by a Serbian student of the heir to the Austrian throne at Sarajevo in the Balkans on June 28, 1914—probably with the connivance of high officials in the Serbian government. Austria on July 23d sent a sharp ultimatum to Serbia with a series of exacting demands. Serbia agreed to most of them, but on July 28th Austria declared war. Thereupon, the two alliances fell into line. Russia interfered on behalf of the Serbs because they were also Slavs, and commenced the mobilization of her army. But her general staff had made but one plan of mobilization—a double one in which troops were to gather on the German frontier as well as on the Austrian. On the last day of July, Germany gave Russia twelve hours to stop mobilizing. Russia kept on, so on August 1st Germany declared war.

The German general staff was in the same fix— they had no plans for a single mobilization either. When troops went to the Russian frontier, they also headed for the French. By August 3d, France was in the war. The least fortified entrance [1] to France was through neutral Belgium. England not only had

[1] See p. 83.

promised to protect Belgian neutrality, but had also made certain definite military and naval agreements with Belgium and France. As a result, England came in on August 4th. Thus, with the temporary exception of Italy, both great alliances were lined up against each other.

CENTRAL POWERS—INTERIOR LINES—As is usual, each side had its distinct advantages. The Central Powers, as their name implies, had the help of "interior lines." [2] They occupied the strip through middle Europe from the Baltic to the Mediterranean, and after Turkey and Bulgaria joined them, across Europe from the Rhine into Western Asia. They could, for instance, shift troops and munitions quickly from the French to the Russian front. Russia, on the other hand, was almost completely cut off from her allies.

ALLIES—SEA POWER—To offset this military advantage, the Allies controlled the seas, for the British Navy was the largest afloat. The Allies were able to draw men, munitions, and supplies from beyond the seas, and at the same time to shut off their enemies from similar aid. This was naturally a tremendous asset.

THE RIVAL ARMIES—The Allies had more men. Germany could mobilize 5,000,000 at once and Austria about 2,000,000. France and Russia could each throw 4,000,000 into the field, although Russia did not have enough equipment for that many. England, with her small regular army, had only 70,000 men available.[3] Germany had more reserves than France. Russia had vast hordes, but they were largely untrained and unequipped. England had practically no reserves ready for overseas duty.

[2] See p. 116.
[3] See p. 110.

As far as quality went, Germany was generally supposed to have the best army in the world, with the French a close second. The war proved that unit for unit, the Germans, French, and English made more efficient soldiers than the Austrians, Russians, and Italians.

THE VARIOUS "FRONTS"—The war was fought in several separate theaters of operations, called "fronts." We shall treat these in turn, keeping in mind the constant interplay between them, and the way in which one affected the other. The most important was the "Western Front," where the French, the English, the Belgians, and later the Americans faced the Germans in Belgium and northern France. Next came the "Eastern Front," where the Russians opposed the Germans and Austrians on their mutual frontiers. Later the "Italian Front" saw the fighting of the Italians and Austrians between the Alps and the Adriatic. Another theater of action was the Balkans. England conducted three separate campaigns against the Turks in Gallipoli, Mesopotamia, and Palestine. Russia also fought the Turks far out in the Caucasus. In the fighting in Africa, the Far East, and the South Seas, most of the German colonies were quickly seized, German East Africa alone holding out until the end of the war.

THE VON SCHLIEFFEN PLAN—All the various great general staffs had carefully drawn up plans during the preceding years.[4] The German plan was largely the work of the late Count von Schlieffen. He knew that when the Germans marched toward Paris, the Russians would start for Berlin. He realized fully that Germany's trump card was speed. Her army could mobilize faster and maneuver more

[4] See p. 138.

rapidly than her neighbors' forces. At the same time, France was quicker at mobilization than Russia, with the creaking, corrupt machinery of her vast empire. So the German staff's plan was to put France out of the fight in a speedy campaign before Russia was ready. Then Russia could be handled at leisure. This idea of concentrating their efforts on one front at a time was tried by the Central Powers throughout the war, as they had interior lines. It was the principle of economy of force, while the Allies opposed it by following the principle of coöperation.[5] That meant simultaneous attacks on several fronts at once in order to prevent their opponents' concentration.

The Western Front in 1914

THE GERMAN ATTACK—In accordance with their plan, the Germans advanced rapidly against France as soon as war was declared. Von Schlieffen intended to hold the eastern part of the Western Front with relatively weak forces and to come crashing through Belgium with a very powerful right wing, so as to encircle the French and crush them from the rear. He chose this Belgian route because it was less strongly fortified. The French had powerful modern fortresses at Belfort, Epinal, Toul, and Verdun, but none behind the frontier of neutral Belgium. They had planned such defenses there also, but were held back by the tremendous cost. The Germans attacked with seven armies, numbered from right to left. The main work fell to the First Army under von Kluck and the Second under von Bülow. The von Schlieffen plan was followed in general, but the chief of staff in 1914, the younger von

[5] See pp. 121, 127.

Moltke, foolishly modified it just enough to cause its failure. Ignoring von Schlieffen's dying injunction to keep the right wing strong, von Moltke weakened it in order to bolster up other parts of the line. This, of course, violated the principle of economy of force.

THE FRENCH FORMATION—The French did not know for some time just what was the German plan. They strung out five thin armies along the line, but kept great numbers of troops together behind these in a "mass of maneuver." This was a sort of defensive "back-field," ready to rush as reinforcements to whichever one of the five armies had to withstand the main German attack.

ABORTIVE FRENCH ATTACK—In spite of the principle of attacking whenever possible, the French should have remained on the defensive, for they had the smaller army. That did not fit their temperament. Their general staff believed in "forward action," so they launched an immediate attack on Alsace-Lorraine, which they longed to recover. The Germans had avoided that eastern region because of the strong French fortresses. The Germans had equally powerful ones there, too, at Metz, Thionville, and Strassburg. The French offensive met with tremendous losses as the machine-guns mowed down their close formations. Then the French saw that their hands were going to be more than full defending France itself, so abandoned any more such attacks for a while.

THE GERMANS IN BELGIUM—Meanwhile the German right wing was crashing into Belgium according to its fast schedule of arriving in Paris in six weeks. But two unforeseen things occurred. The Belgians resisted to their uttermost, and their forts at Liége and Namur stopped the Germans for nearly three weeks.[5a] Heavy howitzers finally demolished these concrete creations. As we recall, the infantry trenches between them had never been dug, although essential in Brialmont's defense plan. By August 23d, the Germans were clear of these fortresses, but the French had had time to strengthen their left with the "mass of maneuver," and the little expeditionary force of England had arrived.

GERMAN PLANS GO WRONG—The Germans crossed into northwestern France and kept going. The English fought an heroic rear-guard action, back from Mons. Both they and the French retreated, giving up a large part of northern France to the enemy. The French seat of government was moved from Paris on September 3d. Then the German plans went wrong. Von Moltke apparently lost control of the vast armies in their rapid advance. We saw that he had already weakened his extreme right wing, which was to envelop the French left. Von Kluck felt that he lacked sufficient force now to swing west of Paris as he was supposed to in order to encircle the French left flank, so he headed southeast of Paris instead. By doing so, he lost contact with the Second Army under von Bülow and exposed his own left flank to the enemy. There was a wide gap in the German lines.

FIRST BATTLE OF THE MARNE—Two French commanders, Gallieni and Foch, were quick to take advantage of this blunder. On September 5th, with the advanced German lines at Meaux only fourteen miles from Paris, the French and British stopped their discouraging retreat. Joffre gave the word for a firm stand near the River Marne. The ensuing First Battle of the Marne was one of the most decisive encounters in world history. The strengthened French left was thrown against the divided German

[5a] See p. 43.

right, which was lucky to escape being cut off, and had to retreat. Fierce fighting took place all along the line, and the German center followed the right in retreating about thirty miles northward to strong positions already prepared on the River Aisne. Here, in the First Battle of the Aisne, they checked the French pursuit. In the heavily fortified region from Verdun eastward the Germans had not advanced far. By a close shave, the initial advantage of Germany's speed had been destroyed, part of northern France regained, and the Allied morale restored.

THE "RACE TO THE SEA"—Now came the "race to the sea." Both sides began to extend their lines northwestward to get around each other's flanks. If the Germans could have reached the Channel ports first, they might still have rolled up the French flank and also threatened England, but the British, French, and Belgians prevented this movement by severe fighting. At Ypres, the old British regular army was nearly wiped out.

UNBROKEN TRENCH LINES—The "open warfare" of maneuver was now over for a long time on the Western Front. There were no more flanks left to turn on either side, as they rested on the North Sea and Switzerland respectively. The enemies faced each other in two solid lines more than 600 miles long. As the armies could no longer get around each other, they tried to go through. The next four years consisted of these rival attempts to break through these lines. At times they bent, but they never broke decisively until the last days of the war in 1918.

NEW FEATURES IN 1914

TRENCH WARFARE—A new and unaccustomed type of fighting resulted. The war on this front became in fact a gigantic siege. Each side "dug in" and formed continuous lines of trenches with intricate systems, somewhat like Vauban's approach to a fortress as we have seen.[6] The strategists had to shelve their practice in the maneuvers of open warfare and adapt themselves to the new conditions. The last year of our Civil War had seen similar fighting around Petersburg and Richmond, but that had been largely forgotten.[7] In order to "break through," the plan was to blast a hole in the opposing trench system with artillery, then to send the infantry through to consolidate the positions, and finally to let loose the cavalry for the purpose of reopening the war of movement. Ammunition and men were lavishly spent to gain a few square miles of shell-torn waste, but the cavalry stage never came.

AVIATION—Even in reconnaissance cavalry was not needed. Its place was taken by aviation, still in its infancy at the outbreak of the war. Planes had first appeared in action in the comic-opera war between Italy and Turkey in 1911–1912, and in the Balkan wars immediately afterward. Now the young aviation corps of the powers were greatly expanded. Each side soon had detailed photographs of the enemy lines. Pursuit planes were developed to check enemy reconnaissance. Finally heavy bombing planes began to drop missiles not only on enemy troops and communications but also on cities far in the rear.

OTHER INNOVATIONS—Other improved features came into general use. Wireless was employed widely even between planes and batteries. Machine-guns

[6] See pp. 62, 63, 80, 88.
[7] See p. 260.

and automatic rifles constantly gained in importance. Hand-grenades were rescued from their long oblivion. The regular rifle became in many cases chiefly a handle for a bayonet, due principally to defective training and a lack of appreciation of its value. The trench systems were protected by barbed wire entanglements, which had to be blasted away before the infantry could attack with success. Quick-firing artillery made possible the "rolling barrage"—a curtain of shells which was kept just ahead of the advancing infantry. The two most novel inventions of the war, poison gas and the tank, did not appear at first. We shall now leave the Western Front, which by the end of 1914 had settled down to its long siege.

THE EASTERN FRONT IN 1914

SPEEDY RUSSIAN ADVANCE—Dramatic events had been going on in the East. It was part of the original Allied plans, we remember, that the Russian "steam-roller" was to advance toward Berlin. Germany estimated that, due to the slow Russian mobilization, it could afford to leave this menace alone until France was out of the way. Instead, the Russians not only began to mobilize before the outbreak of war, but speeded up their preparations to relieve the pressure on France—the first example of the principle of coöperation.

The Eastern Front had three distinct parts, and each presented a different problem. In the north, near the Baltic, was East Prussia, a part of Germany jutting eastward into Russia. Just south of it, adjoining the frontier of Germany on north and west, lay Russian Poland. Below that the Russian territory touched the frontier of Galicia or Austrian Poland. Altogether this Eastern Front was 900 miles long, from the Baltic to the Balkans.

RUSSIANS IN EAST PRUSSIA—The Russians made a double attack, invading both East Prussia and Galicia. Against East Prussia, they sent two armies, totaling about 850,000 men. The Germans had only 200,000 men on hand to check them, since they were applying the principle of economy of force with minimum strength here and maximum in the west. The Russian First Army under Rennenkampf was to attack straight from the east near the Baltic coast. When the German defenders had hurried in that direction, the Second Army under Samsonoff, was to come up from Poland to take the Germans in flank and rear. The Russians had such a slipshod organization, with almost no railroads, that their superior numbers did not matter so much.

HINDENBURG AND LUDENDORFF—According to this plan, Rennenkampf invaded East Prussia on August 16th. The little German force fell back, abandoning considerable territory. The alarmed inhabitants swarmed to Berlin, demanding that something be done. Immediate relief came, not so much from additional troops as from two men who were to be Germany's supreme leaders in the war. The command went to old Hindenburg, a retired general, who knew the whole region like a book. His chief of staff was Ludendorff, who with Foch, is ordinarily given first place among the generals in the war. The two made a remarkable combination.

TANNENBERG—Samsonoff had already started from Warsaw, striking blindly northward on a too-extended front and with no idea of where the enemy was. Hindenburg and Ludendorff took a very long chance by applying the principles of mass and of economy of force to the limit, at the expense of security. But it was a well-considered move. They left only a handful of cavalry to hold Rennenkampf's great army, and turned most of their forces on Samsonoff. They met him in the battle of Tannenberg on August 27th, where they reproduced Hannibal's famous double envelopment of Cannæ. It will be recalled that Hannibal pushed in both wings of a much larger Roman army, surrounded it, and annihilated it.[8] In the same way, the Russian center was allowed to advance, then the Germans drove in both flanks, encircled the main army, and practically wiped it out.

EAST PRUSSIA CLEARED—Hindenburg and Ludendorff then turned on Rennenkampf, who had patiently sat by with some 400,000 men and let his opportunity slip. He was defeated at Allenstein on September 1st. By the middle of the month East Prussia was rid of Russians. According to some Germans, however, this invasion was responsible for the French victory at the Marne. Two army corps were detached from von Kluck's army at a critical moment, although Ludendorff had said he did not need reinforcements, and rushed to the Eastern Front because of the clamor raised at Berlin by prominent residents of Königsberg in East Prussia.

AUSTRIA'S HANDICAPS—The Russian Army had better luck against the Austrian, which was more nearly in its own class. Austria-Hungary was weakened by her large number of different nationalities and languages. Some of her Slavic subjects, in fact, could not be trusted to fight against the Russians. Whole regiments sometimes went over to the enemy. Also the Austrians lacked the excellent organization of their German allies. As a result, the Russians, with their superior numbers, were successful until

[8] See p. 130.

Germans were sent over to stiffen the Austrian front.

RUSSIAN ADVANCE IN GALICIA—Both Russia and Austria planned offensives at the very beginning. Austria invaded Russian Poland, but was driven out almost at once. At the same time, the Austrians were thrown out of little Serbia on the south. Brusiloff's Russian offensive into Galicia against the Austrians had better success, as he took several cities and pushed almost through to the Carpathian Mountains on the boundary of Hungary.

HINDENBURG AGAIN—By October Hindenburg felt that he must do something to strengthen this crumbling Austrian defense. He tried to distract the Russians' attention from Galicia by overrunning the western third of Russian Poland, but failed to capture Warsaw.

SUMMARY OF THE YEAR 1914

Each side had its successes and failures in 1914. Germany had backed the Russian "steam-roller" out of East Prussia. She had come within a few miles of taking Paris and winning the war. Her troops were in possession of northern France, Belgium, and part of Russian Poland. Turkey had come in with her, cutting off Russia from easy communication through the Mediterranean with England and France. But on the other hand, Germany had not achieved the quick, decisive victory she had hoped to win with her rapid mobilization and movement. The Belgian forts had slowed her up, and the First Battle of the Marne had determined that it was to be a long war. Austria had been badly beaten by both Serbia and Russia. Japan had joined the Allies, though all she did was to help plunder Germany's colonial empire. The sea was dominated by the Allies except for a few scattered raiders, as the main German fleet was bottled up at Kiel, its base, by the British Navy.

THE WESTERN FRONT IN 1915

GERMANY ON THE DEFENSIVE—In 1915 the Germans stood on the defensive on the Western Front for the same reason that they were on the defensive at the start of the war on the Eastern Front, namely, economy of force. The Austrian defeats in Galicia made it necessary to send German troops down there. The new German commander, Falkenhayn, felt it wisest to settle the Russian emergency first, trusting that the Germans could hold their own in the west with fewer troops as long as they did not attempt any large-scale offensives.

ALLIES ATTEMPT "BREAK-THROUGH"—On the other hand, the French and English did launch several drives along the Western Front. They were following their favorite principle—coöperation—to relieve pressure on Russia, just as Russia had done for them in 1914. These apparently opposing principles were the natural result of Germany's advantage of interior lines, which made it possible for her to concentrate. Coöperation was the best way for the Allies to oppose it.

But although the Allies tried again and again all year in hopes of really achieving a "break-through" in the west, they met with only local successes. Their heavy casualties were all out of proportion to their meager gains of a few square miles. Besides, the strain on Russia was hardly affected by this activity on the Western Front. The principal attacks were against Neuve Chapelle by the British, in hopes of capturing the industrial and railroad center of Lille;

around Ypres and Vimy Ridge by the British and Canadians; and in the Champagne region by the French.

LACK OF MUNITIONS—The trouble lay in the Allied lack of ammunition and guns. The new trench warfare had put unusual demands upon the artillery because of the need of bombardments and barrages before the infantry attacks. In these various drives the Allies had shot away all their shells before decisive results had been obtained. Ammunition became so scarce that the artillery was limited to four rounds a day. The rest of the time the British replied to the German shelling with rifle grenades. English and French munition factories were working night and day in order that future drives might accomplish more.

THE EASTERN FRONT IN 1915

The German leaders were quicker than the Allies in realizing the necessity of plenty of ammunition if offensives were to mean anything, so they took quantities to the Eastern Front in 1915. The Russians, cut off as they were from Western Europe, were most inadequately supplied. All three parts of the Eastern Front were again involved in the fighting along the 900-mile trench line from the Baltic to Roumania.

RUSSIANS CONTINUE INTO GALICIA—Again, as in 1914, the Russians took the offensive first, invaded East Prussia, and were thrown out by Hindenburg almost on the same ground as before. In Galicia, their offensive was again successful for a while. They finally captured the unpronounceable key fortress of the region, Przemysl, by a long, old-fashioned siege as they lacked artillery to blast

down the walls.[9] After that, they pressed on toward
Cracow, the chief city, and for a while seemed likely
to force their way through the Carpathians into
Hungary. In fact, they did fight through the snowy
passes to the crest of the mountain-range, but there
they were stopped.

GALICIA FREED BY GERMANS—In April the Germans struck. Hindenburg, in supreme command, had
an army in the north, while Mackensen led an
Austro-German army farther south. The Russian
lines in Galicia were almost blasted away by Mack-
enson's furious bombardment between Gorlice and
Tarnow and, like East Prussia in 1914, the region
was soon cleared of the invading armies.

ATTACK ON RUSSIAN POLAND—Russian Poland
still remained as a salient for the Russians, and this
was the next point of attack. Salients were wedges
jutting into the enemy's territory, and they were
common, since trench lines bent, but rarely broke.
They were useful for farther advances, but were
at the same time more vulnerable than straight lines.
The favorite way to deal with a salient was to cut
into it at the corners where it joined the main line,
so that the forces in the wedge would have to retreat
or be captured. Hindenburg struck at the Polish
salient from the north near Prasnysz and Mackensen
from the south near Lublin. The Russians retreated
rapidly with great losses, and abandoned Warsaw.

RUSSIANS BADLY REPULSED—Thus the third great
section of the Eastern Front was clear of Russians,
and the Germans were in Russia itself. The new
trench line by fall was much farther east, running due
south from Riga. It was a tremendous German victory and an equally big loss for the Russians in
morale as well as men and munitions. "Not only was

[9] See p. 86.

it the most disastrous campaign in all history," writes one of the ablest historians of the war, "but the disaster was so great that there could be no comparison with any other campaign."

OTHER FRONTS IN 1915

ITALY JOINS THE ALLIES—The Allies had great hopes when Italy joined them in the spring of 1915. Italy did some sharp bargaining before coming in. Almost all the land that she coveted belonged to Austria. Naturally the Allies could promise this to Italy and the Central Powers would not. So she deserted the Triple Alliance completely. It was hoped that she could attack Austria from the rear to relieve Russia. Most of the Italian-Austrian frontier lay along the mountains of the lower Alps, and an effective invasion of Austria was almost impossible. The Austrians, moreover, held the well-fortified crest of the mountains, and were thus in a better position for an offensive than the Italians. The Italians might go between the mountains and the head of the Adriatic, over the rough Gorizia plateau toward the Austrian seaport of Trieste. Such an approach, however, was exposed to a flank attack from the mountains. These difficulties in the way of an Italian invasion and the fact that Austria was too busy in Galicia for an offensive herself resulted in two comparatively quiet years on the Italian Front. The two armies were of much the same quality. The Austrians could use here the Slavic troops who could not be trusted against the Serbs or Russians. Not until reinforced by stronger allies did either of these two armies make any great progress.

GALLIPOLI—England in 1915 fought her first campaign against Turkey at Gallipoli. She determined to take Constantinople in order to control the entrance to the Black Sea and give Russia a clear route to the Mediterranean. Besides, this capture would also cut off Asiatic Turkey from Europe. The affair was sadly bungled from the start. The Allied generals were reluctant to release men for this "side-show" because, to secure mass on the Western Front, economy of force was essential elsewhere. A most inadequate number were sent to the Dardanelles. Then the Army and the Navy failed to coöperate. The Navy attacked first, but withdrew because of mines without destroying the coast-defenses commanding the straits. They should have waited for troops to land and seize the high ridge of the Gallipoli Peninsula overlooking the Dardanelles and these coast-defenses. By the time that the troops got there, the Turks, under a German general, had so strengthened the fortifications on the Gallipoli Peninsula that this could not be done without the greatest difficulty. The troops did attack, however, in the face of almost insurmountable odds. The Anzacs from Australia and New Zealand won eternal fame by their heroic struggles to gain a foothold on the shore, but there were not enough of them to continue the advance. At the end of a year of continual hardships, this ill-fated expedition withdrew, leaving Russia still isolated by the Turks.

BALKANS—Meanwhile the Central Powers were meeting with success near-by in the Balkans also. The Serbs, who had been so successful in 1914 against their big neighbor, Austria, now found another enemy in their rear. Bulgaria had come into the war on Germany's side. Serbia was completely overrun by these two hostile neighbors. To relieve this Balkan situation, the Allies sent an expedition to the strategically located city of Saloniki. For three years this expedition did nothing. Saloniki belonged to Greece, who kept a big army near-by while she was slowly making up her mind which side to join in the war.

NEW FEATURES IN 1915

POISON GAS INTRODUCED—The Germans had introduced a new element into warfare. In a small offensive at Ypres on April 27th, the Allied defenders were suddenly overcome by a cloud of poisonous chlorine gas, released from tanks by the Germans and blown down on the enemy lines by a favorable breeze. Hundreds died in agony, giving the Germans a clear field for a while. But the Germans had made a serious strategical blunder in wasting this complete surprise on merely a minor objective, when they were not ready to follow up their advantage. Had they saved it for a major offensive like Verdun in the next year, it might have brought them complete victory. The Allies already had crude gas-masks for defense, when they tried it again, and before long were using gas themselves.

GAS WARFARE—From this time on, both sides employed gas extensively. The most deadly varieties were chlorine and phosgene; later mustard-gas, which burned severely, and tear-gas, which caused temporary blindness, were developed. As we saw, gas was used in artillery shells. It put many men out of action, but killed relatively few. It caused 27 per cent of the total American casualties, but less than 4 per cent of the deaths. It hampered tactical efficiency by forcing the use of masks.

SUBMARINES—Just two weeks after the first gas-attack, the British liner *Lusitania* was sunk by a German submarine—an instrument previously of little

BALTIC SEA

RIGA

MEMEL

KONIGSBERG

DANZIG

EAST PRUSSIA

MASURIAN L.S.

ALLENSTINE

VISTULA

THORN

TANNENBERG

PRZASNYSZ

BUG R.

WARSAW

RUSSIAN POLAND

RUSSIA

BREST LITOVSK

PRIPET MARSH

LUBLIN

GERMANY

TARNOW

CRACOW

PRZEMYSL

GORICE

GALICIA

LEMBERG

AUSTRIA-HUNGARY

EASTERN FRONT
SOLID LINE — APRIL 1915
BROKEN LINE — END OF 1915
0 30 60 90 120 150 180 MILES.

RUMANIA

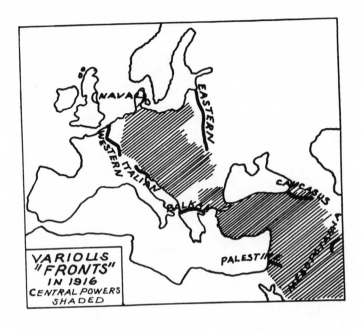

VARIOUS "FRONTS" IN 1916 CENTRAL POWERS SHADED

NAVAL

EASTERN

WESTERN

ITALIAN

BALKAN

CAUCASUS

PALESTINE

MESOPOTAMIA

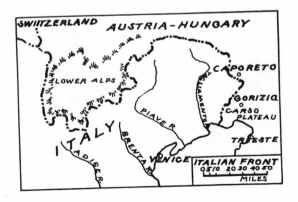

SWITZERLAND AUSTRIA—HUNGARY

LOWER ALPS

CAPORETO

GORIZIA

CARSO PLATEAU

TAGLIAMENTO

ITALY

PIAVE

BRENTA R.

ADIGE R.

VENICE

TRIESTE

ITALIAN FRONT

0 5 10 20 30 40 50
MILES

importance in naval warfare. Germany was able to raid the seas with submarines, although her fleet was bottled up at its base by the British Navy. Scores of these slipped by the Allied blockade and raised havoc with Allied shipping. The submarine warfare increased steadily for two years, annoying neutral traders and alarming England about her food-supply.

SUMMARY OF THE YEAR 1915

The Central Powers definitely improved their situation in 1915. Their concentration on Russia had resulted in victory. The Russian Army was no longer a menace, although Russia's line was still intact. In the Near East, the Central Powers dominated the Balkans with a new ally, Bulgaria. Serbia was out of commission. Russia was still isolated after the disastrous Gallipoli campaign. Italy had joined the Allies, but was not doing much. The Allied triple attack had accomplished little to offset these defeats.

THE WESTERN FRONT IN 1916

As in 1914, Falkenhayn centered his efforts on the Western Front in 1916, confident that the defeated Russians would not bother him that year. The Allies had planned an offensive for the spring in the form of a triple concerted attack on the Western, Eastern, and Italian Fronts, but again the Germans acted too quickly for them.

VERDUN—On February 21st, the Germans utterly surprised the French by a terrific bombardment of Verdun, the key position of the French right flank. With the same powerful artillery as in Poland, the

Germans hoped to blast their way past Verdun for a real "break-through." They knew that after the fall of the Belgian fortresses the Verdun fortifications had been neglected. In spite of the withering fire, the French troops stood fast and abandoned only the outer positions. In contrast to the Belgians at Liége, they had combined the trench and fortress system. Strangely enough, not even the concrete gave way. "They shall not pass" was the vow of the garrison under the able leadership of Petain and later Nivelle. The German artillery mowed down the French infantry until gradually the French brought up enough guns to answer the Germans. Then, in their turn, massed infantry attacks of the Germans were mowed down. Tens of thousands were sacrificed, partly to save the reputation of the Crown Prince, who was in nominal command. The Germans finally gave up in July, when the Allies relieved the city with their long-planned triple attack.

THE SOMME—The main action of this triple attack on the Western Front was known as the Battle of the Somme. It was fought from July to November on the British sector in Flanders. A "break-through" seemed entirely possible at times, for the British now had much more ammunition, but the attack died down in the autumn without accomplishing anything decisive.

WAR OF ATTRITION—The wholesale slaughter at Verdun and also on the Somme caused the fighting to be termed a "war of attrition" or "wearing-down." Brilliant maneuvering had given way to straight killing. Huge forces were shattered against strong positions. The only way to victory seemed to be the destruction of the enemy's man-power. With the larger populations of the Allies plus the recent adoption of universal conscription in England, such attrition would tell more quickly on Germany. It was the same brutal policy Grant had pursued in 1864.[10]

THE EASTERN FRONT IN 1916

RUSSIANS AGAIN IN GALICIA—In her share of the Allied triple attack, Russia surprised the world in June by a magnificent come-back. Six months earlier, her routed armies had been thrown far to the eastward. Falkenhayn, as we know, expected no trouble from that quarter during the year. But, just before the Verdun offensive died down, the Russians made their third attack all along the Austrian line. They wisely did not try East Prussia and the northern German sector again. Brusiloff, again commanding in Galicia, repeated his former gains. Attacking from the Pripet Marshes southward, he advanced steadily throughout the summer and once more almost went over the crest of the Carpathians.

GERMANS AGAIN SAVE AUSTRIA—Again Hindenburg and Ludendorff had to rescue Austria from a perilous position by sending German troops to stiffen her resistance. The Russian offensive lost momentum and practically stopped by the end of the summer. The Russians had shown marvelous bravery, especially considering their handicaps—corruption and treachery behind the lines, and a munitions shortage at the front. Their losses had been enormous, and the Revolution was fast approaching. It was their last appearance in force.

ROMANIA—At the end of August, Romania joined the Allies and prepared to invade Austria-Hungary as a sort of left wing to Brusiloff's army. She came in too late, as the Russians were nearly through and the Germans were free to concentrate on her. The

[10] See p. 258.

Germans overran her in short order, and she had to make a separate peace.

OTHER FRONTS IN 1916

THE ITALIAN FRONT—The plan of the triple Allied attack did not work out on the Italian front either in 1916, as here too the Central Powers got in the first offensive. While the Germans were at Verdun, the Austrians came down from their mountains and made a threatening invasion of northern Italy. Then came the Russian offensive against the Austrians in Galicia—the third side of the triple attack—and that saved Italy. In August, the Italians at last took the offensive, and in three days captured the city of Gorizia. This was their first victory, and its importance was overestimated. A rough plateau was still ahead of them, and by another month their drive had been slowed up.

THE CAUCASUS—Far out in Asia there were two Allied campaigns. The Russians attacked Turkey from the east in the Caucasus and finally took the stronghold of Erzerum. This was too far from the main theater of action to have any decisive influence.

KUT-EL-AMARA—Farther south came an Allied defeat that had a greater moral effect. From India, a British force under Townshend pushed up the Tigris into Mesopotamia in order to police that region and protect the oil-fields. Encouraged by their easy progress, they went too far. Townshend was surrounded by the Turks in the river town of Kut-el-Amara and forced to surrender after a three months' siege.

JUTLAND—The only great naval battle of the

war was fought in the North Sea off Jutland. The German cruiser squadron and battle-fleet came out from its base at Kiel, but were soon located by the British. The running fight on May 31st was a tactical victory for the Germans, who outmaneuvered the British and sank several ships. But the British claimed a strategical victory, for the German fleet never again sallied forth after this battle.

NEW FEATURES IN 1916

TANKS—The Battle of the Somme saw the introduction of a new instrument of war. This was the tank, the "motor fort" moved by caterpillar traction of which we heard in connection with tactics. Tanks made surprise attacks possible by dispensing with preliminary bombardments. They were a big moral as well as a physical support to the infantry. Like gas, tanks produced no decisive results at first, but they did reduce the infantry losses. It was not until late in 1917 at Cambrai that tanks won a victory of their own.

SUMMARY OF THE YEAR 1916

The year 1916 had seen about equal gains and losses on both sides. The Germans had failed at Verdun and the British had gained little on the Somme. The Russians had made big progress against the Austrians again, but were finally stopped by the Germans, who had next put Romania out of the war. President Wilson, when he inquired about possible peace terms at the end of 1916, found that the Allies were determined to fight the war to a finish.

PLANS FOR 1917

For the second time the Allies planned a triple concerted attack on the three main fronts for 1917. They were doomed to disappointment, and 1917 was for them the blackest year of the war. The Eastern and Italian Fronts collapsed, while the repeated Allied efforts on the Western Front accomplished little. The entry of the United States on the Allied side could not for many months offset the loss of Russia.

THE WESTERN FRONT IN 1917

THE HINDENBURG LINE—Early in the year, the British assembled a vast quantity of munitions and men in their sector. But their blow fell on empty air. Hindenburg and Ludendorff were now in chief command of the Germans. They decided that the irregular trench lines in the western half of the front, principally opposite the British, were not worth holding. Instead, they prepared a powerful new line some distance to the rear. It was shorter, and could be defended with fewer men. It was the new type of "elastic defense" which we studied in tactics.[11] No regular narrow line was to be held rigidly; the new positions were deep and yielding. The enemy might make some penetration easily, but unless he did it on a very wide front, he would be caught in flank without accomplishing anything. The Germans retired unmolested to this new "Hindenburg Line" with its concrete "pill-boxes" during February, leaving their old positions defended with a skeleton force. When the British attacked, they pushed this aside and made rapid, almost unopposed advances.

[11] See p. 89.

All seemed to be going well when they suddenly came up against the Hindenburg Line. On April 9th Haig, the British commander, attacked this line in what is called the Battle of Arras. Severe fighting lasted nearly a month until Haig realized the futility of further effort.

NIVELLE'S FAILURE—Meanwhile, the French had launched a great offensive in the center of the Western Front between Soissons and Rheims. This is the same region which we shall study in detail later as the Marne Salient of 1918. Nivelle had replaced Joffre in the French command and had promised great things with this drive, popularly known as the "drive to end the war." This Second Battle of the Aisne was a ghastly failure, for the Germans had been forewarned. They quickly repulsed the attacks, inflicting such heavy casualties that the French abandoned their offensive. Nivelle was replaced by Petain, the original defender of Verdun. The French had hoped for so much from this drive that its failure led to profound depression. Serious mutinies broke out along the French front. By the end of the year, the French morale was somewhat restored when Petain captured the Chemin des Dames, a very strong position in the region of Nivelle's failure.

MESSINES RIDGE AND FLANDERS—The British made three more attacks during the year. At one point their lines were dominated by the Germans on Messines Ridge. The British blasted away the ridge with a million pounds of high explosive, but won only a local success. Then, between August and November, they attacked in the Battle of Flanders at the extreme western end of the line near the sea, hoping, among other things, to get the German submarine bases, Ostend and Zeebrugge. Again it was the usual thing—early gains, heavy losses, and a return to the "war of attrition."

CAMBRAI—In the last days of November they did inflict a big surprise on the Germans in the Battle of Cambrai. Instead of warning the enemy with a preliminary artillery bombardment, they sent a fleet of tanks just ahead of the infantry, breaking down the wire and machine-gun nests. But it was the story of the first German gas-attack repeated. The local success was complete, and the British drove a wedge into the German lines. But they were not prepared to follow their advantage with force. Before the year was over, the Germans had returned to most of their original positions. There seemed to be a deadlock on the Western Front.

THE EASTERN FRONT IN 1917

THE RUSSIAN REVOLUTION—The main event here in 1917 was the collapse of Russia. We recall at what a cost in human life the Russian advances in Galicia had been purchased. The soldiers were now tired of trying to pull down barbed wire entanglements with their bare hands and meeting German machine-guns with clubbed rifles. In March the Czar's government was easily overthrown. The Revolution was so orderly that the Allies took it as a good sign. They felt that the treacherous German influences in Petrograd were ended. Russia might make even greater efforts. But the army discipline went completely to pieces, with the death-penalty for insubordination abolished, and the soldiers debating whether or not to obey orders.

RUSSIA'S LAST GASP—Kerensky, who headed the new government during the summer, stirred up the Army for a final flare of energy. This was Russia's share of the triple Allied attack. Once more a feverish onslaught pushed the Austrians back into Galicia. But again the Germans stiffened the Austrian line and stopped what proved to be Russia's last gasp of effort. The Central Powers did not dare withdraw all their troops yet from the Eastern Front because another flare-up might come at any minute. Yet they did not take the offensive lest they provoke any more revivals in Russia's fast disintegrating army.

RUSSIA OUT—BREST LITOVSK—In November came a more radical revolution in Russia. The Bolshevists or Reds seized control of the government. They believed in peace, and were ready to stop fighting at once. On December 17th, they agreed to an armistice, which was later confirmed in the treaty of Brest Litovsk. Russia withdrew from the war and ceded considerable territory to Germany. The Central Powers now had a vast new region from which to draw supplies. Still more important, Germany was enabled to release some 600,000 men for a concentrated effort on the Western Front. Austria, too, could center her energies on the Italians.

OTHER FRONTS IN 1917

ITALIAN OVERCONFIDENCE—A most surprising collapse occurred on the Italian Front this year, also. The Italians had started the year by making good advances against the Austrians both in the mountains and near the coast, as their part of the Allied triple attack. Cadorna, the commander, went confidently ahead in both regions, but he grew careless. An unprotected gap appeared between the two sections of his army. This did not escape the enemy. By autumn, they were able to withdraw many German and Austrian troops from the collapsing Eastern Front. A huge concentration of men and guns was prepared behind this gap at Caporetto.

CAPORETTO—On October 24th Hindenburg struck. Within three weeks, the Italians lost all they had gained in two and one-half years. Venice itself was threatened by the enemy advance. Only the chance rising of a river to flood height saved the Italians from further disaster. Cadorna was replaced by a new leader, Diaz. Italy, instead of being an asset to distract the enemy from other fronts, now had to be reinforced by her allies.

MESOPOTAMIA—Only from Asia could the Allies draw any comfort. There the British were conducting their second and third campaigns against Turkey. One force, under Maude, invaded Mesopotamia, where Townshend had been captured in 1916. Maude had enough men this time and took Bagdad in March. It was hoped that a Russian Caucasus expedition would join with him to cut Turkey in two, but just then came the Russian Revolution. The British continued on toward the oil-fields of Mosul.

PALESTINE—Meanwhile the British were also invading Palestine under Allenby. They were aided in this by the Arabs, who were roused against their Turkish masters by the famous Lawrence. On December 9th, Jerusalem surrendered to Allenby. Its fall had no great strategical or tactical significance, but the moral effect was considerable at a time when everything else looked black for the Allies.

UNRESTRICTED SUBMARINE WARFARE—The German Navy this same year thought it had found a way to end the war—through *unrestricted* submarine warfare. Having assumed the general military defensive on land, the Germans left the 1917 offensive to the U-boats. They planned to sink every ship inside a danger zone surrounding the British Isles. It was a clever plan, and nearly succeeded. England was absolutely dependent on outside nations for food, so it seemed a chance to starve her into submission. The German submarines had been active, as we know, since 1915, but hitherto they had shown some consideration for neutral rights. Now they simply torpedoed at sight. An appalling amount of British and neutral shipping was sunk.

AMERICA ENTERS THE WAR—This brought America into the war. The nation's indignation had been rising ever since the *Lusitania* was sunk in 1915. President Wilson had written notes in protest, but the sinkings had continued. American ships, cargoes, and lives were lost. The announcement of unrestricted submarine warfare at the beginning of February was accompanied by an insulting provision allowing one American ship a week. Then it was discovered that Germany was plotting in Mexico. On April 6, 1917, the United States declared war on Germany. That did not worry the Germans much for the time being. They knew of our little army and our unpreparedness. They felt that we could not train enough real soldiers to make any difference, and could not get them across the Atlantic anyway. We have seen already how America finally gathered and trained 4,800,000 men.[12] But it was more than a year before the American Expeditionary Force in France saw real action. General Pershing went across with the nucleus of a staff late in May. On October 21st, the first American troops went into training in a quiet sector of the front line, and two days later fired their first shot. But at the close of 1917, there were scarcely 150,-

[12] See pp. 168, 188.

ooo Americans in France, and they were still learning the business of war.

SUMMARY OF THE YEAR 1917

The Allied situation at the end of 1917 was more dismal than it had been at any time in the war. With Russia definitely out, the Central Powers could concentrate their efforts in the west. Italy had proved a broken reed, and had to be helped. Great things had been expected from the drives on the Western Front, but they had failed. England had been threatened with starvation by the unrestricted submarine campaign. The European armies and peoples were thoroughly weary after more than three years of war with no prospect of an early end. With one big nation collapsed, it was a question of how long the others would stand the strain. There was one ray of hope for the Allies—the entrance of the United States. Yet it remained to be seen whether or not she could get adequate trained forces to France in time to offset the additional German troops released by Russia's withdrawal.

THE WESTERN FRONT IN 1918, THROUGH ST. MIHIEL

THE GERMAN "PEACE DRIVE"—Ludendorff hoped to end the war with a gigantic "Peace Drive" in the spring of 1918. The idea was not new—Germany had tried it at Verdun in 1916, and the French in 1917. But Ludendorff had several causes for optimism. In the first place, Germany would have a superiority of numbers on the Western Front. The man-power of France and England was pretty well exhausted after the heavy drives of the preceding year, while Germany had her extra troops released from the Eastern Front. The Germans had, moreover, worked out a new plan of attack. They had already tried the new elastic, deep defense. Now they applied the same principle to the attack. Instead of a concentrated mass attack against the enemy trench system, they practised what was called "infiltration," which we studied under tactics.[13] Under cover of a gas and smoke screen, detached units were to penetrate through and behind the enemy positions. Behind them would be successive waves to go on through, honeycombing the enemy defenses. This combination of numerical superiority and the new system of tactics nearly brought victory. It was a case of "now or never" with the Germans. The population was already beginning to murmur. Only promises of victory held them in line.

1. BATTLE OF PICARDY—The "Peace Drive" started on March 21, 1918, with what Pershing called "by far the most formidable force the world had ever seen." Ludendorff attacked the British in the Somme region. This was near the junction of the British and French lines. If the attack should be successful, communications between those two Allies could be cut, and the British rolled back toward the sea. The sector was held by one weak British army. The first day, its thirty-two divisions were attacked by sixty-four German divisions. The "infiltration" methods broke the British line and left a six-mile gap. The Germans pushed ahead until they had occupied a large salient, threatening the vital railroad center at Amiens. The drive was stopped only when the French threw in the troops they had been saving for a counter-attack. This Battle of Picardy was the most successful of the five German drives between March 21 and July 18, 1918.

[13] See p. 65.

SUPREME ALLIED COMMAND—In the midst of this crisis before Amiens, when it looked as though the British and French lines would be torn apart, the Allies in their peril took a very wise step. For the first time, they selected one supreme commander instead of acting as several separate forces. Marshal Foch, who had shown his ability at the Marne, became generalissimo of the Allied forces with full authority over the national commanders, Petain, Haig, Pershing, and Diaz. He was able to transfer troops of any nation to that part of the line where they were most needed. The principle of simplicity demanded such a step, but it took the Battle of Picardy to enforce it.

2. BATTLE OF THE LYS—The second German attack was the Battle of the Lys from April 9th to 27th. They fell upon the other end of the British lines, near their junction with the Belgians farther west in Flanders. There they drove in a smaller salient. After which there was quiet for a month.

3. THIRD BATTLE OF THE AISNE—On May 27th came the dangerous third attack—the Third Battle of the Aisne. This fell upon the Chemin des Dames between Soissons and Rheims, won by Petain the preceding autumn. Breaking through the supposedly impregnable lines, the Germans advanced almost unopposed for thirty miles in three days until they reached the Marne. Here, at Château-Thierry, they were within striking distance of Paris. It was here that the Americans fought their first major action in checking the advance. We shall study this Marne Salient in detail in the next chapter.[14]

4. NOYON—MONTDIDIER—The fourth German attack, on June 9th, was the least successful of the five. The Marne Salient was too deep and narrow

[14] See pp. 336, 337.

for comfort and safety, so they tried to join it with the Amiens Salient by blows at the northwest corner, between Noyon and Montdidier. They made slight advances, but did not widen the salient. Again there was a month of quiet while they massed all their resources for the final blow.

CRITICAL SITUATION FOR ALLIES—Now that the World War is over and won, the Allied victory may seem to have been a foregone conclusion. But it did not look that way at the Allied headquarters around the 1st of June. There were only 168 Allied divisions to withstand the attacks of 208 German divisions. (The fighting strength of a division was about 10,000 men, except the American division, which numbered 27,000.) The British and French had almost no more reserves. On June 12th, the Allied premiers reported:

"General Foch has presented to us a statement of the utmost gravity . . . as there is no possibility of the British and French increasing the numbers of their divisions, there is great danger of the war being lost unless the numerical inferiority of the Allies can be remedied by the advent of American troops."

AMERICANS AVAILABLE—About 600,000 American troops were then in France, and they kept coming at the rate of about 250,000 a month. Both the Germans and the Allies had been skeptical of the ability of these hastily trained troops. It was thought that they might be as worthless as the Portuguese, who melted away when first attacked. But on May 28th the Americans had shown their mettle by capturing Cantigny in a well-executed local offensive, and during the next week they had helped to check the German advance around Château-

Thierry. Then it was realized that the American forces were more than mere numbers and could be of real value to the Allies.

5. SECOND BATTLE OF THE MARNE—The crisis grew acute on July 15th, when the Germans launched their fifth and final drive to widen the Marne Salient. American troops near Château-Thierry and Rheims, as we shall see later, helped the French to check this in the Second Battle of the Marne.[15]

ALLIED COUNTER-ATTACK—Then the tide turned. On July 18th, Foch launched his great counter-offensive. The opening blow was struck by the Americans and French near Soissons.[16] They imperiled the German communications in the Marne Salient, forcing the Germans to evacuate. It was the beginning of the end. The effect was tremendous in Germany as well as in France. The German Chancellor revealed the importance of that turn of the tide. "At the beginning of July, 1918, I was convinced, I confess it, that before the first of September' our adversaries would send us peace proposals," he said. "We expected grave events in Paris for the end of July. That was on the 15th. On the 18th even the most optimistic among us understood that all was lost. The history of the world was played out in those three days."

REDUCING THE SALIENTS—Once the tide had turned, the Allies kept on advancing. One could not have a better illustration of the principle of movement. Once he had seized the initiative, Foch did not give the Germans a minute's rest. His first plan was to flatten all the salients which the Germans had driven into the Allied line. By the first week in August, the French and Americans had reduced the

[15] See pp. 343–345.
[16] See pp. 345–354.

Marne Salient. On August 8th, the British and French started a drive which recovered what they had lost in the Battle of Picardy in March and April. Later in the month, they regained the land lost in the second German drive on the Lys in Flanders.

AMERICAN FIRST ARMY—The Americans for the first time now secured an official army of their own. This was a result of Pershing's firm stand. The British and French wanted to incorporate the Americans in their own units as replacements. In the emergency of June and July, the Americans had fought wherever they were most needed, some with the British, others with the French. Now, the American First Army was given a sector of its own in the southeastern part of the Western Front. This particular sector was assigned so that the Americans could bring their men and supplies from the ports of southeastern France without disturbing the French and British supply system.

ST. MIHIEL—The first work assigned to this new separate American Army, which included some French under its command, was the reduction of the St. Mihiel Salient just east of Verdun. It had existed since the beginning of the war. With overwhelming numbers, the Americans quickly flattened it on September 12th and 13th. That was the last of the big bulges.

OTHER FRONTS IN 1918

BULGARIA OUT—Germany's allies on the other fronts collapsed before the Western Front finally gave way. The Balkans had been a Central Powers' stronghold throughout most of the war. Serbia had been put out of the fight in 1915 and Romania in

1916. Now Greece had come into the war on the
Allied side and Serbia had revived. The long-idle
Saloniki army, in coöperation with the Greeks and
Serbs, attacked the Bulgarians late in September.
Within a week, Bulgaria had surrendered, the first
of the Central Powers, and signed an armistice on
September 30th.

TURKEY OUT—Turkey followed just a month
later. Allenby's Palestine drive, which had captured
Jerusalem late in 1917, thoroughly routed the Turkish Army in September. Nazareth and Damascus
quickly fell. The British had Turkey at their mercy.
On the last day of October, Turkey surrendered un-
conditionally.

AUSTRIA OUT—Austria was next. The Italians attacked the Austrians late in October. In five days
they had broken the enemy defenses and the Austrians were in full retreat. They, too, signed an
armistice which was a practical surrender on November 3d.

THE FINAL DRIVE ON THE WESTERN FRONT

"THE ADVANCE TO VICTORY"—By the middle of
September, the Allies had wiped out the salients
created by the Germans. Foch now kept straight
on, following literally the principle of movement.
He devised a series of heavy attacks all along the
line, so that the Germans could not concentrate a
defense. In the last week in September, three big
drives started: the Americans in the Meuse-Argonne
region, the French through Champagne, and the
British and Belgians farther to the westward.

THE MEUSE-ARGONNE—The Americans faced
their hardest task in this rugged Meuse-Argonne
region, north of Verdun. It was a long and intricate

DOVER

ANTWERP

OSTEND
BELGIUM
FLANDERS
CALAIS
YPRES
BRUSSELS
BOULOGNE
MONS
ARTOIS
VIMY
ARRAS
CAMBRAI
MAUBEUGE
NAMUR
LIEGE
AIX LA CHAPELLE
COLOGNE
GERMANY
COBLENZ

SOMME
AMIENS

MONTDIDIER
SEDAN

COMPIEGNE
AISNE
SOISSONS
RHEIMS
VERDUN
CHATEAUTHIERRY
CHAMPAGNE
METZ
LORRAINE
PARIS
MEAUX
MARNE
TOUL
STRASSBURG
ALSACE
FRANCE
EPINAL
VOSGES
BELFORT

WESTERN FRONT
BATTLE LINE AT END OF 1916.
(TYPICAL FOR MOST OF WAR)
REGIONAL NAMES UNDERLINED
0   50 100 150 200 250 300
MILES

campaign through rough country with stubborn German resistance all the way, for their vital communications were at stake. The Americans had nearly reached Sedan when the war ended. The French Champagne drive was just to the west of the Americans and reached Sedan. Still farther westward, the British smashed the Hindenburg Line and continued to advance.

GERMAN COLLAPSE AND ARMISTICE—Foch thus had the initiative all along the line. He was at his best in this "forward" type of fighting, and gave the enemy no rest. The German Army as a whole did not collapse. In most cases, it fought stubbornly and heroically all the way back in its long retreat. But behind the Army, the German population revolted. They had been promised victory in the spring, and it had not come. They were "fed up" and disillusioned with the war. President Wilson's Fourteen Points had made them more ready to give in. On November 7th, mutiny broke out in the German Navy at Kiel. Two days later the Kaiser abdicated. The Germans immediately signed an armistice, and on November 11th, at 11 A. M., the fighting of the World War ended.

SUMMARY—Many were surprised that the war stopped so suddenly. The Allies had been making plans for a great drive in the spring of 1919, not realizing that Germany's defenses and morale would crumble so quickly. The outcome of the war had not been a foregone conclusion. Germany had come within an ace of winning it at the very beginning, and the situation in the spring and early summer of 1918 had been equally grave. The millions of fresh American troops took the heart out of the Germans, once it was shown that they could fight. Nevertheless, when one thinks of what the French and English went through for four years, it is idle to boast that "America won the war."

The World War had far surpassed all previous contests in its magnitude. It was a real contest of peoples against peoples. No one man dominated it as Napoleon had the European battle-fields a century earlier. Foch and Ludendorff stand out above the others, but the war was more an endurance contest than a matter of brilliant strategical maneuvering, except for the few months at the very beginning and the end. The long struggle produced many new developments in the art of warfare, and military scientists are still studying and trying to apply its lessons. But above all, the World War was a tremendous catastrophe from which Europe will not recover for many years.

CHAPTER XIV

THE MARNE SALIENT AND ITS
REDUCTION

The American Expeditionary Force received its
real baptism of fire in and around the Marne Salient. This was a huge dent or pocket, roughly
twenty-five miles in width and depth, between Soissons and Rheims in the very center of the Western
Front. The Marne Salient lasted only ten weeks,
but it was decidedly important during its brief existence. It was here that the dramatic turning-point
of the war occurred. In creating the salient, the
Germans threatened to win the war with their last
tremendous efforts. In reducing it, the Allies started
a counter-offensive which ended only with the Armistice. Some 270,000 Americans fought in this Aisne-
Marne area, alongside many French and a few
British and Italians, under French higher command.
The Americans saw action in many parts of the
Aisne-Marne area, but in two places their fighting
had particular significance. Around Château-
Thierry, at the salient's tip, they helped to stop
the Germans both when the salient was created and
again when an attempt was made to extend it. Then
they had a leading part in the Soissons offensive
which marked the beginning of the end for Germany.

The Marne Salient in general and the Soissons

attack in particular will be the subject of this chapter. The Marne Salient seems better suited to such special treatment than the other two great actions of the American Expeditionary Force—the reduction of the St. Mihiel Salient and the Meuse-Argonne offensive. The former had less strategical significance, while the latter was too intricate for adequate description in this short space.

THE FOUR "BATTLES"—The fighting in the Aisne-Marne area included four separate major operations or "battles" between May 27 and August 6, 1918. Their relation to the five German 1918 offensives was as follows:

German Offensives (Popular names)	Aisne-Marne Area (Official U. S. designations)	Dates
1. Battle of Picardy (Amiens)		Mar. 21–Apr. 6
2. Battle of the Lys		Apr. 9–27
3. 3d Battle of the Aisne	1. Aisne Defensive	May 27–June 3
4. Noyon-Montdidier Attack	2. Noyon-Montdidier Defensive	June 9–15
5. 2d Battle of the Marne	3. Champagne-Marne Defensive	July 15–18
	4. Aisne-Marne Offensive	July 18–Aug. 6

Thus, three of the four Aisne-Marne operations were connected with the Germans' final efforts. In the first, they drove in the salient. In the second, the least important, they tried to widen it by blows at the northwest corner. In the third, they made a last immense effort to extend it by blows in the southeast corner and to the eastward. That had scarcely stopped when the Allies began the fourth operation by striking at Soissons and then pushing the Germans out of the salient.[1]

THE AISNE DEFENSIVE—CREATION OF THE SALIENT

THE CHEMIN DES DAMES—Before this fighting started, the battle-line in this area ran fairly straight from Noyon to Rheims. Along the center ran the Chemin des Dames, which the French had captured late in 1917. Their position on this road, five miles north of the Aisne, rested on successive rows of hills and was considered almost impregnable. Foch felt that the Germans would not attack such a strong position, so he stripped it of most of its defenders, sending them westward toward Amiens, where he expected the third German offensive. The Chemin des Dames became a sort of rest sector, guarded by only about eleven tired French and British divisions.

THE SURPRISE ATTACK—But for once Foch guessed wrong. With the greatest secrecy, the Germans massed forty-two divisions and 4,000 guns against this thinly manned sector. The Allies suspected nothing until it was too late to bring up reserves. At dawn on May 27th, the Germans launched an infiltration attack which honeycombed the Allied lines and kept going. By noon, they had crossed the Aisne, and before nightfall had reached the Vesle. The Allied defense was so shot to pieces that the Germans advanced almost unhindered. By

[1] See pp. 328–330.

May 30th, Soissons had fallen. To the southward, the Germans were at the Marne. Thirty miles in three days—that was a record for a Western Front offensive. They had not planned or expected to go so far, but once started, the Marne Salient simply grew.

GRAVE SITUATION FOR ALLIES—The situation could not have been much graver for the Allies. Once at the Marne, the Germans would be able to swing westward toward Paris, fifty miles away. And what was to stop them from doing this? The Allied forces in the area had been too weak to hold the fifty-five miles of straight line between Noyon and Rheims. Now they had ninety miles to guard— two sides of a triangle. Their line was stretched out to the limit. Gaps appeared between the units—the whole defense was in danger of cracking. Reserves were needed desperately. But where could they be had? Foch hurried back the reserves he had massed in the Amiens area, but that took time. France and England had no prospect of raising new divisions.

THE AMERICAN REINFORCEMENT—This was the desperate situation when the Americans came into their first important action. The Allies had a crying need for more men, and there were 600,000 Americans in France. But the Allied high command questioned whether they could be counted upon to hold the line in such a crisis. Just then, the Americans showed that they could. The day after the Germans struck the Chemin des Dames, the American First Division captured Cantigny, just to the westward, and successfully beat off local counterattacks. That settled the question. American divisions could be depended upon to fill in the cracks in the over-taut defense line in the Marne Salient.

SITUATION AROUND CHÂTEAU-THIERRY—Two

American regular divisions were rushed to the vicinity of Château-Thierry, where the Germans were threatening to cross the Marne and to head westward for Paris. One of these divisions was the Second—half regulars and half Marines. It had spent some time in a quiet trench sector near St. Mihiel. The other was the Third, all regulars, who had never even been in the front line. Both of these divisions did important work in stopping the German advance.

THE THIRD AT THE MARNE CROSSINGS—The Third was scattered among the French troops holding the line of the Marne from Château-Thierry to Jaulgonne Bend, six miles eastward. The Germans were trying hard to cross to the south bank of the Marne at both those points. The first unit of the Third to see action was a motorized machine-gun battalion which reached Château-Thierry on May 31st, in time to help the French defend the bridges. Another part of the Third was hurried to Jaulgonne Bend. There, too, they helped the French repel a German crossing.

THE SECOND ON THE PARIS ROAD—Then, just to the northwest of Château-Thierry, it was necessary to plug up the French defense line covering the main highway to Paris, north of the Marne. The Second was thrown across this road. Hastily digging little shelter-pits, they met the Germans with steady rifle-fire. The German offensive finally stopped on the 3d of June. For a while, at least, the Paris road was safe. So, too, was the south bank of the Marne.

BELLEAU WOOD AND VAUX—The Second Division was immediately given a harder job in that same locality. When the drive stopped, the Germans had the advantage of high and wooded ground on either side of the Paris road, particularly at Belleau Wood and on Hill 204 above Vaux. The French high command gave the Second Division the task of improving the line by capturing these points. This took several weeks. On June 4th, the Marine brigade, north of the road, made its famous attack through the wheat-fields toward Belleau Wood, where the German machine-guns took a terrific toll. But the position was finally taken. The brigade of regulars showed equal heroism when they carried Vaux by storm on July 1st. The division suffered nearly 10,000 casualties—almost half its fighting strength. While Belleau Wood has become famous, this work had no great strategical importance. It was a purely local offensive, not a part of the four major operations. A slip of the censor gave the public the impression that all this work around Château-Thierry was done "with the help of God and a few Marines." The Marine brigade did its full share, but so, too, did the regular Army infantry.

THE MARNE SALIENT

A DEEP, NARROW SALIENT—The Marne Salient, or "Château-Thierry Pocket," created by the Third Battle of the Aisne, was a deep and narrow wedge jutting into the Allied lines. If a salient is to be stable and safe, its base should be at least twice its depth. The Marne Salient was roughly twenty-five miles deep on an average, with a base of only thirty-seven miles. The Germans, during the battle, had been able to go forward almost unopposed to the Marne, but on either flank the Allied defenses held fast. The fortress system of Rheims protected the northeast corner, while the dense forest of Compiègne had prevented an advance in the northwest.

NO REGULAR TRENCH SYSTEM—This new section of the battle-line, almost twice as long as the original defenses, did not become a regular, conventional trench system. The Germans, hoping to move on again shortly, did not take the time or trouble to dig elaborate trenches, lay much barbed wire, or construct concrete "pill-boxes" to any extent. They established hundreds of temporary machine-gun nests and artillery emplacements, but the fighting in this area was more open than the trench warfare of the earlier years.

ALLIED ORGANIZATION—The Allies gathered troops around this sector as fast as possible. The three army commanders, Mangin, Degoutte, and Gouraud, on the west, south and east respectively, were all French. So too were the corps commanders until the American First Army Corps was given a sector on July 4th. These corps, each of which had a specific sector, consisted of a headquarters (commander and staff) and certain organic "corps troops" such as artillery, aviation, signal corps, and the like. An "army" was similar, containing at least two corps. Each corps contained at least two divisions, but these were not permanently assigned to it. French, British, American, or Italian divisions might be shifted into or out of a corps as units. The divisions of the different armies were interchangeable since the establishing of supreme Allied command in March. Thus, after Soissons, the American First Division was relieved by Scots, and the Second by French. Some of the American troops were split up into even smaller units than divisions and scattered among the Allied troops around the salient. Pershing's plan for a separate American Army had to be postponed in the emergency. There were altogether about 500,000 Allied troops outside the salient and an equal number of Germans inside.

SERIOUS RAILROAD SITUATION—The trouble was that the Allies did not have men enough for so much space, while the Germans did not have space enough for so many men. The salient had good and bad features for both sides. It gave the Germans a jumping-off place for a new attack across the Marne or toward Paris, and they were also in a position to threaten the important French rail connections to the eastward. But the long, narrow salient also had its disadvantages for them. Their 500,000 men had to be moved, fed, and supplied with munitions over a very inadequate and insecure transportation system. The only railroad leading from the German lines into the salient passed through Soissons, which was dangerously near the Allied lines on the northwest corner. From there a single line ran to Fismes and down almost to the Marne. Gasoline was so scarce that trucks could be used only in emergencies. As a result, most of the supplies had to be hauled with horses or mules. The main highway from Soissons to Château-Thierry ran close to the western face of the salient all the way. The Germans made feverish attempts to remedy this by opening another railroad line into the salient, but there was not time to complete it. This was to have been a "cut-off" from one line north of Rheims to another, west of that city.

NOYON-MONTDIDIER—Naturally, the Germans wanted to widen this dangerous pocket before going farther. Their first attempt was in the northwest corner, where they hoped to join the Marne and Amiens Salients. On June 9th, they launched a heavy attack around Noyon and Montdidier, using tremendous quantities of gas. The American

First Division was on the edge of this offensive. The Germans made little progress and quickly abandoned the effort. After that failure, they were quiet for a month, preparing for their final grand offensive.

The Second Battle of the Marne

THE FINAL GERMAN ASSAULT—Having failed to widen the salient on the west, the Germans now tried the east. Rheims itself was too strongly defended for a direct assault—the Germans remembered Verdun. Therefore, they tried to cut the city off by attacking on both sides. One assault was to be made in Champagne, just to the east of Rheims. The other was to be from inside the salient itself on the southern and eastern sides, to cross the Marne and to attack the Heights of Rheims. They set the date for July 15th, the morning after the French national holiday, for the same reason that Washington picked Christmas for his battle of Trenton. Germany massed all possible resources for this final drive and was highly confident of victory. As a matter of fact, she had a right to be. The Second Battle of the Marne was in many ways as critical for the Allies as the first, four years earlier.

REPULSED IN CHAMPAGNE—In Champagne, the Germans gained almost nothing from Gouraud's Fourth Army. A raid at 9:30 P. M. on July 14th netted prisoners who revealed the hour of the German artillery preparation, the hour of the attack, the nature of the formations and objectives, and other valuable information. Consequently, the Allies were able to anticipate the Germans with an artillery bombardment which caught the attackers before they started. Gouraud had adopted an elastic defense, holding the first lines very lightly, so that the force of the German blow fell on empty air, while their regiments were cut to pieces by heavy fire. The American Forty-second Division, National Guard, was among the defenders.

"THE ROCK OF THE MARNE"—In the other half of the drive, the Germans gained some ground against Degoutte's Sixth Army. Massing nearly all their force against the southeast side of the salient, they pushed part way up the Heights of Rheims and threw ten divisions across the Marne. Two companies of the Twenty-eighth Division, Pennsylvania National Guard, were badly cut up in the course of this. But against the American Third Division, still at its old stand between Château-Thierry and Jaulgonne Bend, the Germans made no gains on the south bank of the Marne. One of its regiments, the Thirty-eighth Infantry, guarded the approaches to two very vital roads. Pershing reported very briefly its achievement:

"A single regiment of the 3rd wrote one of the most brilliant pages in our military annals on this occasion. It prevented the crossing at certain points on its front, while on either flank the Germans, who had gained a footing, pressed forward. Our men, firing in three directions, met the German attacks with counter-attacks at critical points, which succeeded in throwing two German divisions into complete confusion, capturing 600 prisoners."

The Third still boasts of the title "The Rock of the Marne."

THE SALIENT DEEPENED—Within three days, the force of the German drive had died down. They had enlarged the salient, to be sure, but not at the corners. They had simply made it deeper, and it was impossible to get ammunition or food to the ten divisions south of the Marne, for the river was covered by Allied artillery. Those hundred thousand marooned men represented Germany's final offensive effort in the World War. A little more, however, and they might have been marching toward Paris.

THE AISNE-MARNE OFFENSIVE

THE ALLIED COUNTER-OFFENSIVE—Now Foch took the offensive himself. He had anticipated the German drive, and was ready with a counter-attack to drive the Germans out of the salient. Hindenburg and Ludendorff had thrown practically all their reserves into the last attack. Foch had saved such few as he had. These included many new American divisions. The Americans had shown what they could do in quiet sectors and on the defensive, but to use them as "shock troops" seemed to him a gamble. Yet with France and England so drained of man-power, this had to be tried.

OPPORTUNITY AT SOISSONS—The center of interest now shifts to the northwest corner of the salient. While Gouraud's Fourth Army in the east and Degoutte's Sixth Army in the south of the salient were holding back the Germans, "Butcher" Mangin's Tenth Army on the west side of the salient was getting ready for the counter-attack. The Germans had stripped this face of the salient of all but eight divisions in order to concentrate for the attack on the opposite side. The remaining corps commanders protested against holding thirty miles of front with 80,000 men, but to no avail. Foch's plan—some say it was Pershing's suggestion—was to strike at Soissons. If Allied artillery could play on the railroad junction there, the salient would be untenable. He planned therefore to close in on the whole western side of the salient, but the "spear-head" for the critical attack was to be the French Twentieth Corps just southwest of Soissons. If Foch had had twenty more divisions in reserve he would have closed in sharply from Rheims, too, trapping the Germans in the pocket. Under the circumstances, the blow at Soissons was all that he could do.

THE "SPEAR-HEAD" CORPS—Three divisions were picked for shock duty in this Twentieth Corps—one French and two American (First and Second, regulars). A new American corps, just organized, had administrative but not tactical control over the American divisions. The French division was the First Moroccan, one of the "crack" shock divisions of their army. One brigade consisted of the famous Foreign Legion. The other had white officers and African men—and the Germans feared those Senegalese more than any one else on the front, it is said. They used knives, in addition to the conventional instruments of war, and supposedly seldom bothered to take prisoners. This division was picked to set the pace for the two American outfits. Altogether, there were 67,000 men in the corps, four fifths of them Americans, because French divisions were smaller.

SURPRISE APPROACH—A complete surprise had created the Marne Salient and complete surprise was to flatten it again. The tired divisions were brought to the scene of action with the greatest possible speed and secrecy. The First had been around Cantigny for some time, and was anticipating rest behind the lines, while the Second was still tired from its terrific work at Belleau Wood and Vaux. The men of the Second trudged or hustled two whole nights without sleep. On the night of the 17th a violent thunderstorm made marching harder, but prevented the German planes from bombing the crowded road and spreading the alarm. The flashes of lightning on that single road jammed with tanks, artillery, trucks, staff cars, and men revealed that it really was a *world* war. There in Europe, alongside the Frenchmen, were the Americans, the black Senegalese from Africa, and the little Asiatic truck-drivers from Indo-China. They seemed tangled in an inextricable mess—and they all had to be on hand at 4:35 the next morning when the attack started. Some of the infantry actually had to double-time into the battle-line to move off with the others. It was a miracle of management and luck that most of the 67,000 men were not still roaming around the Forest of Retz.

THE LINE-UP—The corps attacked on a five-mile front. The Moroccans were in the center, with a narrower sector than the larger American divisions. On their left (to the north) was the First Division with four regiments in line, and on their right the Second with three in line and one in corps reserve. Other French divisions were on either side of this "spear-head" corps. The French One Hundred and Fifty-third Division, on the left of the First, had a particularly difficult assignment. As we shall see, it failed in this, so that the work of the First was greatly increased.

THE TERRAIN—The attack lay over a plateau five or six miles square. On its western side was the Forest of Retz (or Villers-Cotterets) from the edge of which the attack was launched—the Second actually started their fighting in the woods. On the east, the plateau sloped sharply down into the valley of the little River Crise, which joins the Aisne at Soissons. In that valley ran the railroad from Soissons to

Villers-Cotterets and also, what was more important, the main highway from Soissons to Château-Thierry. One objective of the attack was to cut that road. The other was to gain the edge of the plateau on the heights around the town of Berzy-le-Sec. From there, the artillery could fire upon the roads and railroads in Soissons, scarcely three miles away. This original drive was not planned to capture Soissons itself—only to command it with artillery.

Most of the plateau was covered with wheat-fields, with here and there a stone-walled farm-house or hamlet. At that time, the ripe wheat was about breast-high. The going was fairly good in the center, but on the outer edges of the sector were two ravines which cost the attackers hundreds of lives. The Second Division had to contend with the Vierzy ravine, along which they had to fight they way. It ended in Vierzy, where a railroad tunnel gave the Germans a chance for shelter and reinforcements. Much worse than that was the Missy ravine on the extreme north side of the sector. This ran directly across the path of the left brigade of the First, and of the French One Hundred and Fifty-third, who were on their left. We shall see how this Missy ravine slowed up the whole attack and caused terrific casualties in the infantry of the First.

TAKING A CHANCE—The plan of attack was quite different from the conventional trench fighting which had been in style on the Western Front for three years. No longer were there two strong, elaborate rival trench lines protected by barbed wire nor an overwhelming artillery preparation to blast such semi-permanent defenses to pieces. The whole success of Foch's plan depended on complete surprise. A preliminary bombardment would have given the Germans warning to rush up reinforcements, so it was omitted. Simply a rolling barrage was to keep ahead of the infantry as they advanced. Naturally, this was taking a long chance.

"OPEN WARFARE"—Fortunately for the Twentieth Corps and the Allied cause, the Germans had not yet consolidated their position with regular trenches or barbed wire. The salient was still new, and, as we said, they hoped to be moving on toward Paris soon. They were holding the outer lines lightly, depending on rifle-pits, machine-gun emplacements, and batteries of field artillery scattered among the wheat-fields and the little stone farms. This was an extreme form of "yielding defense" without the concrete fixtures of the Hindenburg Line. To deal with the machine-guns in particular, the Allies depended on their fleet of 300 tanks. Whenever the infantry ran up against a bad machine-gun nest, they were to signal for the nearest tank to crush it. Altogether, it was quite a return to open warfare. The horses of the artillery batteries were kept near-by, ready to gallop ahead to new positions, and even cavalry was ready for the hoped-for "breakthrough."

INITIAL SUCCESS—The rolling barrage started at 4:35 A. M. on July 18th. Those guns sounded the first note in the Allied counter-offensive which was to last without interruption until the Armistice four months later. The infantry started at the same time. The Second at the outset had some rough fighting in the forest, but out in the wheat-fields the going was good. Luckily for the infantry, the surprise was complete. Some of the German batteries were overrun within twenty minutes, almost before they had time to start a counter-barrage. The inner brigade of the First advanced three miles in two hours.

THE TIDE TURNS—Those early hours of the Soissons drive marked the turn in the tide of the World War. General Liggett claims that it is "almost possible to fix the instant if not the acre" of that dramatic turning-point. At 10:30 that morning "the war's great divide was topped" when the French artillery secured a position from which it could fire on the railroad junction at Soissons, and the Americans and Moroccans had swept across the plateau to where they could dominate the Soissons-Château-Thierry road.

GERMAN MACHINE-GUNS—But the Soissons attack was by no means over at 10:30 A. M. on July 18th. The grimmest part of the work was still ahead. The Germans had been caught off their guard with a critical part of the salient undermanned. But once the initial surprise was over, the resistance stiffened. Most deadly of all were the machine-guns, strewn through the wheat and around the ravines, so placed that they supported and protected one another. The machine-gunners were the "suicide outfit" of the German Army. They stuck to their guns until some one finally "got" them, but almost every gun had taken a heavy toll of the advancing brown or gray-blue lines before that happened.

CAVALRY—The Allied advance in the center had been so rapid that it looked as though the long-expected "break-through" had come. For years, the Allies had been looking forward to the day when the artillery and infantry should so thoroughly break down the enemy resistance that the cavalry could be sent through to make rapid advances behind the enemy lines. A force of French cuirassiers now advanced to try this. They trotted through their artillery and then, as they came to the forward infantry lines, made a charge. But the German resistance had not been completely broken. Scores of machine-guns played on the unfortunate horsemen, and only a shattered remnant returned.

SECOND DIVISION—VIERZY RAVINE—The infantry on the outer flanks were having a similar experience in the ravines. The Marine regiment of the Second fought its way along the Vierzy ravine until at nightfall it had reached the line set as that day's objective. But they could not rest securely with that, for the railroad tunnel permitted the Germans to bring up fresh reserves under shelter. So the tired troops, who had been marching and fighting for three days without sleep or adequate food, pushed on until they had taken the town of Vierzy and the other end of the tunnel.

FIRST DIVISION—MISSY RAVINE—Even harder was the lot of the Second Brigade of the First Division around the Missy ravine on the north. The sides of this ravine were so steep that the German machine-guns and artillery placed there were not damaged by the Allied barrage. So, when the Americans approached, they were met with a withering fire. They had to go on, forcing their way through the swampy bottom and up the opposite slope. The tanks could give them no help in such rough terrain, but the infantry finally rushed the German positions and advanced beyond the village of Missy-aux-Bois. This flank brigade could not, however, keep pace with the rest of the corps because the One Hundred and Fifty-third French Division was having even more serious trouble farther down the ravine, where it was deeper. They had not been able to get across. Naturally, the American brigade could not advance with its left flank thus exposed. Consequently, at nightfall on the first day, this extreme left brigade was the only one in the Twentieth Corps which had not reached the assigned objective. The other brigade of the First Division had gone ahead in the center, so it, too, had to look out for an exposed left flank.

RESULTS OF FIRST DAY—The first day, on the whole, had been a decided success. The Americans had covered more than half the plateau, but they had to get it all to make their position secure. That night, the Germans were busy rushing guns and men to the threatened sector, concentrating in particular on the high land between Missy-aux-Bois and Berzy-le-Sec. This was their most sensitive point, because Allied artillery there would completely dominate Soissons.

SECOND DAY—SECOND DIVISION—The second day, July 19th, gave the Allies only a fraction of the gains of the previous day, because of the increased German opposition. The Second Division sent in its reserve regiment, which covered the remaining two miles of the plateau, taking the town of Tigny and reaching the Soissons-Château-Thierry road. The Germans put up a fierce fight at that road, and their counter-attacks drove the Marines back to the edge of Tigny. They were able to hold that position, close enough to the road to prevent any further use of that vital highway to the tip of the salient. That night the Second Division was relieved by the French. Their casualities amounted to nearly 5,000, and they had taken about 3,000 prisoners.

SECOND DAY—FIRST DIVISION—The First Division and the Moroccans also advanced on the 19th, in spite of the increasing German opposition. Again, the exposed outer brigade of the First had the hardest time. The heavy concentration of machine-guns in front of Berzy-le-Sec thinned their ranks rapidly. Tanks were rushed to their assistance, but German field-pieces at point-blank range put the tanks out of commission. The Germans had control of the air and were able to warn their troops of the Allied dispositions. By the end of the second day, the hard-worked brigade of the First had finally reached the town of Ploisy at the head of another nasty ravine. Unlike the Second, the First was not relieved that night. It still had some of its hardest work ahead.

THIRD DAY—CHECK AT BERZY—The program for the third day, July 20th, called for the capture of Berzy-le-Sec by the French One Hundred and Fifty-third, while the First Division was to clear the Ploisy ravine and capture an important knoll in front of Berzy. The Americans accomplished their task in spite of murderous fire from German machine-guns and field-pieces which had been left right out in the front lines. The One Hundred and Fifty-third, however, was unable to take Berzy-le-Sec. The Americans tried late in the afternoon, but were driven back.

FOURTH DAY—BERZY TAKEN—The fourth day, July 21st, saw the task accomplished. The artillery laid a heavy barrage on the town, and, although the German field-pieces fired back at point-blank range, the Americans, led by Brigadier-General Buck and his staff in the front lines, carried it by storm. The Americans and Moroccans continued on across the Château-Thierry road toward Buzancy, which was to fall soon afterward. The attack had attained its objective.

HEAVY CASUALTIES—But the victory had been purchased at a very heavy cost. The First Division had 8,363 casualties, including 1,252 killed. The infantry in particular had suffered. Half its enlisted men and three fifths of its officers had fallen. One company came out of the battle with a private in command, while a young captain was the highest surviving officer in the Twenty-sixth Infantry regiment. This was in keeping with the statistics for the American Expeditionary Force as a whole, which showed that the most perilous occupation of all was that of the infantry officer, and next to him, that of the infantry enlisted man. The division had taken 3,500 German prisoners and seventy-five guns. After another twenty-four hours in the sector, the First was relieved by the Fifteenth Scottish Division on the night of June 22d.

AMERICAN IMPETUOSITY—The Americans had advanced faster than the crack Moroccans, but that had a bearing on their casualty list. It was remarked that the French would take a half-day to capture easily what the Americans would carry with a rush in fifteen minutes, paying the price for their swiftness. General Liggett tells how on the first morning of the attack, some one asked the commander of the Moroccans if things were not going well. *"Mais oui,"* he replied, "I weep for the families and sweethearts of these Americans. See how they go into battle as we did in 1914. My division, the flower of the French army, no longer can keep up with them." Ludendorff too paid tribute to the bravery of the Americans on the offensive, saying also that it was mixed with rashness.

STRATEGIC SIGNIFICANCE—The attack at Soissons, like those at Belleau Wood and Vaux, had been a heroic demonstration of American ability and bravery. But unlike those earlier encounters, it was also of the utmost strategic significance. Foch had stolen the initiative from the Germans and did not give it back. Allied artillery now commanded the railroads in Soissons. The Château-Thierry road had been cut. The Germans were forced to abandon the salient as rapidly as possible. All this happened

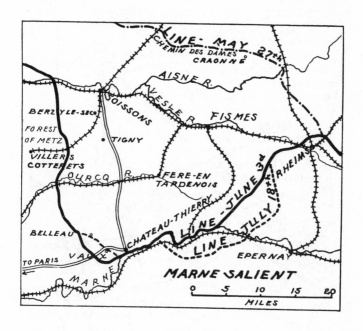

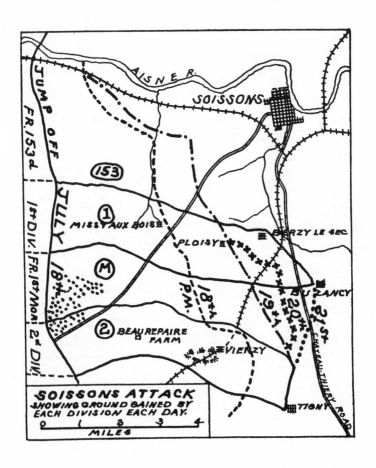

AISNE R.

SOISSONS

JUMP OFF
FR. 153d
JULY 18th
1st DIV. FR. 1st Mor. 2nd Div.

(153)

(1) MISSY AUX BOIS

PLOISY

VERZY LE SEC.

(M)

18th P.M.

19th 20th BUZANCY

21st

(2) BEAUREPAIRE FARM

VIERZY

CHATEAU THIERY ROAD

TIGNY

SOISSONS ATTACK
SHOWING GROUND GAINED BY
EACH DIVISION EACH DAY.

0   1   2   3   4
MILES

within a week after they had launched their own final great offensive. The tide had turned.

REDUCING THE SALIENT—The rest of the story of the reduction of the salient was the Seven Days of 1862 over again. Just as Gaines's Mill determined McClellan's withdrawal, so Soissons forced von Boehm, the German commander, to get out as quickly as possible and with as much as possible. The only difference was that von Boehm *had* to get out, while McClellan merely thought he had to.[2] In each case, there was a stubborn rear-guard action on the part of the withdrawing force, with a series of tactical victories. The Germans wanted to save as much of their material as they could, and the Allies did their best to keep them moving too fast for that. A general pressure was exerted all around the salient, which "collapsed like a punctured balloon." The principal American participation in this was a northwestward drive from the region of Château-Thierry to Fismes on the Vesle. Six divisions took part in this, two at a time. They were the Third and Fourth, regulars, and the Twenty-sixth, Twenty-eighth, Thirty-second, and Forty-second, National Guard. They kept up a constant pressure on the Germans, who resisted stubbornly until they had withdrawn all they could from the threatened region. The first stand was around Le Charmel, to cover the road from Jaulgonne to Fère-en-Tardenois. Then the resistance vanished, to be renewed again at the Ourcq, where the Germans needed five days to evacuate. In spite of repeated American onslaughts, their machine-guns held the position for just five days. Then the line fell back to the Vesle around Fismes, where the German artillery raised havoc until the Americans finally carried the place and sent the Seventy-seventh

[2] See pp. 287–294.

Division, National Army, on across the river. It was Savage Station, Frayser's Farm, and Malvern Hill over again. But the net result was the same. McClellan withdrew from his attack on Richmond, and the Germans abandoned the Marne Salient. By the first week in August, the line ran straight from Rheims to Soissons. The salient had been short-lived, but it had lasted long enough to stage the turning-point of the war and to win a permanent place in American history.

SUGGESTIONS FOR CAMPAIGN REPORTS

One of the most valuable parts of a course in military history is the preparation of a campaign report by every student. This makes it possible for him to study in detail a concrete example of strategy and tactics, and to apply the general principles which he has learned. The reports may be oral or written. In the military history course in the Princeton R. O. T. C. unit, the reports are given orally in groups of about a dozen students. One student delivers an hour's report each week during one term, while the others criticize it. Thus each man becomes acquainted with more than the particular campaign which he himself has studied. The same campaign should not be reported upon more than once in the same group. In other units, where less time is available for this work, written reports may be submitted instead. They should generally be about 3,000 words in length (about ten typewritten pages). The following suggestions will apply equally to oral and written reports.

FINDING THE MATERIAL—After selecting a campaign or operation, the best first step is to consult the encyclopedia, in order to get the setting and the main facts quickly. Information will be found in most cases under the name of the campaign or battle itself, the war in which it occurred, and the principal leaders. Material on Yorktown, for instance, will be found, in the *Encyclopædia Britannica,* under "Yorktown" and also under "American War of Independence," "Washington," "Cornwallis," and "Rochambeau." The next step is to consult the bibliography in this book to find the best readings on the particular campaign and war. To get the proper setting, it is best to look first at one of the general books on the war. The bibliography also indicates the best accounts of the battle or campaign itself, and upon these the main body of the report should be based. These accounts generally include the necessary maps. Finally, the bibliography will also sometimes indicate illustrative material which gives the "atmosphere" of the fighting and can make the report more interesting.

ORGANIZING THE MATERIAL—The report should start with a short introduction showing why the particular campaign is important, and giving its setting in the war in which it occurred. It should compare briefly the ability and reputation of the opposing commanders; the size, quality, and equipment of the rival forces; and any distinctive features of terrain or defense in the theater of operations. The main body of the report should give a clear "play-by-play" account of the campaign itself. This falls into two parts—the strategical approach and the grand tactics of the principal battle or battles. The strategical section should show *why* the campaign was fought and should citicize the manner in which the opposing commanders brought their troops to the scene of action. The tactical study of the battle or siege ought to give clearly the arrangement of the rival forces and criticize the way in which they were handled on the field. Finally, there should be a short conclusion, giving the casualties and, more important, the effects of the campaign or battle on the outcome of the war.

APPLICATION OF PRINCIPLES—The student should indicate during the report, or in a summary at the end, the way in which the various principles of war were applied or violated. One ingenious student listed the nine principles and gave each side a grade in connection with each. There is also an opportunity in the report to mention the stage of development in the art of war—in respect to arms, tactics, fortification, and personnel.

MAPS—Good maps are essential to any study of military operations. Every report should contain at least two. One should show the "grand terrain" on a large enough scale to give the operations their setting in the theater of war and indicate how the armies were brought to the battle-field. The other should indicate the battle-field itself, showing the line-up of the rival forces, significant features of the terrain such as hills and streams, and also fortifications if any. Movements in the course of the action can be indicated by dotted lines, or a series of tactical maps can be made to show the battle at different stages. These maps should be drawn out carefully, and in the case of oral reports, should be drawn on the blackboard or on sheets of cardboard large enough to be clear to the whole group. The use of colors will help greatly in making the maps clear. There should be a distinctive color for each force, and also for streams and the like. On paper, colored crayons or ink can be used; for the blackboard, boxes of chalk in various colors can be purchased for a few cents. At the side of the map should be placed the name and date of the campaign, the names of the leaders on each side, and the strength of the opposing armies.

THINGS TO AVOID—Since the purpose of the report is to bring out clearly the distinctive features of the subject, the student must utilize his time and space to the best advantage. The careless, hastily prepared report simply gives a series of events and details without showing "what it is all about." The various moves must be thought out carefully before starting to write. Care must be taken not to litter up the report with unimportant details. Only the essential places and names should be included. No attempt should be made to insert the name of every regimental commander or every hamlet in the theater of operations. The book which the student consults has a great deal more space available for such minutiæ. The important thing is to make the distinctive features of the strategy and the fighting stand out clearly. Details should be included only when they assist in attaining that end. They should not be dragged in simply to make the report look more learned. Finally, the proper amount of space should be allotted to each part of the report. In a ten-page report, a page and a half should be ample for the introductory material, and a half-page for the conclusion. The remaining eight pages should include the strategical approach and the tactical study. The proportion between those depends on the campaign itself. The following list should be checked up in writing a report:

1. Have you shown the setting and essential details (statistics, dates and the like)?

2. Have you thought out the campaign so as to explain clearly the important strategical and tactical features?

3. Have you arranged the material in proper proportion, centering on the essentials, but giving a short introduction and conclusion?

4. Have you cluttered up the report and maps with un-essential names and places?

5. Have you two maps—one showing the strategical approach and the other the grand tactics of the battle or siege?

6. Have you included any illustrative material to make the report more interesting without sacrificing the proper proportion?

7. Have you applied the Principles of War and shown the stage of development in arms and armies?

SUBJECT FOR REPORTS—The following campaigns, operations, and sieges have been selected as most appropriate for reports. Individual instructors may naturally wish to add or omit certain items. The reports are divided about evenly between European and American military history. They start with the period of modern warfare, though the student can find material of value in the earlier periods, for example in Alexander's conquests, Cannæ, and the Crusades. Naturally, the more recent campaigns are of greater interest from the tactical side, even though the principles of strategy remain unchanged. In the bibliography following this appendix, readings will be found for every item in this list—partly under the war heading, and partly under the individual campaign heading. The special studies in this book—Trenton-Princeton, Peninsula-Shenandoah, and the Marne Salient—are not available for campaign reports.

THIRTY YEARS' WAR, 1618–1648

BREITENFELD, 1631—Swedes under Gustavus Adolphus defeated Imperialists under Tilly. Important as first application of "modern" tactics vs. old "Spanish square."

War of the Spanish Succession, 1701–1713

BLENHEIM, 1704—English and allies under Marlborough and Eugene defeated French. Report should show and explain in detail Marlborough's brilliant march across Europe to catch the French.

Seven Years' War, 1756–1763

ROSSBACH AND LEUTHEN, 1757—Defeat of larger French and Austrian armies by Prussians under Frederick the Great. Strategical study should show use of "interior lines" to catch enemies separated, and tactical study should show "thin line" in action with oblique attack at Leuthen.

QUEBEC, 1759—Brilliant capture of French stronghold in Canada by British under young Wolfe. Interesting for excellent coöperation between army and navy.

American Revolution, 1775–1783

CAMPAIGN AROUND NEW YORK, 1776—Includes victory of British under Howe over Americans under Washington in battle of Long Island, with British occupation of New York.

BURGOYNE'S CAMPAIGN, 1777—Defeat and surrender of British army invading northern New York from Canada—Burgoyne surrounded by Americans under Gates and others. Report should start with Burgoyne leaving Canada and include St. Leger's side expedition, closing with Saratoga.

YORKTOWN CAMPAIGN, 1781—Movements leading to siege and surrender of British under Cornwallis. Allies under Washington and Rochambeau victorious. Report should start with Cornwallis at

Wilmington, N. C., and show surprise concentration of American and French troops. Should also show naval side of operations.

French Revolutionary and Napoleonic Wars, 1793–1815

(Napoleon's First Italian Campaign, 1796–1797, was a masterful application of "interior lines," but was too intricate for satisfactory treatment in a brief report.)

MARENGO, 1800—Napoleon's second successful Italian campaign against the Austrians. Clever strategic maneuvering to get between the enemy and their base. Napoleon careless in battle itself— nearly lost it.

AUSTERLITZ, 1805—Considered by many to be Napoleon's most brilliant work. Defeated combined Austrians and Russians. Report should start with French Army on Channel, showing relation to naval war; then, the dash across Europe, picking off the Austrian Army at Ulm and finally the defeat of the Austrians and Russians at Austerlitz with clever battle tactics.

JENA, 1806—Napoleon put Prussia out of commission in one brief campaign. Report should include twin battle of Auerstadt, where Davoust beat main part of Prussian Army.

SALAMANCA, 1812—Victory of British under Wellington in Peninsular War against French in Spain.

1814 CAMPAIGN—Ranks high in Napoleon's strategical work, though he was finally defeated. Brilliant use of interior lines against vastly superior enemy forces. Included no important battles, so study should be largely strategical.

WATERLOO, 1815—Final defeat of Napoleon by British under Wellington and Prussians under Blücher. Report should include strategy of whole campaign, including actions at Quartre Bras and Ligny.

WAR OF 1812, 1812–1815

INVASION OF CANADA, 1812—Interesting study of how a campaign should *not* be run. Report should show attempted American invasion at Detroit and Niagara, ending with Hull's defeat and surrender of Detroit.

NEW ORLEANS, 1815—Crushing defeat of superior British force by American backwoodsmen and regulars under Andrew Jackson.

MEXICAN WAR, 1846–1848

SCOTT'S CAMPAIGN, 1847—American advance from Vera Cruz to Mexico City in face of superior enemy numbers and strong defenses. Campaign ended war. Devote tactical attention principally to battles in vicinity of Mexico City.

CIVIL WAR, 1861–1865

CHANCELLORSVILLE, 1863—Victory of 65,000 Confederates under Lee and Jackson over 130,000 Union troops under Hooker. Very interesting tactical study.

GETTYSBURG, 1863—Lee's invading army defeated but not crushed by Union under Meade. Turning-point of war. Strategical approach should begin with close of Chancellorsville campaign.

VICKSBURG, 1863—Capture of Confederate

stronghold on Mississippi by Grant after a brilliant campaign. Should deal very briefly with early Union attempts to capture city, concentrating on period after Grant went down the river for fresh start.

WILDERNESS AND COLD HARBOR, 1864—Grant's "attrition" warfare with superior numbers against Lee's superior skill. Should give strategy from crossing of Rapidan to final settling-down before Petersburg and should center on Cold Harbor for tactics.

GEORGIA CAMPAIGN, 1864—Sherman's successful drive through State, cutting off supplies from Confederacy. Falls into three parts—sparring between Sherman and Johnston from Chattanooga to Atlanta; battle of Atlanta; and unopposed devastating "march to the sea" to Savannah.

AUSTRO-PRUSSIAN WAR (SEVEN WEEKS' WAR), 1866

KÖNIGGRÄTZ (ALSO CALLED "SADOWA")—Prussians, under staff leadership of Von Moltke, ended war in brief Bohemian campaign against Austrians and allies. Shows Prussian General Staff's first triumph and also tactical effect of the needle-gun.

FRANCO-GERMAN WAR (FRANCO-PRUSSIAN WAR) 1870–1871

SEDAN, 1870—Another brilliant application of von Moltke's staff work and strategy against unprepared, bewildered French.

SPANISH-AMERICAN WAR, 1898

SANTIAGO (de Cuba)—Principal military engagement of the war. American victory over Spaniards should show operations at El Caney and San Juan Hill, and relation to naval situation.

RUSSO-JAPANESE WAR, 1904–1905

PORT ARTHUR, 1904–1905—Capture of fortified Russian naval base by Japanese in combined naval and military siege operations. Carefully studied by American, British, and other military observers as first trial of modern features—ring fortresses, howitzers, and the like.

MUKDEN, 1904—Japanese victory in field operations, also illustrating new equipment.

WORLD WAR (GREAT WAR, EUROPEAN WAR) 1914–1918

(See text for description of major operations.)

RETREAT FROM MONS, 1914—Heroic rear-guard action of little British expeditionary force in open warfare against German advance.

FIRST BATTLE OF THE MARNE, 1914—One of the decisive battles of history. The report should indicate the defects in the German strategy and the way in which the French took advantage of them. It should show the general German plan of attack.

EAST PRUSSIA, 1914—Germans under Hindenburg and Ludendorff threw out tremendous Russian invading force. Tactical emphasis should be centered on the defeat of Samsonoff at Tannenberg.

GALLIPOLI (DARDANELLES), 1915—Unsuccessful British attempt to force way through straits to Constantinople and Black Sea, with poor coöperation between navy and army. There is an unusual amount of good material on this dramatic campaign.

VERDUN, 1916—The biggest single "battle" of the war—Germans fail to capture French fortress. Combination of trench warfare and regular siege operations.

BATTLE OF THE SOMME, 1916—Example of typical large-scale Western Front offensive of middle period of war—British made some gains at terrific cost.

ST. MIHIEL, 1918—Reduction of important German salient by First American Army first acting as a unit. Included French under American command. Well-organized, powerful offensive.

MEUSE-ARGONNE, 1918—Principal American action in the war, as part of final "drive to victory." Report should center on only one of the three phases, as whole campaign was too intricate for brief treatment.

MESOPOTAMIA, 1916–1918—British operations in Tigris-Euphrates Valley against Turks. Report should start with Townshend's expedition to Kut-el-Amara in 1916 and with occupation of Bagdad.

PALESTINE, 1917–1918—British in Holy Land against Turks. Report should be limited to work of Allenby and Lawrence, omitting earlier Sinai fighting.

EAST AFRICA, 1914–1918—Small scale but very interesting operations against little German force which held out till end of war.

BIBLIOGRAPHY

The books on military matters run into the hundreds of thousands. The number is so tremendous that the general reader needs some guide through the maze. His natural question is "What are the *best* books on this subject?" This bibliography is designed for just such a reader. It makes no pretensions to being complete or to giving the most thorough scientific studies of the various subjects. Also, it is limited to works in English, though many of the most valuable books in military science have not been translated from the original French or German. Finally, it attempts to tell something about the books instead of merely listing them. It is hoped that a bibliography of this sort will prove useful to readers in military science, for little of exactly this sort exists at present.

The books on each subject generally fall into three classes. The first class contains general sketches of the subject, and should be read first to get the proper setting. The second and main class contains the important details of various aspects of the subject. The third class is useful for illustrative purposes, and even historical novels are included under this head. The military or academic titles of the authors have been omitted, as they generally changed later, anyway.

REFERENCE BOOKS—The general reader should appreciate the usefulness of the encyclopedia in getting a start on any subject. Some one has remarked, "It is hard to tell which man is more of a fool—the one who never uses the encyclopedia or the one who never uses anything else." In the historical sketches, the *Britannica* is generally more useful, but its illustrations in the recent period are mainly British. For American military history, the *Americana* and the *International* are often more detailed. Most of the articles contain short bibliographies. The reader will also find E. S. Farrow, *Dictionary of Military Terms* (1918) of great service as a reference book.

History of Warfare—General

The most complete one-volume sketch of the development of the art of war, military and naval, is B. A. Fiske, *The Art of Fighting, Its Evolution and Progress* (1920). Another good survey is F. B. Austin, *The Saga of the Sword* (1929). Much more thorough for the whole period down to the American Revolution is O. L. Spaulding, H. Nickerson, and J. W. Wright, *Warfare, a Study of Military Methods from the Earliest Times* (1924). The most complete study in English is the "Great Captains" series by T. A. Dodge (1892–1907). It consists of *Alexander, Hannibal, Cæsar, Gustavus Adolphus* (two volumes), and *Napoleon* (four volumes). While the main titles indicate only the outstanding leaders, the combined series gives a fairly good running story of the whole progress of military art, and good accounts of most of the battles through the Napoleonic period. The standard work on the medieval period, slighted by Dodge, is C. Oman, *The Art of Warfare in the Middle Ages* (two volumes) (new ed. 1924). The whole evolution of warfare since the early middle ages is included in J. W. FORTESCUE, *History of the British Army* (1897–   ). The fourteen volumes already published carry the story to 1852. FORTESCUE, *Military History* (1913) is an interesting little volume of general lectures. See also H. BELLOC, *Warfare in England* (1912). The broader aspects of war at the end of the nineteenth century are discussed in I. S. BLOCH, *The Future of War, in its Technical, Economic and Political Relations* (tr. 1899). For recent developments, see F. A. VON BERNHARDI, *On the War of Today* (tr. 1913) and *The War of the Future in the Light of Lessons of the World War* (tr. 1921); and B. H. LIDDELL HART, *The Remaking of Modern Armies* (1928). These general works should naturally be consulted in connection with the following special topics.

SMALL ARMS

The most satisfactory history of weapons up to the last half-century is A. DEMMIN, *Weapons of War* (tr. 1869). Other books dealing principally with the pre-gunpowder period are C. BOUTELL, *Arms and Armor* (1871), C. H. ASHDOWN, *British and Foreign Arms and Armour* (1909), and *Handbook of Arms and Armour* (Metropolitan Museum of Art, New York, 1915). For the general reader, the most readable history of firearms will be found in H. S. and E. H. WILLIAMS, *Modern Warfare* (1915). Other books on the subject are W. W. GREENER, *The Gun and its Development* (7th ed. 1899) and C. W. SAWYER, *Firearms in American History,* three volumes (1910–1927). Modern small arms are described in F. H. CALVIN and E. VAILL, *United States Rifles and Machine Guns* (1917) and F. V. LONGSTAFF and A. H. ATTRIDGE, *The Book of the Machine Gun* (1917). See the annual reports of the Chief of Ordnance, United States Army, for details of experiments and developments. See *Britannica,* articles on "Arms and Armour," "Ammunition," "Gun," "Machine Gun," "Rifle," and "Pistol."

ARTILLERY AND EXPLOSIVES

No single volume gives an adequate account of the whole development of artillery. Its start is told in H. W. L. HIME, *The Origin of Artillery* (1915). For guns of the "middle period," see W. E. BIRKHEIMER, *Historical Sketch of the Artillery, U. S. Army* (1884). The general reader will get a good introductory idea of the recent developments in three works of a popular nature: H. S. and E. H. WILLIAMS, *Modern Warfare* (1915); H. VON DEWITZ, *War's New Weapons* (1915) and T. W. CORBIN, *The Romance of War Inventions* (1918). More technical accounts of recent artillery are H. A. BETHELL, *Modern Guns and Gunnery* (1907) and *Modern Artillery in the Field* (1911); and L. E. BABCOCK, *Elements of Field Artillery* (1925). Much information will also be secured from three handbooks recently published by the United States government under the direction of the Chief of Ordnance: *Handbook of Artillery* (1924); *American Coast Artillery Matériel* (1922) and *Military Explosives* (1924). The first of the three includes a brief illustrated historical sketch of the development of artillery from its beginning. An excellent study of modern explosives is A. P. VAN GELDER and H. SCHLATTER, *History of the Explosives Industry in America* (1927). See *Britannica,* "Artillery," "Ammunition," "Explosives," and "Ordnance."

TACTICS

An outstanding book on this subject is A. L. WAGNER, *Organization and Tactics* (new ed. 1912), which traces separately the development of infantry, cavalry and artillery in modern history. It is an official text in the army service schools. There are numerous special studies for each arm, including G. T. DENISON, *The History of Cavalry* (new ed. 1913). German and French studies of tactical developments in the World War are W. BALCK, *Development of Tactics—World War* (tr. 1922) and P. J. L. AZAN, *The War of Positions* (1917) and *The Warfare of Today* (1918). Recent studies by the United States Army Service Schools, based on World War experience, are *Tactics and Technique of the Separate Branches* (1923) and *Tactical and Strategical Studies, Corps and Army* (1922). For the new tactical elements introduced in the World War, see O. STEWART, *Strategy and Tactics of Air Fighting* (1925); J. F. C. FULLER, *Tanks in the Great War* (1920); and, for poison gas, E. S. FARROW, *Gas Warfare* (1920) and V. LEFEBURE, *The Riddle of the Rhine* (1923). See *Britannica,* "Tactics" and separate branches.

FORTIFICATION AND SIEGECRAFT

Most of the technical works in this subject are in French or German, since England and the United States have had less to do with elaborate fortifications. The general reader can get the best idea of the evolution of forts and siege methods from E. E. VIOLLET-LE-DUC, *Annals of a Fortress* (tr. 1875), in which the successive stages from primitive times to the mid-nineteenth century are described in detail as occurring on a particular imaginary spot. T. M. MAGUIRE, *Outlines of Military Geography* (1899) deals with the history of fortifications on the side of strategic significance. A more strictly military work is H. F. THULLIER, *Principles of Land Defense* (1902). Medieval castles are dealt with in A. H. THOMPSON, *Military Architecture in England during the Middle Ages* (1912). Modern fortification is described in G. J. FIEBERGER, *Permanent Fortification* (1900) and *Field Fortifications* (1913), West Point engineering texts; and in T. S. CLARKE, *Fortification* (1907) and J. P. WISSER, *The Tactics of Coast Defense* (1908). The reports of the Chief of Coast Artillery in the United States War Department Annual Reports contain matter of interest. The reader of VIOLLET-LE-DUC will find later illustrative material of a popular nature in E. GILLAT, *The Romance of Modern Sieges* (1909). For a description of a medieval siege, see also C. READE, *The Cloister and the Hearth*.

PERSONNEL AND MILITARY POLICY—GENERAL

The general studies of the problem of securing and training men for an army include C. VON DER GOLTZ, *The Nation in Arms* (tr. 1883); F. N. MAUDE, *Voluntary vs. Compulsory Service* (1897) and *War and the World's Life* (1907); G. C. COULTON, *The Case for Compulsory Military Service, an Historical Review* (1917) and I. S. M. HAMILTON, *The Soul and Body of an Army* (1921). For studies of armies at particular periods, see C. H. FIRTH, *Cromwell's Army* (1902); H. BELLOC, *The Battle of Blenheim* (1911); E. E. CURTIS, *The Organization of the British Army in the American Revolution* (1926); E. UPTON, *The*

Armies of Europe and Asia (1878); C. S. JERRAM, *The Armies of the World* (1900); United States Official, *Strength and Organization of the Armies of France, Germany, Etc. Showing Conditions in July, 1914* (1917). The present status of every army of the world is minutely described in the League of Nations, *Armaments Year Book*. For illustrative material in fiction, see R. KIPLING, *Puck of Pook's Hill* (1904), for a vivid description of the last days of the Roman legion; W. S. DAVIS, *The Beauty of the Purple* (1925), for eighth century Byzantine warfare; FROISSART, *Chronicles* and CONAN DOYLE, *The White Company*, for the Hundred Years' War; and ERCKMAN-CHATRIAN, *The Conscript in 1813* (1889) and *Waterloo* (1893) for Napoleon's army and *The Plebiscite* (1889) for the national army in 1870.

AMERICAN MILITARY POLICY

An excellent and very readable history of American military policy is W. A. GANOE, *The History of the United States Army* (1924). Another good general study is F. L. HUIDEKOPER, *The Military Unpreparedness of the United States* (1915). E. UPTON, *The Military Policy of the United States* (new ed. 1917), the pioneer work on the subject, is the fullest account up to 1862. It is published by the government, as is a brief epitome of the work (1916). Other general books on the subject are W. H. CARTER, *The American Army* (1915) and, more extreme, H. LEA, *The Valor of Ignorance* (1909). The raising of the army in the World War is analyzed well in J. DICKINSON, *The Building of an Army* (1920). The present military system is described in pamphlet form in UNITED STATES ARMY

SERVICE SCHOOLS, *Military Organization of the United States* (1926). Students should also consult the text of the National Defense Act of 1920 and later military legislation (see page 393). A good first-hand picture of nearly all the phases of our Army's peace and war activities during the last half-century will be found in H. L. SCOTT, *Some Memories of a Soldier* (1928). See also C. K. BOLTON, *The Private Soldier under Washington* (1902), E. LONN, *Desertion During the Civil War* (1928), and F. A. SHANNON, *The Organization and Administration of the Union Army, 1861–1865* (1928).

STRATEGY, COMMAND AND STAFFS

One of the best introductions to strategy is W. K. NAYLOR, *Principles of Strategy, with Historical Illustrations* (1921), a text in our Army service schools. Also useful are G. J. FIEBERGER, *Elements of Strategy* (1917), written as a West Point text and G. J. MEYERS, *Strategy* (1928), analyzing naval and military strategy. The United States Army *Field Service Regulations* (1917), should also be consulted. The pithiest statements relating to the methods of waging war will be found in NAPOLEON, *Maxims of War* (tr. 1917). The two old standard pioneer works are C. VON CLAUSE-WITZ, *On War,* three volumes (tr. 1918 and other editions), and A. H. JOMINI, *The Art of War* (tr. 1863). Later standard works are K. ZU HOHENLOHE-INGELFINGEN, *Letters on Strategy,* two volumes (tr. 1898); C. VON DER GOLTZ, *The Conduct of War* (tr. 1896); E. B. HAMLEY, *The Operations of War, Explained and Illustrated* (new ed. 1909); W. H. JAMES, *Modern Strategy* (1908); F. FOCH, *Principles of War* (tr. 1920)

and *Precepts and Judgments* (tr. 1920); F. N.
MAUDE, *The Evolution of Modern Strategy*
(1903); H. M. JOHNSTONE, *The Foundations of
Strategy* (1914); E. A. ALTHAM, *The Principles
of·War Historically Illustrated,* two volumes with
atlas (1914); and W. D. BIRD, *The Direction of
War, a Study of Strategy* (1909).

The German general staff is analyzed in B. VON
SCHELLENDORFF, *The Duties of the General Staff*
(tr. 1914) and S. WILKINSON, *The Brains of an
Army* (1895). The various general staff systems
of the time were described in E. UPTON, *The Armies of Europe and Asia* (1878). Our present staff
system is described in the official *Staff Officers'
Manual,* now in preparation.

Collections of biographies of the great commanders, aside from boys' books of heroes, include T. A.
DODGE, *Great Captains* (Alexander, Hannibal,
Cæsar, Gustavus Adolphus, Frederick the Great,
and Napoleon) (1895), not to be confused with his
longer works; B. H. LIDDELL HART, *Great Captains Unveiled* (Jenghis Khan, Sabutai, Saxe, Gustavus Adolphus, Wallenstein, and Wolfe) (1927);
and N. D'ESTERRE, *Masters of War* (1927). Consult *Britannica,* "Army," "Strategy," and "Staff";
Americana, "Military Science."

WARS, CAMPAIGNS, BATTLES, AND SIEGES

This section is designed particularly for guidance
in the preparation of campaign reports, so it is
limited to the subjects in that recommended list.
It indicates general histories to give the background
of the wars; detailed studies of the military operations themselves; and, occasionally, pertinent illustrative material.

The brief details of all important wars, campaigns, and battles up to the American Revolution will be found in SPAULDING, NICKERSON, and WRIGHT, *Warfare*. The more ample descriptions in the various volumes of DODGE will also be found of value. A good account of all fighting involving England up to 1852 will be found in FORTESCUE, *History of the British Army*. Less detailed treatment of American fighting, through the Spanish War, will be found in M. F. STEELE, *American Campaigns*, two volumes. The second volume contains maps of all important operations. The student should not fail to consult the above four works wherever possible. They will furnish at least minimum accounts of the campaigns, and all necessary maps. They are more useful than the famous E. S. CREASY, *Fifteen Decisive Battles of the World from Marathon to Waterloo* (1851) which has led to a host of "battle books," chiefly for boys. Most of the writers on strategy have analyzed certain campaigns or operations to illustrate their points, and these should be consulted. The *Cambridge Modern History*, twelve volumes and atlas, will furnish a useful, if not readable, background.

Any one desiring to study a campaign in ancient or medieval history will find ample background in SPAULDING, NICKERSON and WRIGHT, with more detailed treatment in DODGE for the ancient period and OMAN for the medieval. This list will begin with the modern period of warfare.

THIRTY YEARS' WAR—S. R. GARDINER, *The Thirty Years' War* (1874); B. H. LIDDELL HART, *Great Captains Unveiled* (1927); *Cambridge Modern History* (*C. M. H.*), IV.

Breitenfeld: DODGE, *Gustavus Adolphus*, I; SPAULDING *et. al.*

WAR OF THE SPANISH SUCCESSION—*C. M. H.*, V.

    Blenheim: FORTESCUE, I; DODGE, *Gustavus Adolphus*, II; H. BELLOC, *The Battle of Blenheim* (1911); SPAULDING *et. al.*

SEVEN YEARS' WAR—*C. M. H.*, VI.

    Rossbach and Leuthen: CARLYLE, *Frederick the Great* (volume varies according to edition); A. H. JOMINI, *Treatise on Grand Military Operations*, I and Atlas (tr. 1865); SPAULDING *et. al.*

    Quebec: FORTESCUE, III; J. S. CORBETT, *England in the Seven Years' War*, two volumes (1907); G. M. WRONG, *The Fall of Canada* (1914); LIDDELL HART, *Great Captains Unveiled;* illustrative: G. PARKER, *The Seats of the Mighty.*

AMERICAN REVOLUTION—The most readable brief account of the military side of the war will be found in G. M. WRONG, *Washington and His Comrades in Arms* (Chronicles of America) (1921). FORTESCUE makes a thorough study, but has a strong anti-American bias. For an interesting study of the combined naval and military operations, with very good maps, see W. M. JAMES, *The British Navy in Adversity* (1926). B. F. LOSSING, *Pictorial Field Book of the American Revolution*, two volumes (1860), is out of date, but gives local details. For general histories of the war, not purely military, see the books of G. O. TREVELYAN, W. H. LECKY, C. H. VAN TYNE, J. FISKE and S. E. MORISON, *Oxford History of the United States* (1927), I. Consult also E. UPTON, *Military Policy of the United States.*

    Long Island (and operations around New York): FORTESCUE, III; STEELE; H. P. JOHNSTON, "Campaign of 1776 around New York" (in *Long Island Hist. Soc. Memoirs* [1877]); and C. F. ADAMS, *Studies Military and Diplomatic, 1775–1865* (1911).

Trenton-Princeton (not available for reports): W. H. STRYKER, *The Battles of Trenton and Princeton* (1898); T. J. WERTENBAKER, "The Battle of Princeton" in *The Princeton Battle Monument* (1922).

Burgoyne's Campaign: FORTESCUE, III; STEELE; H. NICKERSON, *The Turning Point of The Revolution* (1928); W. L. STONE, *The Campaign of Burgoyne* (1871); ADAMS; Illustrative: F. J. HUDLESTON, *Gentleman Johnny Burgoyne* (1927); F. C. L. RIEDESEL, *Letters and Journals* (tr. 1867). For new researches, casting doubt on the "triple plan" theory, see *American Historical Review,* Jan., 1929, p. 353.

Yorktown Campaign: FORTESCUE, III; STEELE; JAMES; H. P. JOHNSTON, *The Yorktown Campaign and the Surrender of Cornwallis* (1881); A. T. MAHAN, *Major Operations of the Navies in the War of Independence* (1903).

FRENCH REVOLUTIONARY AND NAPOLEONIC WARS —For the general history of the period see C. D. HAZEN, *The French Revolution and Napoleon,* or biographies of Napoleon by H. A. L. FISHER, R. M. JOHNSTON, E. LUDWIG, J. H. ROSE (two volumes). For the military side, the most generally useful account is DODGE, *Napoleon* (four volumes).

Marengo: DODGE, I; HAMLEY, *Operations of War.*

Austerlitz: DODGE, I; JAMES, *Modern Strategy.* Illustrative: L. TOLSTOY, *War and Peace.*

Jena: DODGE, II; JAMES; HOHENLOHE-INGELFINGEN, *Letters on Strategy,* I; UNITED STATES GENERAL SERVICE SCHOOLS, *Source Book*

on the Jena Campaign (1922); F. N. MAUDE,
The Jena Campaign (1909).

Salamanca: C. OMAN, *History of the Penin-
sular War* (1902–   ), V; FORTESCUE, VIII;
W. F. P. NAPIER, *History of the Peninsular
War* (1842), IV; W. H. FITCHETT, *How Eng-
land Saved Europe* (1900), III. Illustrative: C.
LEVER, *Charles O'Malley* (1841).

1814 Campaign: DODGE, IV; HAMLEY. Illustrative: ERCKMANN-CHATRIAN, *The Campaign
of 1814.*

Waterloo: DODGE, IV; FORTESCUE, X;
FITCHETT, IV; J. C. ROPES, *The Waterloo Cam-
paign;* G. HOOPER, *Waterloo* (1862); H.
BELLOC, *Waterloo* (1912); HAMLEY; JAMES. Il-
lustrative: V. HUGO, *Les Miserables;* ERCKMANN-
CHATRIAN, *Waterloo.*

WAR OF 1812—The best general account, with
good military descriptions, is in H. ADAMS, *History
of the United States,* VI–VIII (1911). FORTESCUE,
in three volumes on the British Army 1812–1815,
devotes less than one twelfth of his space to the
War of 1812. For the Canadian side, see J. HAN-
NAY, *How Canada Was Held for the Empire*
(1905) and C. P. LUCAS, *The Canadian War of
1812* (1906). See also T. C. SMITH, *Wars between
England and America* (1914); UPTON, *Military
Policy of the United States;* and T. ROOSEVELT,
The Naval War of 1812 (1884).

Invasion of Canada, 1812: H. ADAMS, VI;
FORTESCUE, VIII; STEELE; HANNAY; LUCAS; L.
BABCOCK, *The War of 1812 on the Niagara
Frontier* (1928).

New Orleans: FORTESCUE, X; H. ADAMS,
VIII; STEELE; E. O. ROWLAND, *Andrew Jack-*

son's Campaign against the British (1926); C. F. ADAMS, *Studies Military and Diplomatic.*

MEXICAN WAR—The most thorough modern work is J. H. SMITH, *The War with Mexico,* two volumes (1919). For a briefer and very readable account, see N. W. STEPHENSON, *Texas and the Mexican War* (Chronicles of America) (1921). Contemporary accounts include W. SCOTT, *Memoirs,* two volumes (1862).

Scott's Campaign: SMITH, II; STEELE; SCOTT; R. SEMMES, *Campaign of General Scott* (1852); E. D. MANSFIELD, *Life and Military Services of General Scott* (1862); and G. B. MCCLELLAN, *Mexican War Diary* (1917).

CIVIL WAR—The best brief, accurate, and readable accounts are in S. E. MORISON, *Oxford History of the United States,* II, and W. C. H. WOOD, *Captains of the Civil War* (Chronicles of America) (1921). More detailed one-volume accounts are W. B. WOOD and J. E. EDMONDS, *A History of the Civil War in the United States* (1905); and J. F. RHODES, *History of the Civil War* (1917). For a still more detailed account, see J. C. ROPES and W. R. LIVERMORE, *The Story of the Civil War,* four volumes (1895–1913). One of the outstanding books on the first half of the war is G. F. R. HENDERSON, *Stonewall Jackson and the American Civil War,* two volumes (1898). This has long been used as a text in the British military schools. Briefer, but also excellent, are two other English works, F. B. MAURICE, *Robert E. Lee, the Soldier* (1925) and *Statesmen and Soldiers of the Civil War* (1926). A. L. CONGER, *President Lincoln as a War Statesman* (1916) is an illuminating study. Among the great number of memoirs, the most valuable are

U. S. GRANT, *Personal Memoirs,* two volumes (1885–1886); W. T. SHERMAN, *Memoirs,* two volumes (1886); and E. P. ALEXANDER, *Military Memoirs of a Confederate* (1907). STEELE, *American Campaigns* is especially full on the Civil War and has good maps.

The student should also be acquainted with three extensive works which will furnish detailed illustrative material for every campaign: *Battles and Leaders of the Civil War. (The Century Co. Book of the War),* four volumes (1887–1889), a collection of articles written by men who had actually taken part in the various operations—not always reliable as sources; F. T. MILLER, ed., *The Photographic History of the Civil War,* ten volumes (1911), a remarkable collection of contemporary photographs; and finally, the tremendous official collection of orders, reports, and the like in *The War of the Rebellion: a Compilation of the Official Records of the Union and Confederate Armies,* 128 volumes (1880–1901). For a "sugar-coated" but reliable picture of the fighting around Virginia, see the novels M. JOHNSTON, *The Long Roll* and *Cease Firing,* and J. BOYD, *Marching On.* In the following campaign references, only the books having a special bearing on the campaign named will be noted —the student should consult the general works also.

Peninsula and Shenandoah (not available for reports): HENDERSON, *Stonewall Jackson* is a masterpiece on this subject. See also United States General Staff, *Source Book on the Peninsula Campaign.*

Chancellorsville: HENDERSON, *Stonewall Jackson,* II; A. DOUBLEDAY, *Chancellorsville and Gettysburg* (1882); J. BIGELOW, *The Campaign of Chancellorsville* (1910); T. A. DODGE, *The*

Campaign of Chancellorsville (1881); *Battles and Leaders,* III.

Gettysburg: F. A. HASKELL, *The Battle of Gettysburg* (Wisconsin Historical Commission) (1908); DOUBLEDAY; HENDERSON, *The Science of War; Battles and Leaders* III.

Vicksburg: GRANT, *Personal Memoirs,* I; SHERMAN, *Memoirs,* I; A. T. MAHAN, *The Gulf and Inland Waters* (1883); *Battles and Leaders* III.

Wilderness and Cold Harbor: HENDERSON, *The Science of War;* A. A. HUMPHREYS, *The Virginia Campaigns of 1864-65* (1882); GRANT, II; *Battles and Leaders,* IV.

Georgia Campaign: SHERMAN, II; *Marching with Sherman* (1927); *Battles and Leaders,* IV.

AUSTRO-PRUSSIAN WAR—For general background, see lives of Bismarck by E. LUDWIG and C. G. ROBERTSON; C. D. HAZEN, *Europe since 1815* (1924).

Königgrätz: A. L. WAGNER, *The Campaign of Königgrätz* (1889); H. M. HOZIER, *The Seven Weeks' War* (1867); G. J. R. CLUNICKE, *The Campaign in Bohemia* (1907)

FRANCO-GERMAN WAR—For general background, see same as above and P. GUEDALLA, *The Second Empire* (1922).

Sedan: G. HOOPER, *The Campaign of Sedan* (1887); VON MOLTKE, *The Franco-German War.*

SPANISH-AMERICAN WAR—For a good brief account, see C. R. FISH, *The Path of Empire* (Chronicles of America) (1921); H. C. LODGE, *The War with Spain* (1899).

Santiago: H. H. SARGENT, *Campaign of Santiago de Cuba* (1908); A. L. WAGNER, *Report of the Santiago Campaign* (1908); J. WHEELER,

The Santiago Campaign (1899); T. ROOSEVELT, *The Rough Riders* (1899). For Spanish side, see J. MULLER Y TEJEIRO: *Battles and Capitulations of Santiago de Cuba* (1899).

RUSSO-JAPANESE WAR—The best general account is I. A. S. HAMILTON, *A Staff Officer's Scrap Book,* two volumes (1905–1907). The most thorough account is the British *Official History (Naval and Military) of the Russo-Japanese War,* three volumes (1910–1920), with a case of loose maps for each volume. See also the *Reports of Military Observers attached to the armies in Manchuria during the Russo-Japanese War,* five parts, United States General Staff, 1906.

Port Arthur: See above and F. VILLIERS, *Port Arthur, Three Months with the Besiegers* (1905).

Mukden: See above and F. PALMER, *With Kuroki in Manchuria* (1905); A. K. KUROPATKIN, *The Russian Army and the Japanese War,* two volumes (1909).

WORLD WAR—The number of books already written on the World War is tremendous. Many of them have had only transient value, being written to keep the public informed as the war went along. It will be a long time yet before thorough and complete histories can be written, but a few of the present books stand out as most useful for the general reader. For one-volume presentations, the most satisfactory are T. G. FROTHINGHAM, *A Guide to the Military History of the World War* (1920); C. J. H. HAYES, *A Brief History of the Great War* (1920); A. F. POLLARD, *Short History of the Great War* (1920); and H. C. O'NEILL, *A History of the War* (1920). The first two are American, the others English. The most useful book for strategical and tactical study is C. R. HOWLAND, *A Military History of the World War*, two volumes (1923). It is based on lectures at the Army General Service Schools and gives an excellent analysis, with application of the principles of war. The second volume is a portfolio of 150 loose maps on subjects from the most general to the local tactical situations. Probably the best of the longer complete histories is J. BUCHAN, *History of the Great War*, four volumes (1921). B. H. LIDDELL HART, *Reputations Ten Years After* (1928) is a series of clever studies of the leaders, which has aroused much dispute. For pictures of what went on "behind the scenes," read C. à C. REPINGTON, *The First World War*, two volumes (1920); W. L. S. CHURCHILL, *The World Crisis*, five volumes (1923–1928); J. DE PIERREFEU, *Plutarch Lied*, (tr. 1924) and T. J. MASSON, *Without Censor* (1928).

The most ambitious and thoroughgoing study of the war so far is the British official *History of the Great War, Based on Official Documents, by the Direction of the Historical Section of the Committee of Imperial Defense*. So far, four volumes have appeared on *Military Operations, France and Belgium*, 1914–1915, compiled by J. E. EDMONDS. In addition are C. R. ASPINALL, *Gallipoli*, and F. J. MOBERLY, *The Campaign in Mesopotamia, 1914–1918*, three volumes (1922). New volumes will probably appear steadily. They are accompanied by excellent maps.

Several books on special features of the war, aside from those which will be mentioned in connection with particular campaigns, deserve particular attention. Prominent among these are the memoirs of the three outstanding German leaders: P. VON HINDENBURG, *Out of My Life* (tr. 1920); E. VON

LUDENDORFF, *My War Memories (Ludendorff's Own Story)* two volumes (tr. 1920); and E. VON FALKENHAYN, *The German General Staff and its Decisions (German General Headquarters and Its Critical Decisions) 1914–1916* (tr. 1920). The field diary of Crown Prince Rupprecht of Bavaria is now being translated. For the Eastern Front, see A. W. F. KNOX, *With the Russian Army, 1914–1917* (1921) and M. HOFFMAN, *The War of Lost Opportunities* (tr. 1920). For the Turkish campaigns, see L. VON SANDERS, *Five Years in Turkey* (tr. 1927) and E. DANE, *British Campaigns in the Nearer East, 1914–1918,* two volumes (1919). The final period of the war is told in F. B. MAURICE, *The Last Four Months* (1919). See also H. H. SARGENT, *Strategy on the Western Front* (1920); D. W. JOHNSTON, *Topography and Strategy in the World War* (1917), and numerous books on the war referred to in the earlier sections of this bibliography. For illustrative material from the standpoint of the man in the trenches, read H. BARBUSSE, *Under Fire* (tr. 1917); D. HANKEY, *The Student in Arms* (1916), ANON., *The Cannoneers Have Hairy Ears* (1927), J. B. WHARTON, *Squad* (1928), and E. M. REMARQUE, *All Quiet on the Western Front* (tr. 1929).

On American military participation in the war, the most useful short works are T. J. FROTHINGHAM, *The American Reinforcement in the World War* (1927); S. THOMAS, *The History of the A. E. F.* (1920); J. A. DE CHAMBRUN and C. DE MARENCHES, *The American Army in the European Conflict* (1919); A. W. PAGE, *Our 110 Days' Fighting* (1920); and J. C. WISE, *The Turn of the Tide* (1920). The student should also consult the *Final Report of General J. J. Pershing* (1919), and will find a great deal of very useful material in the *Guide to The American Battle Fields in Europe* (1927), prepared by the American Battle Monuments Commission, with numerous illustrations and three large-scale maps. The actual fighting is vividly described in D. VAN EVERY, *The A. E. F. in Battle* (1928) and J. W. THOMASON, *Fix Bayonets!* (1926). The memoirs of American commanders include H. LIGGETT, *Commanding an American Army* (1925) and *The A. E. F., Ten Years Ago in France* (1928); R. L. BULLARD, *Personalities and Reminiscences of the War* (1925); J. T. DICKMAN, *The Great Crusade* (1927); and J. G. HARBORD, *The American Expeditionary Forces* (1929). One of the most interesting little volumes of official statistics ever written is L. P. AYRES, *The War with Germany, a Statistical Summary* (1919). The Historical Section of the Army War College has prepared several excellent short monographs. There are numerous divisional, regimental and regional histories of unequal value. The series of monographs now being prepared by the Second Division is of high quality.

The Retreat from Mons: J. E. EDMONDS, "Official History," I; F. B. MAURICE, *Forty Days in 1914;* A. VON KLUCK, *The March on Paris and the Battle of Marne* (tr. 1920); LUDENDORFF; FALKENHAYN; J. FRENCH, *1914* (1920); A. CORBETT-SMITH, *The Retreat from Mons* (1916); G. S. GORDON, *Mons and the Retreat* (1918).

First Battle of the Marne: EDMONDS, MAURICE, KLUCK, LUDENDORFF, FALKENHAYN; A. CORBETT-SMITH, *The Marne—and After* (1917); LIDDELL HART, *Reputations Ten Years After* (1927).

East Prussia: LUDENDORFF, HINDENBURG,

388 INTRODUCTION TO MILITARY HISTORY

KNOX; P. PARES, *Day by Day with the Russian Army* (1917).

Gallipoli: ASPINALL, "Official History"; I. S. M. HAMILTON, *A Gallipoli Diary* (1918); VON SANDERS; CHURCHILL, II; DANE; W. D. PULESTON, *The Dardanelles Expedition* (1927) with seventy excellent maps; also books by C. E. CALLWELL, A. N. H. HERBERT, H. W. NEVINSON, and N. L. WILKINSON. For a vivid description, see J. MASEFIELD, *Gallipoli* (new ed. 1927).

Verdun: EDMUNDS, "Official History"—in preparation; H. DUGARD, *The Victory of Verdun* (tr. 1917); H. BORDEAUX, *The Last Days of Fort Vaux* (tr. 1917).

Mesopotamia: MOBERLY, "Official History"; DANE; C. V. E. TOWNSHEND, *My Campaign in Mesopotamia* (1919); C. E. CALLWELL, *Life of Sir Stanley Maude* (1920); E. CANDLER, *The Long Road to Baghdad*, two volumes (1919): A. T. CLARK, *To Bagdad with the British* (1918); K. ROOSEVELT, *War in the Garden of Eden* (1919).

Palestine: DANE; VON SANDERS, A. BOWMAN-MAINFOLD, *An Outline of the Egyptian and Palestine Campaigns* (1922); V. GILBERT, *Romance of the Last Crusade* (1913); A. AARONSOHN, *With the Turks in Palestine* (1917); W. T. MASSEY, *The Desert Campaigns* (1918); T. E. LAWRENCE, *Revolt in the Desert* (1927); L. J. THOMAS, *With Lawrence in Arabia* (1924); R. GRAVES, *Lawrence and the Arabian Adventure* (1928); LIDDELL HART, *Reputations Ten Years After*.

Battle of the Somme: EDMONDS, "Official History," in preparation; G. A. B. DEWAR and J. BORASTON, *Sir Douglas Haig's Command*, two

volumes (1921); A. CONAN DOYLE, *British Campaigns in Europe* (1928).

East Africa: O. VON LETTOW-VORBECK, *The
War in Africa* (1918); E. DANE, *British Cam-
paigns in Africa* (1919); C. P. FENDALL, *The
East African Force* (1921); F. B. YOUNG,
Marching on Tanga (1927).

Marne Salient (not available for report):
See general works on A. E. F. and MAURICE, The
Last Four Months. Also, United States Army
Service Schools, "The German Offensive of July 15,
1918" (*Marne Source Book*) (1923); and
United States War Department Historical Sec-
tion, General Staff, *The Aisne and Montdidier-
Noyon Operations* (1922).

St. Mihiel: See general works on A. E. F., and
United States War Department Historical Section, General Staff, *St. Mihiel* (1922).

Meuse-Argonne: See general works on A. E.
F., and United States War Department Historical Section, General Staff, *Meuse-Argonne* (1921)
and *Blanc-Mont* (1921).

SUGGESTED RESERVE LIST

(The following list includes many of the most interesting general works on military history. These might well be placed on open reserve shelves in the library wherever practicable.)

Austin, F. B.—*The Saga of the Sword.*

Ayers, J. G.—*The War with Germany, a Statistical Summary* (United States official).

Balck, W.—*Development of Tactics—World War.*

Battles and Leaders of the Civil War, 4 vols.

Corbin, T. W.—*War's New Weapons.*

Dodge, T. A.—*Great Captains.*

—— —*Gustavus Adolphus,* 2 vols.

—— —*Napoleon,* 4 vols.

Farrow, E. S.—*Dictionary of Military Terms.*

Fiske, B. A.—*The Art of Fighting.*

Fortescue, J. W.—*History of the British Army,* v. 3.

Frothingham, T. G.—*Guide to the Military History of the World War.*

—— —*American Reinforcement in the World War.*

Ganoe, W. A.—*History of the United States Army.*

Grant, U. S.—*Personal Memoirs.*

Hayes, C. J. H.—*Brief History of the World War.*

Henderson, G. F. R.—*Stonewall Jackson and the American Civil War,* 2 vols.

Hindenburg, P. von—*Out of My Life.*

Howland, G. R.—*Military History of the World War.*

Jerram, C. S.—*The Armies of the World.*

League of Nations—*Armaments Year Book.*

Liddell Hart, B. H.—*Great Captains Unveiled.*

—— —*Remaking of Modern Armies.*

—— —*Reputations Ten Years After.*

Miller, F. T., ed.—*Photographic History of the Civil War,* 10 vols.

Napoleon—*Maxims of War.*

Naylor, W. K.—*Principles of Strategy.*

Oman, C.—*Art of Warfare in the Middle Ages,* 2 vols.

Pershing, J. J.—*Final Report* (United States official).

Rhodes, J. F.—*History of the Civil War.*

Spaulding, O. L., Nickerson, H., and Wright, J. W.— *Warfare.*

Steele, M. F.—*American Campaigns,* 2 v.

Stephenson, N. W.—*Texas and the Mexican War* (Chronicles of America).

Thomas, S.—*History of the A. E. F.*

United States, American Battle Monuments Commission— *Guide to the American Battlefields in Europe.*

——, Chief of Ordnance—*Handbook of Artillery.*

Upton, E.—*Military Policy of the United States.*

Van Every, D.—*The A. E. F. in Battle.*

Viollet-le-Duc, E. E.—*Annals of a Fortress.*

Wagner, A. L.—*Organization and Tactics.*

Williams, H. S. and E. H.—*Modern Warfare.*

Wood, W. B., and Edmonds, J. E.—*A History of the Civil War in the United States.*

Wood, W. C. H.—*Captains of the Civil War* (Chronicles of America).

Wrong, G. M.—*Washington and His Comrades in Arms* (Chronicles of America).

THE NATIONAL DEFENSE ACT OF 1920

WITH SUPPLEMENTARY LEGISLATION

EXTRACTS FROM THE OFFICIAL TEXT [1]

Be it enacted by the Senate and House of Representatives of the United States of America in Congress assembled, That the Army of the United States shall consist of the Regular Army, the National Guard while in the service of the United States, and the Organized Reserves, including the Officers' Reserve Corps and the Enlisted Reserve Corps.

SEC. 2. COMPOSITION OF THE REGULAR ARMY—The Regular Army of the United States shall consist of the Infantry, the Cavalry, the Field Artillery, the Coast Artillery Corps, the Air Service, the Corps of Engineers, the Signal Corps, which shall be designated as the combatant arms or the line of the Army; the General Staff Corps; the Adjutant General's Department; the Inspector General's Department; the Judge Advocate General's Department; the Quartermaster Corps; the Finance Department; the Medical Department; the Ordnance Department; the Chemical Warfare Service; the officers of the Bureau of Insular Affairs; the officers and enlisted men under the jurisdiction of the Militia Bureau; the chaplains; the professors and cadets of the United States Military Academy; the present military storekeeper; detached officers; detached enlisted men; unassigned recruits; the Indian Scouts; the officers and enlisted men of the retired list; and such other

[1] Copies of the complete text, 70 pages in length, can be purchased from the Government Printing Office. All extracts here given are from the Act of June 4, 1920, unless otherwise indicated.

officers and enlisted men as are now or may hereafter be provided for. Except in time of war or similar emergency when the public safety demands it, the number of enlisted men of the Regular Army shall not exceed two hundred and eighty thousand, including the Philippine Scouts.

NOTES.—From the War Department appropriation act of June 30, 1922, to that of April 15, 1926, the total authorized number of enlisted men, not including the Philippine Scouts, was annually fixed at 125,000. The number was not fixed in the War Department appropriation act of February 23, 1927.

For change of title of Air Service to Air Corps, see act of July 2, 1926.

SEC. 3. ORGANIZATION OF THE ARMY—The organized peace establishment, including the Regular Army, the National Guard and the Organized Reserves, shall include all of those divisions and other military organizations necessary to form the basis for a complete and immediate mobilization for the national defense in the event of a national emergency declared by Congress. The Army shall at all times be organized so far as practicable into brigades, divisions and army corps, and whenever the President may deem it expedient, into armies. For purposes of administration, training and tactical control, the continental area of the United States shall be divided on a basis of military population into corps areas. Each corps area shall contain at least one division of the National Guard or Organized Reserves, and such other troops as the President may direct. The President is authorized to group any or all corps areas into army areas or departments.

SEC. 3A. THE INITIAL ORGANIZATION OF THE NATIONAL GUARD AND THE ORGANIZED RESERVES—In the reorganization of the National Guard and in the initial organization of the Organized Reserves, the names, numbers, and other designations, flags, and records of the divisions and subordinate units thereof that served in the World War between April 6, 1917, and November 11, 1918, shall be preserved as such as far as practicable. Subject to revision and approval by the Secretary of War, the plans and regulations under

which the initial organization and territorial distribution
of the National Guard and the Organized Reserves shall
be made, shall be prepared by a committee of the branch or
division of the War Department General Staff, hereinafter
provided for, which is charged with the preparation of plans
for the national defense and for the mobilization of the
land forces of the United States. For the purpose of this
task said committee shall be composed of members of said
branch or division of the General Staff and an equal number of reserve officers, including reserve officers who hold
or have held commissions in the National Guard. Subject
to general regulations approved by the Secretary of War,
the location and designation of units of the National Guard
and of the Organized Reserves entirely comprised within the
limits of any State or Territory shall be determined by a
board, a majority of whom shall be reserve officers, including reserve officers who hold or have held commissions in
the National Guard and recommended for this duty by
the governor of the State or Territory concerned.

SEC. 4. OFFICERS—Officers commissioned to and holding
in the Army the office of a general officer shall hereafter
be known as general officers of the line. Officers commissioned to and holding in the Army an office other than
that of general officer, but to which the rank of a general
officer is attached, shall be known as general officers of the
staff. . . . Major generals of the line shall be appointed
from officers of the grade of brigadier general of the line,
and brigadier generals of the line shall be appointed from
officers of the grade of colonel of the line whose names are
borne on an eligible list prepared annually by a board of not
less than five general officers of the line, not below the grade
of major general: . . .

Officers of all grades in the Infantry, Cavalry, Field Artillery, Coast Artillery Corps, Corps of Engineers, and
Medical Department; officers above the grade of captain
in the Signal Corps, Judge Advocate General's Department, Quartermaster Corps, Ordnance Department and
Chemical Warfare Service, all chaplains and professors, and
the military storekeeper shall be permanently commissioned

in their respective branches. All officers of the General Staff Corps, Inspector General's Department, Bureau of Insular Affairs and Militia Bureau shall be obtained by detail from officers of corresponding grades in other branches. Other officers may be either detailed, or with their own consent, be permanently commissioned, in the branches to which they are assigned for duty. . . .

SEC. 5. GENERAL STAFF CORPS—The General Staff Corps shall consist of the Chief of Staff, the War Department General Staff and the General Staff with troops. The War Department General Staff shall consist of the Chief of Staff and four assistants to the Chief of Staff selected by the President from the general officers of the line, and eighty-eight other officers of grades not below that of captain. The General Staff with troops shall consist of such number of officers not below the grade of captain as may be necessary to perform the General Staff duties of the headquarters of territorial departments, armies, army corps, divisions, and brigades, and as military attachés abroad. In time of peace the detail of an officer as a member of the General Staff Corps shall be for a period of four years, unless sooner relieved, and such details shall be limited to officers whose names are borne on the list of General Staff Corps eligibles. . . .

The duties of the War Department General Staff shall be to prepare plans for national defense and the use of the military forces for that purpose, both separately and in conjunction with the naval forces, and for the mobilization of the manhood of the Nation and its material resources in an emergency, to investigate and report upon all questions affecting the efficiency of the Army of the United States, and its state of preparation for military operations; and to render professional aid and assistance to the Secretary of War and the Chief of Staff.

All policies and regulations affecting the organization, distribution, and training of the National Guard and the Organized Reserves, and all policies and regulations affecting the appointment, assignment, promotion, and discharge of reserve officers, shall be prepared by committees of appropriate branches or divisions of the War Department General Staff, to which shall be added an equal number of reserve officers, including reserve officers who hold or have held commissions in the National Guard, and whose names are borne on lists of officers suitable for such duty, submitted by the governors of the several States and Territories. . . .

The duties of the General Staff with troops shall be to render professional aid and assistance to the general officers over them; to act as their agents in harmonizing the plans, duties, and operations of the various organizations and services under their jurisdiction, in preparing detailed instructions for the execution of the plans of the commanding generals, and in supervising the execution of such instructions.

The Chief of Staff shall preside over the War Department General Staff and, under the direction of the President, or of the Secretary of War under the direction of the President, shall cause to be made, by the War Department General Staff, the necessary plans for recruiting, organizing, supplying, equipping, mobilizing, training, and demobilizing the Army of the United States and for the use of the military forces for national defense. He shall transmit to the Secretary of War the plans and recommendations prepared for that purpose by the War Department General Staff and advise him in regard thereto; upon the approval of such plans or recommendations by the Secretary of War, he shall act as the agent of the Secretary of War in carrying the same into effect. Whenever any plan or recommendation involving legislation by Congress affecting national defense or the reorganization of the Army is presented by the Secretary of War to Congress, or to one of the committees of Congress, the same shall be accompanied, when not incompatible with the public interest, by a study prepared in the appropriate division of the War Department General Staff, including the comments and recommendations of said division for or against such plan, and such pertinent comments for or against the plan as may be made by the Secretary of War, the Chief of Staff, or individual officers of the division of the War Department General Staff in which the plan was prepared. . . .

SEC. 5A. Hereafter, in addition to such other duties as may be assigned him by the Secretary of War, the Assistant Secretary of War, under the direction of the Secretary of War, shall be charged with supervision of the procurement of all military supplies and other business of the War Department pertaining thereto and the assurance of adequate provision for the mobilization of matériel and industrial organizations essential to war-time needs. . . .

Under the direction of the Secretary of War chiefs of branches of the Army charged with the procurement of supplies for the Army shall report direct to the Assistant Secretary of War regarding all matters of procurement. He shall cause to be manufactured or produced at the Government arsenals or Government-owned factories of the United States all such supplies or articles needed by the War Department as said arsenals or Goverment-owned factories are capable of manufacturing or producing upon an economical basis. . . .

SEC. 5B. THE WAR COUNCIL—The Secretary of War, the Assistant Secretary of War, the General of the Army, and the Chief of Staff shall constitute the War Council of the War Department, which council shall from time to time meet and consider policies affecting both the military and munitions problems of the War Department. Such questions shall be presented to the Secretary of War in the War Council, and his decision with reference to such questions of policy, after consideration of the recommendations thereon by the several members of the War Council, shall constitute the policy of the War Department with reference thereto.

. . . .

SEC. 24A. PROMOTION LIST—For the purpose of establishing a more uniform system for the promotion of officers, based on equity, merit, and the interests of the Army as a whole the Secretary of War shall cause to be prepared a promotion list, on which shall be carried the names of all officers of the Regular Army and Philippine Scouts below the grade of colonel, except officers of the Medical Department, chaplains, professors, the military storekeeper and certain second lieutentants of the Quartermaster Corps herein-after specified. The names on the list shall be arranged, in general, so that the first name on the list shall be that of the officer having the longest commissioned service; the second name that of the officer having the next longest commissioned service, and so on. . . .

SEC. 24D. TRANSFER OF OFFICERS—Upon his own application any officer may be transferred to another branch without loss of rank or change of place on the promotion list.

SEC. 24E. APPOINTMENT OF OFFICERS—Except as otherwise herein provided, appointments shall be made in the grade of second lieutenant, first, from graduates of the United States Military Academy; second, from warrant officers and enlisted men of the Regular Army between the ages of twenty-one and thirty years, who have had at least two years' service; and, third, from reserve officers, and from officers, warrant officers and enlisted men of the National Guard, members of the Enlisted Reserve Corps and graduates of technical institutions approved by the Secretary of War, all between the ages of twenty-one and thirty years. . . .

. . . .

SEC. 27. ENLISTMENTS—Hereafter original enlistments in the Regular Army shall be for a period of one or three years at the option of the soldier, and reënlistments shall be for a period of three years. . . .

In addition to military training, soldiers while in the active service shall hereafter be given the opportunity to study and receive instruction upon educational lines of such character as to increase their military efficiency and enable them to return to civil life better equipped for industrial, commercial, and general business occupations. Civilian teachers may be employed to aid the Army officers in giving such instruction, and part of this instruction may consist of vocational education either in agriculture or the mechanic arts. . . . (1916)

. . . .

SEC. 37. OFFICERS' RESERVE CORPS—For the purpose of providing a reserve of officers available for military service when needed there shall be organized an Officers' Reserve Corps consisting of general officers of sections corresponding to the various branches of the Regular Army, and of such additional sections as the President may direct. The grades in each section and the number in each grade shall be as the President may prescribe. Reserve officers shall be appointed and commissioned by the President alone, except general officers, who shall be appointed by and with the advice and consent of the Senate. Appointment in every case shall be for a period of five years, but an appointment in force at the outbreak of war or made in time of war shall continue in force until six months after its termination. Any reserve officer may be discharged at any time in the discretion of the President. A reserve officer appointed during the existence of a state of war shall be entitled to discharge within six months after its termination if he makes application therefor. In time of peace a reserve officer must at the time of his appointment be a citizen of the United States or of the Philippine Islands, between the ages of twenty-one and sixty years. Any person who has been an officer of the Army at any time between April 6, 1917, and June 30, 1919, or an officer of the Regular Army at any time may be appointed as a reserve officer in the highest grade which he held in the Army or any lower grade. Any person commissioned in the National Guard and recognized as a National Guard officer by the Secretary of War may upon his own application be appointed as a reserve officer in the grade held by him in the National Guard. No other person shall in time of peace be originally appointed as a reserve officer of Infantry, Cavalry, Field Artillery, Coast Artillery, or Air Service in a grade above that of second lieutenant. In time of peace appointments in the Infantry, Cavalry, Field Artillery, Coast Artillery, and Air Service shall be limited to former officers of the Army, officers of the National Guard recognized as such by the Secretary of War, graduates of the Reserve Officers' Training Corps, as provided in section 47b hereof, warrant officers and enlisted men of the Regular Army, National Guard, and Enlisted Reserve Corps, and persons who served in the Army at some time between April 6, 1917, and November 11, 1918. Promotions and transfers shall be made under such rules as may be prescribed by the President, and shall be based so far as practicable upon recommendations made in the established chain of command. So far as practicable reserve officers shall be assigned to units in the locality of their places of residence. Nothing in this Act shall operate to deprive a reserve officer of the reserve commission he now holds. Any reserve officer may hold a commission in the National Guard without thereby vacating his reserve commission. (1922)

SEC. 37A. RESERVE OFFICERS ON ACTIVE DUTY—To the extent provided for from time to time by appropriations for this specific purpose, the President may order reserve officers to active duty at any time and for any period; but except in time of a national emergency expressly declared by Congress, no reserve officer shall be employed on active duty for more than fifteen days in any calendar year without his own consent. A reserve officer shall not be entitled to pay and allowances except when on active duty. When on active duty he shall receive the same pay and allowances as an officer of the Regular Army of the same grade and length of active service, and mileage from his home to his first station and from his last station to his home, but shall not be entitled to retirement or retired pay.

SEC. 38. COMMISSIONS OF RESERVE OFFICERS—All persons appointed reserve officers shall be commissioned in the Army of the United States. Officers of the National Guard, federally recognized as such under the provisions of this Act, who are appointed reserve officers under the provisions of section 37 of this Act, shall be appointed for the period during which such recognition shall continue in effect and terminating at the expiration thereof in lieu of the five-year period hereinbefore prescribed, and in time of peace shall be governed by such special regulations appropriate for this class of reserve officers as the Secretary of War may prescribe. (1924)

   .   .   .   .

SEC. 40. RESERVE OFFICERS' TRAINING CORPS—ORGANIZA-
TION—The President is hereby authorized to establish and
maintain in civil educational institutions a Reserve Officers'
Training Corps, one or more units in number, which shall
consist of a senior division organized at universities and
colleges granting degrees, including State universities and
those State institutions that are required to provide instruction in military tactics under the Act of Congress of July
2, 1862, donating lands for the establishment of colleges
where the leading object shall be practical instruction in
agriculture and the mechanic arts, including military tactics,
and at those essentially military schools not conferring academic degrees, especially designated by the Secretary of War
as qualified, and a junior division organized at all other
public and private educational institutions, and each division shall consist of units of the several arms, corps, or
services in such number and such strength as the President
may prescribe: *Provided,* That no such unit shall be established or maintained at any institution until an officer of
the Regular Army shall have been detailed as professor of
military science and tactics, nor until such institution shall
maintain under military instruction at least one hundred
physically fit male students, except that in the case of units
other than infantry, cavalry, or artillery the minimum
number shall be fifty: *Provided further,* That except at
State institutions described in this section, no unit shall be
established or maintained in an educational institution until
the authorities of the same agree to establish and maintain
a two years' elective or compulsory course of military training as a minimum for its physically fit male students, which
course, when entered upon by any student, shall, as regards
such student, be a prerequisite for graduation unless he is
relieved of this obligation by regulations to be prescribed
by the Secretary of War.

SEC. 40A. RESERVE OFFICERS' TRAINING CORPS COURSES—
The Secretary of War is hereby authorized to prescribe
standard courses of theoretical and practical military training for units of the Reserve Officers' Training Corps, and
no unit of such corps shall be organized or maintained at

any educational institution the authorities of which fail or neglect to adopt into their curriculum the prescribed courses of military training or to devote at least an average of three hours per week per academic year to such military training, except as provided in section 47c of this Act.

SEC. 40B. PERSONNEL FOR DUTY WITH RESERVE OFFICERS' TRAINING CORPS—The President is hereby authorized to detail such numbers of officers, warrant officers, and enlisted men of the Regular Army, either active or retired, as may be necessary for duty as professors of military science and tactics, assistant professors of military science and tactics, and military instructors at educational institutions where one or more units of the Reserve Officers' Training Corps are maintained.

· · · · · · · · ·

SEC. 47. SUPPLIES FOR RESERVE OFFICERS' TRAINING CORPS—The Secretary of War, under such regulations as he may prescribe, is hereby authorized to issue to institutions at which one or more units of the Reserve Officers' Training Corps are maintained such public animals, transportation, arms, ammunition, supplies, tentage, equipment, and uniforms belonging to the United States as he may deem necessary, and to forage at the expense of the United States public animals so issued, to pay commutation in lieu of uniforms at a rate to be fixed annually by the Secretary of War, and to authorize such expenditures from proper Army appropriations as he may deem necessary for the efficient maintenance of the Reserve Officers' Training Corps. He shall require from each institution to which property of the United States is issued a bond in the value of the property issued for the care and safe-keeping thereof, except for uniforms, expendable articles, and supplies expended in operation, maintenance, and instruction, and for its return when required.

SEC. 47A. RESERVE OFFICERS' TRAINING CORPS CAMPS—The Secretary of War is hereby authorized to maintain camps for the further practical instruction of the members of the Reserve Officers' Training Corps, no such camps to be maintained for a longer period than six weeks in any one year, except in time of actual or threatened hostilities; to transport members of such corps to and from such camps at the expense of the United States so far as appropriations will permit, to subsist them at the expense of the United States while traveling to and from such camps and while remaining therein so far as appropriations will permit, or in lieu of transporting them to and from such camps and subsisting them while en route, to pay them travel allowances at the rate of 5 cents per mile for the distance by the shortest usually traveled route from the places from which they are authorized to proceed to the camp and for the return travel thereto, and to make the payment of travel allowances for the return journey in advance of the actual performance of the same, and to admission to military hospitals at such camps, and to furnish medical attendance and supplies; to use the troops of the Regular Army, and such Government property as he may deem necessary, for the military training of the members of such corps while in attendance at such camps; and to prescribe regulations for the government of such camps.

SEC. 47B. APPOINTMENT OF GRADUATES OF RESERVE OFFICERS' TRAINING CORPS AS RESERVE OFFICERS—The President alone, under such regulations as he may prescribe, is hereby authorized to appoint as a reserve officer of the Army of the United States any graduate of the senior division of the Reserve Officers' Training Corps who shall have satisfactorily completed the further training provided for in section 47a of this Act, or any graduate of the junior division who shall have satisfactorily completed the courses of military training prescribed for the senior division and the further training provided for in section 47a of this Act, and shall have participated in such practical instruction subsequent to graduation as the Secretary of War shall prescribe, who shall have arrived at the age of twenty-one years and who shall agree, under oath in writing, to serve the United States in the capacity of a reserve officer of the Army of the United States during a period of at least five years from the date of his appointment as such reserve officer, unless sooner discharged by proper authority: *Provided,* That no reserve officer appointed pursuant to this Act shall be entitled to retirement, or to retired pay, and shall be eligible for pension only for disability incurred in line of duty in active service or while serving with the Army pursuant to provisions of this Act.

SEC. 47C. PAY AND COMMUTATION OF SUBSISTENCE, RESERVE OFFICERS' TRAINING CORPS—When any member of the senior division of the Reserve Officers' Training Corps has completed two academic years of service in that division, and has been selected for advanced training by the president of the institution and by the professor of military science and tactics, and has agreed in writing to continue in the Reserve Officers' Training Corps for the remainder of his course at the institution, devoting five hours per week to the military training prescribed by the Secretary of War, and has agreed in writing to pursue the course in camp training prescribed by the Secretary of War, he may be furnished at the expense of the United States commutation of subsistence at such rate, not exceeding the cost of the garrison ration prescribed for the Army, as may be fixed by the Secretary of War, during the remainder of his service in the Reserve Officers' Training Corps, not exceeding two years. . . .

SEC. 47D. TRAINING CAMPS—The Secretary of War is hereby authorized to maintain, upon military reservations or elsewhere, schools or camps for the military instruction and training, with a view to their appointment as reserve officers or noncommissioned officers, of such warrant officers, enlisted men, and civilians as may be selected upon their own application; to use for the purpose of maintaining said camps and imparting military instruction and training thereat, such arms, ammunition, accoutrements, equipments, tentage, field equipage, and transportation belonging to the United States as he may deem necessary. . . .

.   .   .   .

SEC. 55. THE ENLISTED RESERVE CORPS—The Enlisted Reserve Corps shall consist of persons voluntarily enlisted therein. The period of enlistment shall be three years, except in the case of persons who served in the Army, Navy, or Marine Corps at some time between April 6, 1917, and November 11, 1918, who may be enlisted for one-year periods and who, in time of peace, shall be entitled to discharge within ninety days if they make application therefor. Enlistment shall be limited to persons eligible for enlistment in the Regular Army who have had such military or technical training as may be prescribed by regulations of the Secretary of War. All enlistments in force at the outbreak of war, or entered into during its continuation, whether in the Regular Army or the Enlisted Reserve Corps, shall continue in force until six months after its termination unless sooner terminated by the President.

SEC. 55A. ORGANIZATION OF THE ENLISTED RESERVE CORPS—The President may form any or all members of the Enlisted Reserve Corps into tactical organizations similar to those of the Regular Army, similarly armed, uniformed, and equipped, and composed so far as practicable of men residing in the same locality, may officer them by the assignment of reserve officers of the Regular Army, active or retired, and may detail such personnel of the Army as may be necessary for the administration of such organizations and the care of Government property issued to them.

.   .   .   .

SEC. 57. COMPOSITION OF THE MILITIA—The militia of the United States shall consist of all able-bodied male citizens of the United States and all other able-bodied males who have or shall have declared their intention to become citizens of the United States, who shall be more than eighteen years of age and, except as hereinafter provided, not more than forty-five years of age, and said militia shall be divided into three classes, the National Guard, the Naval Militia, and the Unorganized Militia. (1916)

SEC. 58. COMPOSITION OF THE NATIONAL GUARD—The National Guard shall consist of regularly enlisted men who upon original enlistment shall be not less than eighteen nor more than forty-five years of age, or who in subsequent en-

THE NATIONAL DEFENSE ACT OF 1920

listments shall not be more than sixty-four years of age,
organized, armed, and equipped as hereinafter provided, and
of commissioned officers and warrant officers between the
ages of twenty-one and sixty-four years. (1925)

SEC. 59. EXEMPTIONS FROM MILITIA DUTY—The Vice
President of the United States; the officers, judicial and
executive, of the Government of the United States and of the
several States and Territories; persons in the military or
naval service of the United States; customhouse clerks; persons employed by the United States in the transmission of
the mail; artificers and workmen employed in the armories,
arsenals, and navy yards of the United States; pilots; mar-
iners actually employed in the sea service of any citizen or
merchant within the United States, shall be exempt from
militia duty without regard to age, and all persons who because of religious belief shall claim exemption from military
service, if the conscientious holding of such belief by such
person shall be established under such regulations as the
President shall prescribe, shall be exempted from militia
service in a combatant capacity; but no person so exempted
shall be exempt from militia service in any capacity that the
President shall declare to be noncombatant. (1916)

SEC. 60. ORGANIZATION OF NATIONAL GUARD UNITS—
Except as otherwise specifically provided herein, the organization of the National Guard, including the composition of all
units thereof, shall be the same as that which is or may hereafter be prescribed for the Regular Army, subject in time of
peace to such general exceptions as may be authorized by the
Secretary of War. And the President may prescribe the particular unit or units, as to branch or arm of service, to be
maintained in each State, Territory, or the District of
Columbia in order to secure a force which, when combined,
shall form complete higher tactical units. (1916)

SEC. 61. MAINTENANCE OF OTHER TROOPS BY THE
STATES—No State shall maintain troops in time of peace
other than as authorized in accordance with the organization
prescribed under this Act: *Provided,* That nothing contained
in this Act shall be construed as limiting the rights of the
States and Territories in the use of the National Guard

408 INTRODUCTION TO MILITARY HISTORY

within their respective borders in time of peace: *Provided
further,* That nothing contained in this Act shall prevent the
organization and maintenance of State police or constabulary.
(1916)

SEC. 62. NUMBER OF THE NATIONAL GUARD—The number of enlisted men of the National Guard to be organized
under this Act within one year from its passage shall be for
each State in the proportion of two hundred such men for
each Senator and Representative in Congress from such State,
and a number to be determined by the President for each
Territory and the District of Columbia, and shall be increased each year thereafter in the proportion of not less than
fifty per centum until a total peace strength of not less than
eight hundred enlisted men for each Senator and Representative in Congress shall have been reached. . . . (1916)

. . . .

SEC. 70. Men enlisting in the National Guard of the several
States, Territories, and the District of Columbia, shall sign
an enlistment contract and subscribe to the following oath
of enlistment: "I do hereby acknowledge to have voluntarily
enlisted this —— day of ——, 19—, as a soldier in the
National Guard of the United States and of the State of
——, for the period of three (or one) year —, under the
conditions prescribed by law, unless sooner discharged by
proper authority. And I do solemnly swear that I will bear
true faith and allegiance to the United States of America and
to the State of ——, and that I will serve them honestly and
faithfully against all their enemies whomsoever, and that I
will obey the orders of the President of the United States
and of the governor of the State of——, and of the officers
appointed over me according to law and the rules and Articles of War."

. . . .

SEC. 73. FEDERAL OATH FOR NATIONAL GUARD OFFICERS—
Commissioned officers of the National Guard of the several
States, Territories, and the District of Columbia now serving
under commissions regularly issued shall continue in office,
as officers of the National Guard, without the issuance of new

commissions: *Provided,* That said officers have taken, or shall take and subscribe to the following oath of office: "I, ——, do solemnly swear that I will support and defend the Constitution of the United States and the constitution of the State of ——, against all enemies, foreign and domestic; that I will bear true faith and allegiance to the same; that I will obey the orders of the President of the United States and of the governor of the State of ——; that I make this obligation freely, without any mental reservation or purpose of evasion, and that I will well and faithfully discharge the duties of the office of —— in the National Guard of the United States and of the State of —— upon which I am about to enter, so help me God." (1916)

. . . .

SEC. 74. QUALIFICATIONS FOR NATIONAL GUARD OFFI-CERS—Persons hereafter commissioned as officers of the National Guard shall not be recognized as such under any of the provisions of this Act unless they shall have been selected from the following classes, and shall have taken and subscribed to the oath of office prescribed in the preceding section of this Act; officers or enlisted men of the National Guard; officers, active or retired, reserve officers, and former officers of the Army, Navy, or Marine Corps, enlisted men and former enlisted men of the Army, Navy, or Marine Corps who have received an honorable discharge therefrom; graduates of the United States Military and Naval Academies; and graduates of schools, colleges, universities, and officers' training camps, where they have received military instruction under the supervision of an officer of the Regular Army who certified their fitness for appointment as commissioned officers; and for the technical branches or Staff Corps and departments, such other civilians as may be specially qualified for duty therein.

. . . .

SEC. 91. DISCIPLINE TO CONFORM TO THAT OF REGULAR ARMY—The discipline (which includes training) of the National Guard shall conform to the system which is now or may hereafter be prescribed for the Regular Army, and the training shall be carried out by the several States, Territories, and the District of Columbia so as to conform to the provisions of this Act. (1916)

. . . .

SEC. 93. INSPECTIONS OF THE NATIONAL GUARD—The Secretary of War shall cause an inspection to be made at least once each year by inspectors general, and if necessary by other officers, of the Regular Army, detailed by him for that purpose, to determine whether the amount and condition of the property in the hands of the National Guard is satisfactory; whether the National Guard is organized as hereinbefore prescribed; whether the officers and enlisted men possess the physical and other qualifications prescribed; whether the organization and the officers and enlisted men thereof are sufficiently armed, uniformed, equipped, and being trained and instructed for active duty in the field or coast defense, and whether the records are being kept in accordance with the requirements of this Act. The reports of such inspections shall serve as the basis for deciding as to the issue to and retention by the National Guard of the military property provided for by this Act, and for determining what organizations and individuals shall be considered as constituting parts of the National Guard within the meaning of this Act. (1916)

SEC. 94. ENCAMPMENTS AND MANEUVERS—Under such regulations as the President may prescribe the Secretary of War is authorized to provide for the participation of the whole or any part of the National Guard in encampments, maneuvers, or other exercises, including outdoor target practice, for field or coast-defense instructions, either independently or in conjunction with any part of the Regular Army. . . . (1916)

. . . .

SEC. 100. DETAIL OF OFFICERS OF REGULAR ARMY TO DUTY WITH THE NATIONAL GUARD—The Secretary of War shall detail officers of the active list of the Army to duty with the National Guard in each State, Territory, or District of Columbia, and officers so detailed may accept commissions in the National Guard, with the permission of the President and terminable in his discretion, without vacating their commissions in the Regular Army or being prejudiced in their relative or lineal standing therein. The Secretary of War may, upon like application, detail one or more enlisted men of the Regular Army with each State, Territory, or District of Columbia for duty in connection with the National Guard. But nothing in this section shall be so construed as to prevent the detail of retired officers as now provided by law. (1916)

SEC. 101. NATIONAL GUARD, WHEN SUBJECT TO LAWS GOVERNING REGULAR ARMY—The National Guard when called as such into the service of the United States shall, from the time they are required by the terms of the call to respond thereto, be subject to the laws and regulations governing the Regular Army, so far as such laws and regulations are applicable to officers and enlisted men whose permanent retention in the military service, either on the active list or on the retired list, is not contemplated by existing law. (1916)

SEC. 111. NATIONAL GUARD WHEN DRAFTED INTO FEDERAL SERVICE—When Congress shall have authorized the use of the armed land forces of the United States for any purpose requiring the use of troops in excess of those of the Regular Army, the President may, under such regulations, including such physical examination, as he may prescribe, draft into the military service of the United States, to serve therein for the period of the war or emergency, unless sooner discharged, any or all members of the National Guard and of the National Guard Reserve. All persons so drafted shall, from the date of their draft, stand discharged from the militia, and shall be subject to such laws and regulations for the government of the Army of the United States as may be applicable to members of the Army, whose permanent retention in the military service is not contemplated by law, and shall be organized into units corresponding as far as practicable to those of the Regular Army or shall be otherwise assigned as the President may direct. The commissioned officers of said organizations shall be appointed from among the members thereof; officers with rank not above that of colonel to be appointed by the President alone, and all other officers to be appointed by the President by and with the advice and consent of the Senate. Officers and enlisted men while in the service of the United States under the terms of this section shall have the same pay and allowances as officers and enlisted men of the Regular Army of the same grades and the same prior service. On the termination of the emergency all persons so drafted shall be discharged from the Army, shall resume their membership in the militia, and, if the State so provide, shall continue to serve in the National Guard until the dates upon which their enlistments entered into prior to their draft, would have expired if uninterrupted.

.   .   .   .

SEC. 120. PURCHASE OR PROCUREMENT OF MILITARY SUPPLIES IN TIME OF ACTUAL OR IMMINENT WAR—The President, in time of war or when war is imminent, is empowered, through the head of any department of the Government, in addition to the present authorized methods of purchase or procurement, to place an order with an individual, firm, association, company, corporation, or organized manufacturing industry for such product or material as may be required, and which is of the nature and kind usually produced or capable of being produced by such individual, firm, company, association, corporation, or organized manufacturing industry.

Compliance with all such orders for products or material shall be obligatory on any individual, firm, association, company, corporation, or organized manufacturing industry or the responsible head or heads thereof and shall take precedence over all other orders and contracts theretofore placed with such individual, firm, company, association, corporation, or organized manufacturing industry, and any individual, firm, association, company, corporation, or organized manufacturing industry or the responsible head or heads thereof owning or operating any plant equipped for the manufacture of arms or ammunition or parts of ammunition, or any necessary supplies or equipment for the Army, and any individual, firm, association, company, corporation, or organized manufacturing industry or the responsible head or heads thereof owning or operating any manufacturing plant, which, in the opinion of the Secretary of War shall be capable of being readily transformed into a plant for the manufacture of arms or ammunition, or parts thereof, or other necessary supplies or equipment, who shall refuse to give to the United States such preference in the matter of the execution of orders, or who shall refuse to manufacture the kind, quantity, or quality of arms or ammunition, or the parts thereof, or any necessary supplies or equipment, as ordered by the Secretary of War, or who shall refuse to furnish such arms, ammunition, or parts of ammunition, or other supplies or equipment, at a reasonable price as determined by the Secretary of War, then, and in either such case, the President, through the head of any department of the Government, in addition to the present authorized methods of purchase or procurement herein provided for, is hereby authorized to take immediate possession of any such plant or plants, and through the Ordnance Department of the United States Army to manufacture therein in time of war, or when war shall be imminent, such product or material as may be required, and any individual, firm, company, association, or corporation, or organized manufacturing industry, or the responsible head or heads thereof, failing to comply with the provisions of this section shall be deemed guilty of a felony, and upon conviction shall be punished by imprisonment for not more than three years and by a fine not exceeding $50,000.

SEC. 127A. MISCELLANEOUS PROVISIONS—In time of war any officer of the Regular Army may be appointed to higher temporary rank without vacating his permanent commission, such appointments in grades below that of brigadier general being made by the President alone, but all other appointments of officers in time of war shall be in the Officers' Reserve Corps.

Unless special assignment is made by the President under the provisions of the one hundred and nineteenth article of war, all officers in the active service of the United States in any grade shall take rank according to date, which, in the case of an officer of the Regular Army, is that stated in his commission or letter of appointment, and, in the case of a reserve officer or an officer of the National Guard called into the service of the United States, shall precede that on which he is placed on active duty by a period equal to the total length of active Federal service and service under the provisions of sections 94, 97, and 99 of this Act which he may have performed in the grade in which called or any higher grade. When dates of rank are the same, precedence shall be determined by length of active commissioned service in the Army. When length of such service is the same, officers of the Regular Army shall take rank among themselves according to their places on the promotion list, preceding reserve and National Guard officers of the same date of rank and length of service, who shall take rank among themselves according to age. (1925)

INDEX